Approaches to Teaching the Works of Charles W. Chesnutt

Approaches to Teaching the Works of Charles W. Chesnutt

Edited by

Susanna Ashton

and

Bill Hardwig

The Modern Language Association of America
New York   2017

MLA and the MODERN LANGUAGE ASSOCIATION are trademarks
owned by the Modern Language Association of America.
For information about obtaining permission to reprint material from
MLA book publications, send your request by mail (see address below)
or e-mail (permissions@mla.org).

Library of Congress Cataloging-in-Publication Data

Names: Ashton, Susanna, 1967– editor. | Hardwig, Bill editor.
Title: Approaches to teaching the works of Charles W. Chesnutt /
edited by Susanna Ashton, Bill Hardwig.
Description: New York : The Modern Language Association of America, 2017. |
Series: Approaches to teaching world literature, ISSN 1059-1133 ; 149 |
Includes bibliographical references and index.
Identifiers: LCCN 2017038786 | ISBN 9781603293310 (hardback) | ISBN 9781603293327 (paper)
Subjects: LCSH: Chesnutt, Charles W. (Charles Waddell), 1858–1932—Study and
teaching (Higher) | BISAC: LANGUAGE ARTS & DISCIPLINES / Study &
Teaching. | LITERARY CRITICISM / American / African American.
Classification: LCC PS1292.C6 Z55 2017 | DDC 813/.4—dc23
LC record available at https://lccn.loc.gov/2017038786

Approaches to Teaching World Literature 149
ISSN 1059-1133

Cover illustration of the paperback and electronic editions:
A Negro church in a cornfield in Manning, South Carolina. Photograph
by Marion Post Wolcott, June 1939. Library of Congress, Prints and
Photographs Division, FSA-OWI Collection, LC-DIG-fsac-1a34294.

Published by The Modern Language Association of America
85 Broad Street, suite 500, New York, New York 10004-2434
www.mla.org

CONTENTS

INTRODUCTION

Biography

Charles Waddell Chesnutt (1858–1932) was brought up with advantages unknown to most Reconstruction Era children of color. He was born in Ohio, the son of free and light-skinned parents, and, although money was scarce, his family was well off in comparison with so many African Americans living in slavery or penury in Southern states. An incident from his father's life, however, suggests how real the suffering of African Americans was to the Chesnutt family, and the manner in which the incident was resolved may have planted in young Charles an early respect for the power of linguistic and transcriptive flexibility, as well as a commitment to social and racial justice.

As Chesnutt's daughter tells it, a runaway slave was recaptured outside Oberlin, Ohio, in 1856. Word quickly spread that slave catchers and a United States marshal were taking advantage of the 1850 Fugitive Slave Act to return the runaway in exchange for a hefty reward or, at the least, a finder's fee. A quickly assembled posse of both white and black abolitionists chased down the wagon with the captured slave, and, after successfully overtaking the wagon, the abolitionists unchained the slave and quickly hustled him off to the networks of the Underground Railroad. When this action was reported, a local judge found himself trying several black and white men (including Chesnutt's father) on the charge of violating the Fugitive Slave Act. Sympathetic to their cause and having a distaste for the controversial fugitive slave laws with their draconian punishments, the judge manufactured excuses to let off as many of the rescuing posse as possible. The judge released Chesnutt's father on the grounds that the writ of arrest read "Andrew Chestnut" and not "Andrew Chesnutt" (H. Chesnutt 3). The shifting *t* in the father's name had, surprisingly, been the means of his liberation.

Family lore about this event lauded the considerable courage of Chesnutt's father in risking his own life and security to free another person. It also spoke to the support that legal justice could provide as well as the dangers of its frequent absence. This family story further emphasized that much depended on transcription and its ability to reflect, if not reality, then a perception of reality that might be used to one's advantage. We should not be surprised, therefore, to see how Chesnutt's life shaped an artist with both a careful ear and a careful imagination. He was raised to understand that manipulating language could be a means to gain power and even alter one's destiny. Transcribing life stories with precision but also with a willingness to reshape language to one's benefit thus became a hallmark of one of the most remarkable writers in American literature.

Born in 1858 to Ana Maria Chesnutt and Andrew Jackson Chesnutt, in Cleveland, Ohio, Charles W. Chesnutt belonged to one of the rare American families of African ancestry who chose to return to the South at the end of the Civil War. As a light-skinned child, he could plausibly have passed as white, but he always chose to resolutely identify himself as a person of color or, as he once put it, as "a voluntary Negro" (Rampersad), to face the hypocrisy, cruelties, and opportunities offered by the vicissitudes of America's color line. In 1866 the Chesnutts moved to Fayetteville, North Carolina, to be closer to their extended families there. Young Charles was fortunate enough to be educated at the Howard School (which later became Fayetteville State University). His talents were soon recognized, and he began a career as a teacher and school administrator.

Despite successfully rising in his responsibilities and job titles from school to school in the South, Chesnutt felt that his future lay elsewhere. Living and working among communities devastated by the Civil War and the brutal nature of failed Reconstruction, he was profoundly affected by the promise of social, political, and cultural equality: a dissonance that he later wove into a unique insider-outsider perspective in his writings about the South. He saw a future for himself as a man of business, or perhaps a man of letters, up north. Thus, with a new wife, Susan Perry, whom he married in 1878, and a growing family to care for, he moved to New York City to pursue a reporting and business career. But he was soon drawn back to Ohio, where there were better opportunities. By 1883 he and his family had established themselves in Cleveland, and he began a study of law. Although he passed the bar exam in 1887, he was unable to secure full-time legal work and was therefore forced to rely on his stenographic skills for a steady income.

This seemingly indefatigable man, while pursuing his legal and stenographic careers, was also honing his literary skills. He had already published a few small pieces here and there, but in the mid 1880s his public image quickly increased when his various short stories were taken up by the vast S. S. McClure syndicate. He rose to national prominence with the publication of "The Goophered Grapevine" in the *Atlantic Monthly* in 1887. The success of the reception of this tale spurred him to produce more stories in the framework of his unique notion of what antebellum plantation tales might be for a racially fraught, progressive era. Even as he practiced his stenography business, Chesnutt found time to write many of his most important stories, including "The Goophered Grapevine" and "Po' Sandy," which later were included in *The Conjure Woman*, a collection set in postbellum North Carolina and published in 1899 by Houghton Mifflin. That year also saw him publish a biography of Frederick Douglass and *"The Wife of His Youth" and Other Stories of the Color Line*, a collection of tales set in Ohio that deal less with the life of freed people in the rural South and more with the delicate balance it took to walk the color line of the genteel and often fair-skinned class of African Americans in the Northern states. Buoyed by the critical and modest commercial success of these works, Chesnutt sold his stenography business so that he could, finally, lead the life of a full-time writer.

Over the next few years, he produced speeches, letters, journals, stories, and novels in a seemingly frenzied pace, although many of his works did not find a publisher during his lifetime. His novel *The House behind the Cedars* (1900) was published by Houghton Mifflin during this time, and *The Marrow of Tradition*, his novel depicting the Wilmington "riots" of 1898, quickly followed (1901).

Chesnutt became increasingly involved in politics and social commentary, and the next few years saw him writing newspaper articles and social commentary about American race relations and the appeal and challenges posed by Booker T. Washington. Despite his admiration for Washington, he was drawn to a different vision of how America might confront its multiracial future, which he articulated when he addressed the anti-Washington factions at the annual conference of the Niagara Movement in 1908. He expressed his objections to Washington's assimilationist policies most succinctly in a letter to Washington in 1903:

> I have no faith in the Southern people's sense of justice so far as the Negro's rights are concerned. . . . I feel deeply on this subject. I want my rights and all of them and I ask no more for myself than I would demand for every Negro in the South. If the white South will continue to ignore the Constitution and violate the laws, it must be with no consent of mine, and with no word that can be twisted into the approval or condonation of their unjust and unlawful course.   (*"To Be"* 181–82)

Chesnutt had long acknowledged that his literary career was not going to support his family (he returned to his stenography business in 1902). Although he continued to write, it was with less encouragement and fewer commercial successes than his explosive debut at the turn of the century might have predicted. His writing didn't always seem in keeping with the youthful energy of the black writers during the heyday of the 1920s, yet his status as an éminence grise of the Harlem Renaissance was marked by his receiving the 1928 Spingarn Medal from the National Association for Colored People for extraordinary achievement in African American literature. In 1932 he died and was buried in Cleveland.

The story of Chesnutt is most remarkable for how many lives he led. His complexity is reflected by the difficulty scholars have had to secure a particular perspective on him and by how different these perspectives are. There are titles that present him as a seminal black author (J. Noel Heermance's *Charles W. Chesnutt, America's First Great Black Novelist*), as a multiracial activist (Helen M. Chesnutt's *Charles Waddell Chesnutt: Pioneer of the Color Line*), and as an exemplar of particular political movements (Ernestine Pickens's *Charles W. Chesnutt and the Progressive Movement*). Tess Chakkalakal's forthcoming Chesnutt biography will situate him in the world of American arts and letters. But most scholars seem to have thrown up their hands in bemused acknowledgment that he was too diverse to be categorized. Thus much of the best writing about his life can be found in the volumes of his own collected work, such as *Charles W. Chesnutt: Essays and Speeches* and *"To Be an Author": Letters of Charles W. Chesnutt, 1889–1905*.

Chesnutt and the Plantation Tradition

Given his multifaceted professional history and his evolving literary style, it is not surprising that readers have responded to his fiction in numerous ways. The style of this fiction—especially of his early work, with its wry humor and at times gentle charm—often belies the fiction's explorations into historical terror and political commentary. Readers have been grappling with this conundrum since he began publishing. Part of the challenge of reading and teaching his work is undoubtedly his complex relation to what we often call the plantation tradition. This term describes the movement of post-Reconstruction white Southern writers who sought to romanticize the antebellum South and to rewrite the legacy of this slaveholding culture in an era (the 1880s and 1890s) that was losing citizens with strong personal memories of the region before the Civil War. Thomas Nelson Page, a white Virginian who wrote dialect stories about pre- and postwar race relations, is often seen as the chief architect of the plantation tradition. His stories typically gloss over the conflicts both in his time, the post–Reconstruction Era, and in the antebellum South to create a romanticized version of the Old South. Barbara Ewell and Pamela Glenn Menke describe Page's recuperation of the prewar plantation culture: "Page created an idealized antebellum world in which that society could be positively experienced and publicly exonerated. In it, cheerfully loyal slaves were part of an extended family in which aristocratic cavaliers lived by a code of honor" (xlvii). Other white authors in the plantation tradition also wrote in African American dialect, most famously Joel Chandler Harris, with his Uncle Remus stories.

While some of Page's fiction shows more nuance and conflict than perhaps readers expect (the story "No Haid Pawn" [162–86] offers such a case), most of his fiction and poetry relies on heavily romanticized accounts of the slaveholding South. Most troubling for readers then and now is his tendency to narrate these tales of idealized plantations through the voices of black characters extolling the virtues of the plantations on which they lived and the kindness and generosity of the owners of those plantations. His lengthy dialect story "Meh Lady: A Story of the War," originally published in *The Century* in 1886, offers one such example (78–139). In this tale, the narrator, Billy, recounts the war bravery and heroic battlefield death of the son of the plantation owner, Marse Phil, as if Billy were a family member: "We bury him in de gyardin dat evenin', and dyar warn' 'nough gent'mens in de county to be he pall-bearers, so de hands on de place toted him, and it ease' me might'ly to git meh arm under him right good, like when he wuz a little chap runnin' 'roun' callin' me 'Unc' Billy,' and pesterin' me to go fishin'" (88). At the story's conclusion, as the chaos surrounding the war subsides, Billy makes a comparison between the story's postwar peace and the prewar days on the plantation: "I sort o' got to studyin', an hit 'pear like de plantation 'live once mo', and de ain' no mo' scufflin', an' de ole times done come back ag'in" (138).

Needless to say, Chesnutt's entry into the literary realm through the use of dialect tales, which had many of the superficial markers of the plantation tradition, was a vexed and complicated undertaking. His conjure tales had a mixed reception over the decades, but Chesnutt was always clear about his investment in using dialect fiction to provide a counternarrative to the racist work of Page, Harris, and others writing in the plantation tradition. In a 1901 letter to Booker T. Washington about the value of literature as a means of political resistance, he wrote, "[T]he medium of fiction offers a golden opportunity to create sympathy throughout the country for our cause. It has been the writings of Harris and Page and others of that ilk which have furnished my chief incentive to write something upon the other side of this very vital question" ("*To Be*" 176).

Chesnutt's stories offer a consistent criticism of the vision of antebellum slave culture expressed in most of Page's work. Take, for instance, "Po' Sandy," which was first published in the *Atlantic Monthly* in 1888. This tale's speaker, Julius McAdoo, relates a story about Sandy, who through conjuring has been turned into a tree by his wife, Tenie, so that he can escape the horrors of being enslaved. In what must be seen as a metaphor for the greed and destruction of slave society, a slave owner later cuts down the tree that Sandy has become in order to make a new kitchen for his house. Julius narrates the scene in graphic detail: "Dey started de saw up agi'n, en cut de log up inter bo'ds en scatlin's right befo' [Tenie's] eyes. But it wuz might hard wuk; fer of all de sweekin', en' moanin', en groanin', dat log done it w'iles de saw wuz' a cuttin' thoo it" (*Conjure Woman* 52). The reader cannot help but see Sandy in the log, and the horrible noises the saw makes while cutting the log become a vocalization of his agony, all of which is witnessed by a horrified Tenie. After the conclusion of Julius's tale, a white Northern listener, Annie, seems to have a fundamentally altered vision of the cruelty of slavery: "What a system it was . . . under which such things were possible! Poor Tenie" (53). Even if Annie doesn't believe the conjuring story, she has learned much about the horrors of slavery, especially the inhumanity of the treatment of slaves and the suffering caused by the separation of loved ones. Readers debate whether Chesnutt's dialect voices sound similar to Page's, but Chesnutt's politics are always working to undermine the romantic tales of antebellum plantation fiction. His plantations are run by greedy and cruel owners, and those who are enslaved, however deferential they act toward their masters, are always searching for freedom, for ways to improve their condition.

As Kenneth Warren reminds us, the plantation tradition rewriting of the slaveholding South had not only consequences for the legacy of the Old South but also a significant stake in the era during which this fiction was produced: "Romanticized views of blacks . . . could . . . serve the need of political and social conservatives who wished to discredit or roll black civil rights gains.

The happy-go-lucky darky images of the antebellum South could be contrasted favorably to the images of impoverished, potentially dangerous blacks of post-Reconstruction" (119). How people felt about the plantation tradition had a lot to say about how they felt about post-Reconstruction racial history. In part because readers did not initially know Chesnutt's biography and because no African American writers had previously been published in *The Atlantic Monthly*, his early work was often seen as belonging to the plantation tradition and not as a counternarrative to it. The contemporary reviews of that fiction were full of such assumptions. The New Orleans *Daily Picayune* commented, "The stories are well written, showing familiarity with the whimsicalities and comicalities of negro character, and a subtle perception of the poetry and romance often hidden in their hearts" (qtd. in Ellison and Metcalf 4–7). The *Book Buyer* compared Chesnutt with Paul Laurence Dunbar, commenting on their "simplicity" and stating that Chesnutt's work exhibited "the playfulness of a child" (Cary 27). The *Los Angeles Times* similarly remarked that the tales "are full of the unconscious humor, the darky belief in the supernatural, the darky mingled child-likeness and shrewdness" ("Some Tales" 14).

As a result of this consistent misinterpretation of his work, the social criticism of Chesnutt became more pointed as he continued to publish and as his identity as an African American author became more widely known. Not surprisingly, there were many white Americans who subsequently changed their minds about him. William Dean Howells, as a prime and often cited case in point, supported Chesnutt's career in his early years but wavered when Chesnutt's work shed the ironic mask of the plantation frame. Howells apparently appreciated Chesnutt most when he could be placed in a familiar and nonthreatening genre. In his review of Chesnutt's *The Marrow of Tradition*, a novel depicting the tragedy of the Wilmington "race riots" (what some might call the Wilmington coup d'état) and the irreconcilable hypocrisies of American racist power, Howells noted that Chesnutt "stands up for his own people with a courage which has more justice than mercy in it. The book is, in fact, bitter, bitter. There is no reason why it should not be so, if wrong is to be repaid with hate, and yet it would be better if it was not so bitter" ("Psychological Counter-current").

Howells acknowledged that "it cannot be said that either his aesthetics or ethics are false" and stated in no uncertain terms, "No one who reads the book can deny that the case is presented with great power." Thus the charge that Howells abandoned or turned on Chesnutt isn't entirely just. Nor can we use Howells as a stand-in for all readers of the period. William L. Andrews has pointed out that Chesnutt's later work, especially *The Marrow of Tradition*, was recognized as "not the work of an apprentice," even by Southern critics of the time (*Literary Career* 204). Nonetheless, Chesnutt's work at the turn of the century was directly competing with some of the most popular and virulently racist literature of all time, such as Thomas Dixon's best-selling novels *The Leopard's Spots* (1902) and *The Clansman* (1905), which appealed to a segment of the white popular imagination through its own brand of reconstructed history, sentimentalism, and plotlines emphasizing African American inferiority. Chesnutt's style of social commentary in his fiction had trouble gaining a foothold in that market. American readers were not able to embrace Chesnutt on the terms he had set, and so his reputation suffered in the decades that followed.

Chesnutt's history of political engagement also runs against the grain of an easy narrative of unambiguous trajectories of progress or liberalism. Because Chesnutt was a writer not known at first to be of color, his sudden rise as a black author writing literature understood by some to be too accommodating of white racial attitudes didn't always endear him to literary scholars wanting a more direct confrontation with a racist culture. Chesnutt's long commitment to political engagement is indisputable, yet his sympathetic relationship to Washington, who in 1905 appointed him to the Committee of Twelve for the Advancement of the Interests of the Negro Race might seem to align Chesnutt with the Tuskegee machine or political factions associated with Washington. Indeed, Chesnutt visited Tuskegee in 1901 and wrote with both admiration for the impressive social achievements he observed there and concern about the political price paid for them. This overture to Washington, coupled with his criticism of many of Washington's policies, demonstrates Chesnutt's thoughtful approach, his refusal to be defined by one school of thought or political movement.

Chesnutt worked with Washington on social issues but at the same time considered himself a friend and ally of W. E. B. Du Bois, who in turn thought much of Chesnutt. In 1908 Chesnutt addressed the annual conference of the Niagara Movement, a radical civil rights organization founded by Du Bois in opposition to Washington's politics of accommodation. By 1910, Chesnutt was working to help launch what was to become the NAACP, and he proudly identified himself as an early member who went on to serve on the association's General Committee. He continued to write pieces and deliver speeches regularly decrying disenfranchisement and social policies supporting segregation. Along with both Washington and Du Bois, he lobbied to suppress the publication of William Hannibal Thomas's 1901 book *The American Negro*, an infamously vicious work by an African American that claimed that black people were inherently inferior. As the twentieth century moved ahead, Chesnutt not only published stories and essays in *The Crisis*, the official mouthpiece of the NAACP and edited by Du Bois, but also frequently offered Du Bois advice about literary submissions to *The Crisis* and the state of African American literature generally. In his "Postcript" column for the *Crisis* magazine of January 1933, Du Bois eulogized him as "the dean of Negro literature" (20).

Part One

MATERIALS

Critical Reception

While Chesnutt is now firmly established in our collective canon of American literature, his place in it was not always a certainty. One can track the increasing visibility and popularity of his literature through its growing representation in anthologies. For example, the Chesnutt selections in the *Norton Anthology of American Literature* have gone from the sole inclusion of his most famous dialect story, "The Goophered Grapevine" (in editions 1–4, years 1979–94), to "The Goophered Grapevine" and a story of the color line, "The Wife of His Youth" (editions 5 and 6, years 1998 and 2000). The seventh and eighth editions of the anthology (2007, 2012) added another short story, "The Passing of Grandison," and an essay on racial dynamics and the publishing community, "A Defamer of His Race." Such an increased profile in a prominent anthology signals a recognition of the importance of Chesnutt's work.

The revived teaching interest in Chesnutt's fiction can be traced back to critical work from the middle of the twentieth century. Groundbreaking monographs that focused on his biography, such as Helen M. Chesnutt's *Charles Waddell Chesnutt: Pioneer of the Color Line* (1952) and J. N. Heermance's *Charles W. Chesnutt: America's First Great Black Novelist* (1974), helped set the stage for what we might think of as the Chesnutt renaissance of the 1970s. In the late 1960s and the 1970s there was nearly ten times more published work on Chesnutt than in the previous three decades combined. This scholarship was reviewed and published principally in journals founded by African American academic organizations and dedicated to the work of African American authors. The *College Language Association Journal* and the *Negro American Literature Forum* (which later became the *Black American Literature Forum* and today is the *African American Review*) led the way in reintroducing the reading and scholarly public to Chesnutt's ideas and writing. Interest in the work of Chesnutt during this time was energized by the work of scholars such as Trudier Harris, Robert Hemenway, Myles Hurd, and Sylvia Lyons Render, who wrote a biography of Chesnutt for the Twayne's United States Authors series and who compiled much of Chesnutt's short fiction in a collection published by Howard University Press. For scholars interested in the history of the reception of Chesnutt's work, Curtis W. Ellison and E. W. Metcalf's *Charles W. Chesnutt: A Reference Guide* (1977) provides invaluable references to and descriptions of post-Reconstruction reviews of Chesnutt's work that appeared in the national, regional, and local press.

Since the 1980s, the momentum of this renaissance has remained and branched out to include numerous approaches to Chesnutt's writing. From monographs such as William Andrews's *The Literary Career of Charles W. Chesnutt* (1980) and Ernestine Pickens's *Charles W. Chesnutt and the Progressive Movement* (1994) to wider critical studies, such as Houston Baker's *Modernism and the Harlem Renaissance* (1987), Eric Sundquist's *To Wake the Nations: Race in the Making of American Literature* (1993), and Richard Brodhead's *Cultures of Letters: Scenes of Reading and Writing in Nineteenth-Century America* (1993), Chesnutt has been increasingly placed in the fabric of African American and American literature. As several of our survey respondents noted, Sundquist's seminal study *To Wake the Nations* accorded Chesnutt a status that markedly exceeded the height of fame Chesnutt enjoyed in his lifetime. In his chapter "Charles Chesnutt's Cakewalk," which constitutes nearly a third of his seven-hundred-page book, Sundquist asserts that Chesnutt belongs among the major American fiction writers of the nineteenth and twentieth centuries. Sundquist places Chesnutt's work alongside that of Nat Turner, Frederick Douglass, Herman Melville, Martin Delany, Mark Twain, and W. E. B. Du Bois—in other words, alongside the authors who made the most incisive contributions to the national discourse about race in that period.

Perhaps the most significant contribution of *To Wake the Nations* is the larger premise that white culture simply does not exist apart from black culture. Sundquist sees Chesnutt as an artist working at the level of and in dialogue with craftsmen such as Twain and Du Bois, not as a local color author who reworked Thomas Nelson Page's dialect tales. Most significant, Sundquist highlights how Chesnutt's work, with its fraught interplay of form and racial themes, demonstrates how American writing must be understood as arising from interwoven traditions.

With the groundwork of established scholarship firmly in place, the interest in Chesnutt's work has blossomed in recent decades with more than 250 publications attending to Chesnutt listed in the *MLA Bibliography* between 2000 and 2016. This scholarship is showcased in prominent periodicals such as *PMLA, The African American Review, The Southern Literary Journal, American Literary Realism,* and *American Literary History*. Dissertations and monographs on Chesnutt's work and life also continue to appear with increasing frequency. Werner Sollors's reappraisal of Chesnutt in his *African American Writing: A Literary Approach* (2016) offers one of the most consequential recent interventions with his chapter "The Goopher in Charles W. Chesnutt's Conjure Tales: Superstition, Ethnicity, and Modern Metamorphoses," a study that deeply embeds Chesnutt not just in literary history but also in cultural history. Yet another direction in the field of contemporary Chesnutt studies is signaled by one of this volume's contributors, Gregory Laski, whose *Untimely Democracy: The Politics of Progress after Slavery* (2017) characterizes Chesnutt as a "prophet of pessimism" who speaks to the nation's failure to live up to its democratic ideals. It is clear that scholarly interest in Chesnutt remains vibrant and expansive.

With the appearance of a Library of America edition of Chesnutt that collects selected stories, novels, and essays (*Charles W. Chesnutt: Stories* [2002]); a Norton Critical Edition of his conjure stories (2011) and of *The Marrow of Tradition* (2012); scholarly editions of his journals (1993), letters (1997), and essays and speeches (1999); as well as new versions of out-of-print or previously unpublished novels, teachers and students now have the access to primary texts and the critical resources that allow them to explore his literature and its context in much greater detail than ever before.

At least part of Chesnutt's growing popularity can be attributed to the impressive variety of his literary and scholarly production. Its artistic and intellectual range is remarkable: numerous short stories, several novels, a biography of Frederick Douglass, and dozens of literary essays and speeches. His fiction moved in the modes of local color fiction, realism, naturalism, the gothic, and arguably even magic realism, and the topic of his essays ranged from racial segregation to education to politics to the law. As many scholars have noted, his literary work was divided between an overt concern with race and the treatment of race with extreme subtlety, if treated at all. In this latter category are the works often labeled as Chesnutt's Northern fiction, which were generally not as popular with the public. This fiction includes several short stories, the recently published novels *A Business Career* and *Evelyn's Husband*, and the yet unpublished *The Rainbow Chasers*.

One must also consider Chesnutt's presence in national and popular culture through his syndication in newspapers and periodicals across the country. As Charles Johanningsmeier has determined, because Chesnutt worked with McClure's, the dominant United States newspaper syndication company, his short stories likely reached hundred of thousands of readers across America on a regular basis for decades. Research tools only recently available to scholars, which will now allow digitized searching over many more periodicals and newspapers than Johanningsmeier could possibly have managed back in 1999, are surely going to teach us more about Chesnutt's reading audience and the different contexts in which his works were shaped. We understand his influence in terms of the high art venues of *The Atlantic Monthly* or the East Coast publishing establishment, but the future of Chesnutt studies will indubitably reveal new cultural contexts for assessing his work.

Available Editions

Because the available editions of Chesnutt's work have expanded exponentially since the 1990s, it can be a challenge to choose an edition to teach. In determining which editions to recommend, we strove to include books that provide helpful critical materials but are also affordable.

For Chesnutt's early fiction, the Penguin Classics edition *Conjure Tales and Stories of the Color Line* (1992) contains a critical introduction by William Andrews and all the stories from Chesnutt's first book of dialect tales (*The Conjure Woman*) and his second book ("*The Wife of His Youth*" *and Other Stories*). The collection includes two popular stories that did not appear in either book ("Dave's Neckliss" and "Baxter's Procrustes"). For teachers wanting to focus exclusively on the conjure tales, we recommend *The Conjure Woman and Other Conjure Tales*, which has a critical introduction by Richard Brodhead and contains seven additional conjure tales not included in the Penguin edition. The Norton Critical Edition of the conjure stories, edited by Robert Stepto and Jennifer Rae Greeson, contains the most resources for teachers and students (*Conjure Stories*). Teachers looking for the least expensive text for students should consider the Dover Thrift version of selected conjure tales and stories of the color line (*Tales*).

Chesnutt's first published novel, *The House behind the Cedars*, is available in many editions. We recommend the Penguin Twentieth Century Classics version, with an introduction by Donald B. Gibson. The University of Georgia Press also offers an edition, with a forward by William L. Andrews.

The best version of Chesnutt's most important novel, *The Marrow of Tradition*, is undoubtedly the Penguin Twentieth Century Classics edition, which offers a critical introduction by Eric Sundquist. Two other editions append considerable critical resources to the novel: the Norton Critical Edition, edited by Werner Sollors, contains wonderful selections of historical context and an historical overview of the critical reception of the novel since its original publication in 1901; the Bedford Cultural Edition of *Marrow*, edited by Nancy Bentley and Sandra Gunning, provides critical essays arranged by theme: "Caste, Race, and Gender after Reconstruction," "Law and Lawlessness," "The Wilmington Riot," and "Segregation as Culture: Etiquette, Spectacle, and Fiction."

For teachers seeking a comprehensive treatment of Chesnutt's work, we recommend the Library of America's collection. It contains *The Conjure Woman*, *The Wife of His Youth*, *The House behind the Cedars*, *The Marrow of Tradition*, uncollected stories, and selected essays. Although the cost of this edition is prohibitive for many teaching situations, teachers will find this book invaluable for their scholarship and teaching preparation. For teachers looking for a wide variety of Chesnutt's work in a less comprehensive format, there is *The Portable Charles W. Chesnutt*, which is edited by Andrews. In this collection there are short stories, *The Marrow of Tradition*, and three essays, "What Is a White Man?," "The Disfranchisement of the Negro," and "Post-Bellum—Pre-Harlem." For the last novel that Chesnutt published in his lifetime, *The Colonel's Dream*, we recommend the edition edited by R. J. Ellis.

Chesnutt's lesser-taught novels have been reappearing in print (and in some cases appearing in print for the first time) over the past two decades. The University of Illinois Press published a version of *Mandy Oxendine* with a forward by Andrews and an introduction by Charles Hackenberry. There are two editions of *Paul Marchand, F.M.C.*, one from the University of Mississippi, with an introduction by Matthew Wilson, and one from Princeton, with an introduction by Dean McWilliams. The University of Mississippi Press also brought out an edition of *A Business Career* and *Evelyn's Husband*, both with an introduction by Wilson. *The Quarry*, with an introduction by McWilliams, is available from Princeton University Press. Those open to using online versions (for class preparation or to assign to students) should be aware that the complete copies of many of Chesnutt's works (*The Colonel's Dream, The Conjure Woman, Frederick Douglass, The House behind the Cedars, The Marrow of Tradition,* and *"The Wife of His Youth" and Other Stories of the Color Line*) are available at the University of North Carolina's *Documenting the American South* Web site.

Archive Resources for Teachers

Chesnutt scholars have long benefited from his meticulous correspondence and the careful curation of his manuscripts by his family, archivists, and Chesnutt himself, who was always concerned with documenting his own legacy and development. Instructors are unlikely to turn to archival research for their teaching preparation, but it is helpful to know where the richest and most extensive collections of Chesnutt materials can be found. Many institutions have good finding aids, helpful links, and instructional materials developed to support their special collections. Since Chesnutt's business career and personal life were so intertwined with his literary craft, accessing images or copies of his stenography and photographs of him and his family can greatly enhance discussions of race, class, and culture of the time in which he wrote.

Fisk University's John Hope and Aurelia Franklin Library's Special Collections and Archives, located in Nashville, Tennessee, is the largest and best-known repository of Chesnutt materials. The Charles Waddell Chesnutt Collection here contains material beginning in 1864. Highlights are typewritten manuscripts, personal and business correspondence, notebooks and a journal, as well as photographs of Chesnutt, his family, and many prominent acquaintances.

Other major repositories of Chesnutt materials are the Western Reserve Historical Society and the Cleveland Public Library, both located in Cleveland. The Western Reserve Historical Society's collection is strong, not surprisingly, in materials related to his Ohio business career, which informed much of his literary work. Personal and business correspondence, clippings, copies of speeches, and other miscellany can be found here. The Cleveland Public Library holds numerous photographs of the Chesnutt family, many of which are readily available at cplorg.cdmhost.com/cdm/search/collection/p4014coll12.

Fayetteville State University's Charles W. Chesnutt Library features a Special Collections and Archives Library with detailed digital finding aids that can direct a reader to several of his letters online. While they hold over nineteen boxes of Chesnutt-related material, including correspondence, clippings, family deeds, wills, and other miscellany, there is some overlap with the collections at Fisk (see library.uncfsu.edu/archives/about-special-collections/finding-aid-for-charles-w-chesnutt).

Other letters and materials can be found in collections held by the Library of Congress, the Pennsylvania State University, Cornell University Library's James Lowell Gibb's Collection, the NAACP's Cleveland Branch, the University of Arkansas's David W. Mullins Library, and the Booker T. Washington collection held by Duke University. These collections all have Chesnutt archival material that might be of interest to students and instructors.

Chronology

1858	20 June. Charles Waddell Chesnutt is born to Ana Maria Chesnutt and Andrew Jackson Chesnutt in Cleveland, Ohio.
1866	The family moves to Fayetteville, North Carolina, his parents' home town.
1867	He begins to attend the Howard School.
1871	His mother dies.
1872	He starts work as an assistant teacher at the Howard School. He sells his first story to a weekly newspaper.
1873–76	He works as an assistant to the principal of the Peabody School in Charlotte, North Carolina. He teaches during the summer, unhappily, at various rural schools in North and South Carolina. He keeps a journal chronicling his extensive studies and begins his study of shorthand.
1877	He accepts a position as assistant principal of the State Colored Normal School in Fayetteville.
1878	He marries Susan W. Perry.
1879	His daughter Ethel is born.
1880	He becomes the principal of the State Colored Normal School. His daughter Helen is born. In his journal, he describes his commitment to writing as a "high, holy purpose" (*Journals* 139).
1883	He moves to New York City to work as a reporter for the Dow, Jones, and Company news agency. His son Edwin is born. In November he moves to Cleveland, where he begins work for the Nickel Plate Railroad.
1885	He begins studying law. He sells the short story "Uncle Peter's House" to the S. S. McClure syndicate. Other stories soon follow.
1887	He passes the bar exam but cannot make a living as a lawyer and thus works primarily as a stenographer. "The Goophered Grapevine" appears in the *Atlantic Monthly*.

1888   "Po' Sandy" is published in the May issue of the *Atlantic Monthly*.

1889   He launches his own stenography practice. He publishes "The Conjurer's Revenge," "Dave's Neckliss," "The Sheriff's Children," and other stories.

1890   His daughter Dorothy is born.

1898   He writes *A Business Career* but is unable to find a publisher for it.

1899   *The Conjure Woman* is published by Houghton Mifflin. His biography of Frederick Douglass is published by Smith, Maynard. *"The Wife of His Youth" and Other Stories of the Color Line* is published by Houghton Mifflin. He sells his stenography business in order to pursue full-time writing.

1900   *The House behind the Cedars* is published by Houghton Mifflin. The manuscript of his novel *The Rainbow Chasers* is rejected. His essay series The Future American runs in the *Boston Evening Transcript*, 18 August–1 September.

1901   He travels to North Carolina to research the 1898 Wilmington riots. *The Marrow of Tradition* is published by Houghton Mifflin. He meets with Booker T. Washington at Tuskegee and reports on Washington's project, with both appreciation and criticism, in *The Cleveland Leader*.

1902   He is blackballed from Cleveland's Rowfant Club on the basis of race (he satirizes the club in his 1904 story "Baxter's Procrustes"). Returns to working as a lawyer, stenographer, and notary public.

1903   He writes *Evelyn's Husband* but is unable to find a publisher for it.

1905   *The Colonel's Dream* is published by Doubleday, Page.

1908   He addresses the annual conference of the Niagara Movement (precursor of the NAACP, founded by Monroe Trotter and W. E. B. Du Bois).

1910   He is admitted to the Rowfant Club.

1912   He tours Europe with his daughter Helen.

1915   He protests screenings of the controversial film *The Birth of a Nation*.

1919   His collection of dialect stories *Aunt Hagar's Children* is rejected by Small, Maynard, and Company.

1920   His father dies.

1921   *The House behind the Cedars* runs as a serial in *The Chicago Defender*.

1924   The film version of *The House behind the Cedars*, directed by Oscar Micheaux, is released.

1927   The film version of *The House behind the Cedars* is initially banned by the Virginia Board of Censors for its depiction of race relations.

1928   He is awarded the Spingarn Medal by the NAACP for his extraordinary achievements in African American literature.

1932   He dies on 15 November.

1952   His biography *Charles W. Chesnutt: Pioneer of the Color Line* is published by his daughter Helen.

1974   His uncollected stories are published in *The Short Fiction of Charles W. Chesnutt* (Howard UP).

1997   *Mandy Oxendine*, a novella he wrote in the 1890s but was never published in his lifetime, is published by the University of Illinois Press.

1999   His novels *Paul Marchand, F.M.C.* and *The Quarry*, both rejected in the 1920s, are finally published by Princeton University Press.

2001   Library of America publishes *Charles W. Chesnutt: Stories, Novels, and Essays*.

2002   *The Chronicle of Higher Education* reports that he is the second most represented author at the American Literature Association conference, behind only Walt Whitman.

2005   *A Business Career* and *Evelyn's Husband*, neither published during his lifetime, are published by the University of Mississippi Press.

2010   *Mrs. Darcy's Daughter*, his only known play, never published in his lifetime, is published in the journal *Modern Language Studies*.

Part Two

APPROACHES

The Challenge of Teaching Chesnutt:
An Introduction to the Essays

Charles W. Chesnutt began his teaching career in the 1870s, working in rural schools for ex-slaves and their children in North Carolina. A Northern-born, upwardly mobile African American with a bookish bent and a slight build, he had a hard time of it. At best, he noted in his journal of 10 August 1874, he was able "to manage to manage." Yet there were "hard cases" among his students, and he did not find that teaching came easily (*Journals* 45).

It is notable, then, that this self-taught scholar included along with his nightly reading of Voltaire, Quintillian, and Dickens, the study of teaching. In his journal he writes about *The Theory and Practice of Teaching; or, The Motives and Methods of Good Schoolkeeping*, by David Perkins Page, an influential educator and principal of the State Normal School of New York. Chesnutt recognized that a teacher who truly wishes to help students must learn not just from his own experiences but from the experiences of others as well.

Eight years after this ruminating journal entry, the speech that Chesnutt delivered to the North Carolina State Teachers Educational Association, entitled "Methods of Teaching," was more assured. In it, he expressed an optimism in the future of education and the teaching profession:

> The world is yet in its infancy and a thousand years hence our knowledge will seem as crude, our methods as imperfect as those of the middle age appear to us. *Sursum corda!* ["Lift up your hearts"] my fellow workers! The perfect school, and the perfect teachers will yet exist, if not in this world, in a higher sphere, where the stores of infinite knowledge will be placed at our disposal, and we shall have an eternity in which to learn them. (51)

It is with this spirit of collegial support that we introduce this volume of essays to address issues and approaches to teaching selected works from Chesnutt's oeuvre.

Examining the history of the reception of Chesnutt's work gives us a spectacular example of how canon formation evolves according to both historical vicissitudes and contemporary notions of literary merit. Some essays in this collection outline for teaching purposes the very telling and particular historical relation that Chesnutt had with print culture. His popularity in today's classrooms arises in part from his insightful description of race, culture, and power relations in America at the end of the nineteenth century and the beginning of the twentieth. These issues were painful ones when he published his work, and they continue to be painful today. Keeping in mind this troubled history, this collection offers several strategies to help teachers negotiate this chapter of the sensitive yet vital history of oppression and prejudice in the United States.

In teaching Chesnutt's work, we encounter clear examples of how literature is, in many ways, what we make of it or how we present it. Students easily see how his stature at the beginning of the twentieth century was followed by his disappearance in terms of reprints and scholarly attention for most of the century. What, then, do we make of his ascendancy today in both the academy and in popular culture more broadly (in 2008 he appeared on a commemorative United States postal stamp)? Much of it is part and parcel of the solidification of African American studies in the academy, but the especially dramatic vicissitudes of his career and the history of his reception raise compelling questions for students about what is at stake in reading, editing, printing, and assigning particular writers. Chesnutt's oeuvre demonstrates, perhaps better than any other work currently appearing in American literature anthologies, the fraught and mercurial contingencies of aesthetic value.

The very vicissitudes of Chesnutt's life and writing make it a joy to teach his work, and the story of his reception and reputation reminds us that literary interpretations always have been and always will be biased, even by readers who pride themselves on keen and just perceptions. How are our own readings of Chesnutt tied to our particular twenty-first-century moment? What does it mean to have an evolving relation to a body of work? Was William Dean Howells ever able to go back to the *Conjure Tales* and Chesnutt's other plantation fiction and see these works as the resistant and defiant texts so many critics see today?

Some of the challenges Chesnutt poses for us now, in particular his use of dialect, were not unfamiliar to readers of his time, and the challenges he posed to his contemporary audiences remain challenges now. What is justice? Can there be reparation? Who controls a story, the author or the readers? What are the differences and similarities between class and caste? How are we haunted by the land and the landscape of American slavery, and how do we perpetuate that haunting? Audiences felt those questions then as we do now, and teachers will do well to reckon with such questions and harness them for the classroom.

Chesnutt often writes about painful issues in United States history that can be sensitive to address in a classroom—lynching, rape, human degradation in slavery, offensive racial stereotypes and language, and the constant burdens of nineteenth- and twentieth-century racism. Most of his writing presents formal challenges to teachers as well. His transcription of thick dialect, his complex use of narrative framing (especially in his conjure tales), his careful engagement of history and culture, and his complicated relation to the periodicals and publishing houses of his day can be difficult to incorporate into the classroom.

There is always the risk of flattening out the vibrancy of his work, of unintentionally reducing a sophisticated body of literature to, on the one hand, mere politics or, on the other, simplistic storytelling. Chesnutt stands as a great ethical thinker for students to engage and contemplate. Discussions of race often combine with questions for students about the role of literary forms, the goals and failures of high art, and other such vexed issues that aren't always immediately apparent to them. This collection seeks to offer practical suggestions and innovative strategies to walk teachers through these questions, so that they bring them into their courses when teaching the work of Charles W. Chesnutt.

Navigating through This Collection of Essays

This volume is organized to facilitate quick consultation by instructors in a hurry as well as to provide deeper and more sustained suggestions, ideas, and perhaps even cautionary tales for those seeking to plan and adapt different approaches for syllabus development and long-term exploration. All the essays offer content for short-term and long-term goals, and we have structured our volume to enable reference by work as well as by conceptual or thematic approach.

Since Chesnutt's use of dialect is steadily cited by scholars and instructors of Chesnutt as being the greatest challenge to teaching his fiction, in our opening unit two experienced scholars offer entries into the subtle sophistication of his linguistic representation. Drawing on linguistics, stenography, and poetics, they provide resources for teachers. The units that follow are divided both by genre and text and should open possibilities for provocative juxtapositions as well as sustained analyses of individual works.

The units overlap in topic, to be sure—the essays that focus on the short stories, for example, present critical and analytical context that would be useful for the teaching of Chesnutt's novels and essays. There is no denying what our instincts tell us and what the survey made in preparation for this volume has revealed: some of Chesnutt's works are more featured than others in the cultural and educational scene today and therefore merit more attention in the classroom. The growing popularity of *The Marrow of Tradition* in courses on literary realism, African American studies, and the American novel is so striking, for example, that this volume has several essays that discuss it. For another example, although some faculty members are weaving considerations of Chesnutt's biographical writing and posthumously published novels into their courses, we allocated little space for the analysis of these materials. Fortunately Chesnutt's oeuvre is so varied that each unit demonstrates the diversity of the works themselves. Less commonly taught works, such as *The Colonel's Dream* and "Aunt Mimy's Son," are featured alongside the better-known works, such as the conjure tales, in order to illuminate productive juxtapositions.

Different Ways to Group the Essays

Obviously, questions of race and United States racial history inform every essay in the collection and doubtless will shape the approach of instructors. Some essays more than others, however, grapple with the fraught dynamics of power and color in Chesnutt's work. For a teacher seeking to foreground this approach, the essays by Bauer, Sawaya, Moody-Turner, Gordon-Smith, Parham, Zeigler, and Lewis all present Chesnutt's acute attention to racial dynamics in concise and thought-provoking ways.

The facts of Chesnutt's life lend themselves to rich classroom connections and can provoke unexpected critical and historical context for the long arc of writing in the American experience. In the essays by Sussman, Koo, Gleason, Pickens Glass, Sawaya, Lewis, and Wagner-McCoy, aspects of Chesnutt's career that can inspire students to explore that life further are discussed.

The teacher interested in Chesnutt's engagement with other literary models and authors and in intertextual play should look at the essays by Ingle, Robbins, Bauer, Yothers, and Adams, which use writers such as Pauline Hopkins, Edgar Allan Poe, Walter Scott, Mark Twain, as well as historical journalism, to broaden the kinds of questions that can be asked in a college class on Chesnutt. There are essays that focus more specifically on literary methodology, such as realism, American magic realism and fantasy, the romance, the gothic, and genre analysis (Ingle, Adams, Simmons).

One could explore the issue of reader response to Chesnutt's literature through the essays by Koo, Glass, Yothers, and J. Miller. The essays that situate Chesnutt's literary contributions in historical contexts, such as the Wilmington race riots, eugenics, publishing history, legal theory, and Jim Crow America, are by Bauer, Adams, Mariano, Pickens Glass, Gordon-Smith, Laski, and Koo. To explore the relevance of Chesnutt today, one should look at the essays by Robbins, Gleason, Parham, Yothers, and Lewis, which challenge students with conversations about racial violence, the challenges of democracy, the literal and figurative borders of our nation, and, in the essays by Gordon-Smith and Parham, the literal and figurative borders of our own bodies.

There are essays particularly relevant to graduate teaching (Gleason, Robbins, Adams, Wagner-McCoy) and targeted more to undergraduate teaching (Glass, Harding, Ingle, Bauer, Parham, J. Miller, Laski, Yothers, Lewis). There are essays dedicated to teaching Chesnutt to special student populations and in special courses (Bauer, J. Miller, Laski, Yothers, Parham, Lewis, Simmons). There are essays that concern the media, both contemporary and historical (Koo, Sussman, Parham). There are essays that deal explicitly with how Chesnutt negotiates gender and sexuality (Harding, Wagner-McCoy).

While all the essays provide models for questions and class discussion topics, some concern themselves with modeling special activities and exercises. Gleason, for one, has students sketch out maps of Chesnutt's figurative and literal terrain, and Ziegler has students actually enact the drama of various scenes and dialogues. Miller gets his students to try their hands at nineteenth-century-style transcription, and Gordon-Smith shows his students how to search the Internet for references to race and disability and report on their findings in order to open up sensitive discussions of eugenics.

One wonderful aspect of Chesnutt's work is how it proves fruitful on examination in so many different contexts, courses, and theories. While Chesnutt published little after 1905 and passed away in 1932, his literature continues to give to us, as we find new ways to teach his work to new generations of students.

Toward a Usable Dialect:
Chesnutt's Language in the Classroom

Jeffrey W. Miller

When I first began teaching *The Marrow of Tradition*, I found that the first day of discussion was dominated by the book's opening chapter, even when the assignment included additional chapters. This is because the chapter provides important exposition voiced by "Mammy" Jane, whose speech Chesnutt renders in heavy dialect. My students recognized that information was being conveyed but often could not decipher it because of their inexperience with reading dialect literature. Specifically, as residents of the Pacific Northwest, they had little personal involvement with Southern dialect. I provided the needed translations— that is, we went over the narrative that Jane relates and together reconstructed its plot. This method was effective in the short term but did not help my students understand the dialogue of Josh Green or Jerry Letlow later in the book.

Furthermore, Chesnutt's language is so intertwined with his literary art that I do not think a reader who is missing what some of the main characters are saying can come to a considered analysis of the novel. The next time I taught *Marrow*, I began to develop a few exercises to help students see why Chesnutt chose to write using dialect and to acquaint them with his contemporaries who also wrote in dialect. As the students became more familiar with the language, they began to understand many other, related issues in Chesnutt's work. In short, these exercises made them more careful readers of Chesnutt and, by extension, of literature in general.

What follows is an account of the assignments I developed, in the hope that other teachers might be able to adapt them for use in their classrooms. I use the example of *Marrow* throughout, as it is the Chesnutt text I have taught most frequently, but this pedagogy is relevant to any of his dialect literature. Focusing on the dialect in his work has two benefits for undergraduate students: it helps them understand difficult material, and it provides a framework in which they can explore the complex themes and issues of Chesnutt's fiction. I see my approach to dialect in Chesnutt as holistic.

This essay details four interrelated assignments. The first three were devised to help students decipher Chesnutt's dialect; the fourth involves a particular discussion that resulted from this focus on dialect and language. Helpful practices in deciphering dialect are transcription, comparison, and recitation. Figuring out how written dialect works at a fundamental level makes it possible to explore more complex issues in Chesnutt's work—the issue, for example, of the relation between race and class. I also find that the concrete nature of dialect counters students' tendency toward abstraction. Students are quick to point out the different dialects of William Miller and Josh Green in *Marrow*, but they generally do not distinguish among the dialects of Josh, Jerry, and Jane. I ask them to look for differences in the way these characters use language and consider the extent to which those differences communicate aspects of racial or class-based identity.

A few days before we begin reading Chesnutt, I ask students to think about the relation between spoken English and written English. I point out that much of the literature we read utilizes so-called Standard English in dialogue at the expense of realism. If we listen to any person talking, we see that he or she rarely speaks in complete sentences or even complete words. Elisions are frequent, and interjections are common. It is important that my students recognize that Chesnutt's use of dialect was deliberate. I show them how he described writing dialect, and I ask them to listen to speech and transcribe it into writing.

From Chesnutt's nonfiction we read an excerpt of his explanation of how to be a law reporter and an excerpt of his letter to Walter Hines Page explaining his choices when writing in dialect. I like telling my students that many writers work traditional jobs in order to pay their bills. Herman Melville was a customs inspector, Wallace Stevens an insurance executive. Chesnutt had many jobs, but the most relevant to his dialect writing was his work as a stenographer and his creation of a stenography business. In "Some Requisites of a Law Reporter," he emphasizes the particular skills required in this work:

> The natural qualifications requisite for a successful law reporter are easily disposed of. Quickness of apprehension—the ability to "catch-on" quickly—is one; a reporter must understand, superficially at least, what is going on, and he has no time to study it out. Good hearing is another. When one is listening merely to understand, one word or sentence explains another; but when listening to record, each word, at least each sentence, must explain itself, and therefore must be heard distinctly. Quickness of movement is equally essential; the reporter who takes down correctly a rapid cross-examination has not a second to lose. His work must be even.

> The regularity of the piston stroke of an engine would hardly be sufficient to characterize it; it must be rather the steady flow of a stream of water, which pauses only when the initial pressure is interrupted.
>
> (*Selected Writings* 40–41)

Students know that recording, both audio and video, is a twentieth-century development but often do not appreciate the many ways in which oral speech needed to be translated into the written word on a daily basis when Chesnutt lived. Insightful students might notice that his choice of metaphor indicates that he saw stenography as organic (a stream of water) rather than mechanical (a piston stroke), which suggests a view of the skill as an art rather than a science.

Chesnutt writes about dialect and its literary transcription in a letter to Page, who was the editor of the *Atlantic Monthly* and the future partner of Doubleday, a firm that would publish some of Chesnutt's fiction:

> Speaking of dialect, it is almost a despairing task to write it. What to do with the troublesome r, and the obvious inconsistency of leaving it out where it would be in good English, and putting it in where correct speech would leave it out, how to express such words as "here" and "hear" and "year" and "other" and "another," "either" and "neither," and so on, is a "'stractin'" task. The fact is, of course, that there is no such thing as a Negro dialect; that what we call by that name is the attempt to express, with such a degree of phonetic correctness as to suggest the sound, English pronounced as an ignorant old southern Negro would be supposed to speak it, and at the same time to preserve a sufficient approximation to the correct spelling to make it easy reading.   (*"To Be"* 105)

The key here is the attempt to "suggest the sound" when writing dialect. Many students are struck by his claim that he is trying to write English as spoken by an "ignorant old southern Negro" and wonder why he seems so condescending. This is a great question, but at this point I usually defer it, asking them to think about his point of view as he depicts these characters in his fiction. Does the character of Jane in *Marrow*, for instance, fit this description? To what extent does Chesnutt depict her as ignorant? Is she a character or a caricature? These questions can be explored in more depth as we read further into the novel.

Transcription

Next we try our hands at writing dialect. I ask students to listen to the spoken word and transcribe it into writing. I tell them to be prepared to defend their orthographic and grammatical choices. One preparation for such an assignment might be to ask them to go out into the world and listen. However enlightening and interesting this exercise might be, it is also fraught with ethical complications. Students might get into tense situations with people who feel that their privacy is being violated. Also, my university's Institutional Review Board has rules governing field research with human subjects that make this exercise impractical.

I prefer a more controlled environment, and given the availability of online audio and video archives, such an environment is easy to create. The assignment could be homework or conducted in the classroom. An instructor could direct students toward a particular narrative or ask them to find something on their own. I generally offer a short recording (one or two minutes) and ask students to transcribe it in class. I loop it so that it repeats four or five times, then ask for three or four examples from the class and prompt students to comment on the differences and similarities between them.

Although there are many oral narratives available on the Internet, I like the Library of Congress *American Memory* site (memory.loc.gov/). Several of the WPA interviews with former slaves are available for downloading or streaming. I prefer to let the students read the transcription first, because the Library of Congress transcriptions are conservative: grammar is not corrected, but there is generally no attempt to approximate speech through orthography or other changes. For instance, the transcription for Alice Gaston includes the following sentence: "And I can remember when my missus used to run in the garden, from the Yankees and tell us if they come, don't tell them where they at." One could transcribe this sentence with a greater emphasis on the sounds that Gaston produces and be a bit more creative with orthography, employing the practices common in nineteenth-century dialect literature: "And I can rahmembah when muh missus use'ta run in de gyarden, from de Yankees an' tell us if dey come, don' tell dem where dey at."

Students almost always observe that transcription is difficult work. Keeping up with the recording, even when it is repeated several times, brings home Chesnutt's point that "quickness of movement" is an important skill for stenographers. If classroom technology allows, it is useful to provide the standard transcription while the students listen, with the understanding that they will adapt it along the lines that I adapted Gaston's sentence above. Modeling the exercise first is also helpful.

I make clear that it is a rare speaker who speaks in Standard English. One might illustrate this fact by playing an excerpt of a speech by John F. Kennedy. This president of the United States represents the epitome of mainstream success, yet his Boston accent is conspicuous and clearly nonstandard. One of my favorite moments is his call to go to the moon: "We choose to do these things not because they ah easy, but because they ah hod."

This exercise is intended not to create stenographers but to show students that writing dialect is integral to Chesnutt's literary project, that Chesnutt did not undertake it lightly, and that it is difficult work that has no rigid structures or obvious right answers.

Comparison

I give students this list of quotations from Chesnutt's contemporaries for them to see the range of dialect writing in the nineteenth century:

> Mark Twain, *Adventures of Huckleberry Finn* (1885): Yo' ole father doan' know yit what he's a-gwyne to do. Sometimes he spec he'll go 'way, en den agin he spec he'll stay. De bes' way is to res' easy en let de ole man take his own way. Dey's two angels hoverin' roun' 'bout him.
>
> Joel Chandler Harris, *Uncle Remus* (1881): Brer Fox went ter wuk en got'im some tar, en mix it wid some turkentime, en fix up a contrapshun w'at he call a Tar-Baby, en he tuck dish yer Tar-Baby en he sot 'er in de big road, en den he lay off in de bushes fer to see what de news wuz gwine ter be.
>
> Thomas Nelson Page, "Marse Chan" (1884): Yes, dat you! You gittin' deaf as well as bline, I s'pose! Kyarnt heah me callin', I reckon? Whyn't yo' come on, dawg?
>
> William Dean Howells, *A Hazard of New Fortunes* (1890): Ah-h-h-h-h, my dear poy! my gong friendt! my-my—Idt is Passil Marge, not zo? . . . It sheers my hardt to zee you. But you are lidtle oldt, too? Twenty-five years makes a difference. Ah, I am gladt! Dell me, idt is Passil Marge, not zo?
>
> Sarah Orne Jewett, *Country of the Pointed Firs* (1896): Your bo't ain't trimmed proper, Mis' Todd! . . . You're lo'ded so the bo't'll drag; you can't git her before the wind, ma'am. You set 'midships, Mis' Todd, an' let the boy hold the sheet 'n' steer after he gits the sail up; you won't never git out to Green Island that way. She's lo'ded bad, your bo't is,— she's heavy behind's she is now!

We talk about how some of the changes these writers make to Standard English are orthographic rather than phonetic—along the lines of the homophones that Chesnutt points out in his letter to Walter Hines Page. I ask students to indicate spellings that differ from Standard English but do not appear to suggest alternative pronunciation. They often notice, for instance, that Thomas Nelson Page spells "dog" as "dawg," that Jewett uses "bo't" for "boat," and Harris has "w'at" for "what" and "contrapshun" for "contraption." James Weldon Johnson calls this practice "clumsy [and] outlandish" in his preface to the *Book of American Negro Spirituals* (44), but it is common among dialect writers. Once students develop an eye for this sort of substitution, they usually observe that Chesnutt also employs it. For example, Jane and other characters say "w'en" for "when" and "wuz" for "was."

We discuss other ways in which these samples align, including the *d* for *t* or *th* substitution that Twain, Harris, and Page use to represent African American speech ("de news") and that Howells uses to represent German American speech ("dell me"). The point here is not to parse all these samples for fine distinctions but instead offer some context for Chesnutt's work and to give students a sense of the range of possibility in dialect writing.

Recitation

I incorporate recitation into our dialect work—the reading of passages aloud in class. Students tend to resist it, as they initially think they sound ridiculous. Some, regardless of their own ethnic identity, recognize that reading African American dialect carries connotations of caricature and racism. Those well-versed in American history find in this exercise troubling echoes of minstrelsy. For these reasons, reading aloud is on a volunteer basis, and we talk about why we are doing it. Most of the time, the resistance is minor (a few nervous laughs) and relatively short-lived. Students need to realize that their discomfort may be an essential prelude to an understanding of Chesnutt's work.

In his influential reading of *Marrow*, Eric Sundquist claims that Tom's imitation of Sandy at the cakewalk provides a lens by which we can view the many layers of racial performance in the novel (*To Wake* 273). That is, the question of what it means to act (talk?) black is at the heart of Chesnutt's literary project. Asking students to perform the novel's dialect (and performing it myself) may generate discomfort, but the discomfort can lead to productive discussions about race, language, and authenticity. Some relevant questions for these discussions: To whom does language belong? Is Chesnutt's use of dialect an appreciation of African American vernacular or an appropriation of it? How does his use differ from that of his white contemporaries?

Dialect as Discussion Starter

The focus on dialect opens up to the relation in Chesnutt's work between race and class. If I ask students to identify the class distinctions in *Marrow*, they are likely to note the obvious vocational difference between William Miller and Josh Green: one is a doctor, the other a laborer. But there are many other indications of class and caste in *Marrow* (and, indeed, in much of Chesnutt's work), and I have found that analyzing the dialect of the characters is a good way to begin that discussion.

Students are asked to find evidence in the dialect to support their observations of differences between Miller and Green—concrete details in the manner in which the two characters use language. By the time the class works through the transcription, comparison, and recitation exercises, they are attuned to how speech can be rendered by the written word and are ready to use it in their analyses.

I close this essay with a list of questions I have used with success in past discussions:

> How do the conversations between Miller and Green differ from the narrative frame of "The Goophered Grapevine" (given by the narrator and Julius)? What sort of social hierarchies emerge in this comparison?
>
> Compare how Miller and Burns chat on the train in chapter 5 to one of the Miller-Green conversations. How does their language use relate to their relationships?
>
> How do Jerry and Jane use language, and how does this use reflect their social positions?
>
> How is the speech of Carteret, Belmont, and McBane rendered, and how does their speech reflect their social positions?
>
> How do the expectations of the listeners in Chesnutt's dialogue shape the speech patterns of the speakers?
>
> Why is Tom's "darky dialect" as Sandy at the cakewalk not quoted by the narrator but merely described? ([ed. Sundquist] 118)
>
> How does Chesnutt's usage of dialect compare with Miller's philosophy of racial difference in chapter 5 ("personally, and apart from the mere matter of racial sympathy, these people [African American farm laborers] were just as offensive to him as to the whites in the other end of the train" [82])? In other words, it is possible to identify Miller as an elitist? Is Chesnutt also an elitist? In a broader sense, how is dialect used in literature related to democracy (especially in *Marrow*, the most explicitly political of Chesnutt's books)?

Releasing the Linguistic Shackles: Chesnutt's Verbal and Nonverbal Discourse

Mary E. Brown Zeigler

Aun' Peggy with Henry through Uncle Julius, "The Goophered Grapevine": "Nex' spring, w'en de sap commence' ter rise in de scuppernon' vime, Henry tuk a ham one night . . . ober ter Aun' Peggy's. . . . En bein' ez he fotch her de ham, she fix' it so he kin eat all de scuppernon' he want."
(*Conjure Woman* 38)

Liza Jane with Mr. Ryder, "The Wife of His Youth": "I'd know 'im 'mongs' a hund'ed men. Fer dey wuz n' no yuther merlatter man like my man Sam, an' I could n' be mistook. I's toted his picture 'roun' wid me twenty-five years." (*Portable Charles W. Chesnutt* 66)

Dasdy with Aunt Zillpha, "How Dasdy Came Through": "What's de matter wid yer, Dasdy?" asked Aunt Zilpha, looking up from the washtub at her good-looking daughter. "Dey ain't nuthin' de matter wid me," replied Dasdy, slamming her iron viciously on the ironing board . . . under a skillful hand. (249)

What do these three Chesnutt characters—Aun' Peggy, Liza Jane, and Dasdy—have in common? All these women are seriously involved in something important in their lives, and they all express family and community connections through both verbal and nonverbal communication. It is also apparent, from their discourse, that their families and communities are similar: the similarities in pronunciation (*de ham, de matter, wid me, dey*), the word form variation (*fotch, be mistook, ain't*), and the word choice, including Southernisms (*commence ter, toted*).[1] The verbal mode of communication is enhanced by the nonverbal message sender, such as body action ("slamming her iron viciously"). These Southern, African American characters may entertain us with their way of communicating, but many people disapprove of their language. Some may say to such a speaker, "Don't talk like that!" or "That's funny but you shouldn't really talk that way!" This objection is made now, and it was made in the nineteenth and early twentieth centuries during Chesnutt's time. Why then did Chesnutt use this means of discourse to deliver his community messages?

When this discourse is considered systematically, linguistically, students and teachers together can better understand his literary strategy. A simple step-by-step approach offers a way to learn about both Chesnutt's language and literature, for literature is language.

A Step-by-Step Approach to Teaching Chesnutt's Discourse

For teachers unfamiliar with Chesnutt's work and for students who are being introduced to it, I recommend that in this approach only one of these Chesnutt stories—"The Goophered Grapevine," "The Wife of His Youth," "How Dasdy Came Through"—be used. To address the verbal and nonverbal messaging in a story that relies heavily on dialect, we should ask, How does Chesnutt show respect for his community speakers at the same time that he makes their speech entertaining for his audience? This step-by-step approach to dealing with his vernacular will help students and teachers:

1. Read it.
2. Write it.
3. Speak it.

Step 1: Read It

Read through the story and ask, as you read, What is the message? How is it delivered? What are the place, the people, and the situation of the story? After reading, focus on a passage; examine how Chesnutt uses both verbal and nonverbal techniques to deliver his people's messages.

> AUN' PEGGY:
> Dey wuz a conjuh 'oman livin' down 'mongs' de free niggers on de Wim'l'ton Road, en all de darkies fum Rockfish ter Beaver Crick wuz feared er her. . . . Mars Dugal' hearn 'bout Aun' Peggy's doin's, en begun to flect whe'r er no he couldn't git her ter he'p him. . . . De' nex' dey Aun' Peggy come up ter de vimya'd. . . . She sa'ntered 'roun' 'mongs' de vimes, en tuk a leaf fum dis one, en a grape fum dat one, en a grape-seed fum anudder one; en den a little twig fum here, en a little pinch er dirt fum dere . . . en den fill' de bottle wid scuppernon' wine. W'en she got de gopher all ready en fix', she tuk 'n went out in de woods en buried it under de root uv a red oak tree, en den come back en tole one er de niggers she done goophered grapevimes.   (36–37)

It is important that Uncle Julius reports Aun' Peggy's actions. He is the insider man in charge for the community. His pronunciation gives strength with the consonant sounds—*d*- instead of *th*-, as in *dey* ("they"), *de* ("the"), *dat* ("that")—and with consonant reductions, such as *dey* ("there"), *'oman* ("woman"), *'mongs'* ("amongst"), *fum'* ("from"), and *'nex'* ("next"). The vowel sounds represented in the respellings provide the variation between the Northern and the Southern: *wuz* ("was" [like Southern *hug*, Northern *wall*]). Aun' Peggy, as described by Julius, is involved in the doing that controls the community in which she lives. She is the ultimate insider, having unspoken knowledge of the laws of nature. She seems to perform without hesitation the tasks requested of her and for which she is compensated. The verb *conjuh* (*conjure* and *conjuring*) is related to the accomplishment of the impossible ("Conjure"). It is synonymous with magic because of its association with supernatural powers and beings. Aun' Peggy, the conjure woman, delivers the supernatural power of cultural self-identity.

Even though he renders Aun' Peggy through Julius's dialect, Chesnutt clearly presents her as the highest accomplisher of the community.

> LIZA JANE:
> "Good-afternoon, madam," he said. "Good-evenin', suh," she answered, ducking suddenly with a quaint curtsy. Her voice was shrill and piping, but softened somewhat by age. "Is dis yere whar Mistuh Ryduh lib, suh?" she asked, looking around her doubtfully, and glancing into the open window. . . . "Yes! . . . I am Mr. Ryder. Did you want to see me?" "Yas, suh, ef I ain't 'sturbin' of you too much. . . . 'Scuse me, suh, . . . 'scuse me, suh, I's lookin' for my husban'. I heered you wuz a big man an' had libbed heah a long time, an' I 'lowed you wouldn't min' ef I'd come roun' an' ax you ef you'd ever heered of a merlatter man by the name er Sam Taylor 'quirin' roun' in de chu'ches ermongs' de people fer his wife 'Liza Jane?" She . . . went away, after thanking him warmly. . . . As she walked down the street with mincing step, he saw several persons whom she passed turn and look back at her with a smile of kindly amusement.   (63, 66)

In this passage, Liza Jane connects her outsider self with her insider heart. Her way of speaking—"like down in the old plantation days"—and her means of adornment—"she looked like a bit of the old plantation life"—register her message with Mr. Ryder. She demonstrates the head and the heart of his theory of self-worth: "'With malice towards none, with charity for all,' we must do the best we can for ourselves and those who are to follow us. Self-preservation is the first law of nature" ("*Wife*" 61). She pursues self-preservation no less than he does. His poetic connection with the British poet Lord Alfred Tennyson reminds him of his antebellum past and gives him hope for his postbellum future. Although Chesnutt renders the speech of Liza Jane in dialect, she also enacts Tennyson's message.

As she is leaving to return to her acquaintances, Mr. Ryder writes the address of where she is staying on the flyleaf of his Tennyson volume and, when she has gone, rises to his feet and stands looking after her curiously. As she walks down the street "with mincing step," he sees that several people whom she passes turn and "look back at her with a smile of kindly amusement." Liza Jane moves in an emotionally stirred yet politely refined manner that emphasizes and displays her feelings. Dancing for joy, performing a victory shout inherited from her African ancestors, she demonstrates her discourse style and its captivating nonverbal delivery.

> DASDY:
> Dasdy prayed mechanically but her heart was not in it; and she went home in a worse frame of mind than that in which she had gone to church. The next day she had the conversation with her mother, and this good old woman persuaded her to go to church and continue her prayers. "Try to get through dis week, Dasdy. De big baptizin' gwine ter come off next Sunday, and ef I was you I rudder be baptized at a big baptizin'." "I feel dat I'm gwine ter git through dis night," said Dasdy firmly. . . . At the church . . . somebody started one of the popular and stirring revival songs. During this hymn Dasdy was observed to slip from the seat where she was kneeling and fall to the floor, where she lay at full length, and half closed eyes, moaning and groaning, with occasional writhings and spasmodic movements of the limbs. "Sister Dasdy Williams under conviction," ran round the room. . . . "I b'leeve she's comin' through," said one sister, breathlessly. . . . Suddenly Dasdy sprang to her feet, her face beaming. Uttering a loud shout she jumped straight up and down for a dozen times. "Glory!" she cried; "oh, so happy! Praise de Lamb!" She threw her arms out sidewise . . . , still shouting . . . , and established her reputation for piety by the fine exhibitions of shouting she gave on that occasion.   (251–52)

Dasdy's discourse with her mother and with herself demonstrates the connection between the verbal and the nonverbal in her language community. When her mother says, "Try to get through dis week," the *get through* seems to mean "become finished" or "completed," as in attending a church service to the end. But when Dasdy replies, "I'm gwine ter git through," the stress indicated in the pronunciation delivers a different meaning. The hard voiced rhythmic velar stop [g] in her "gwine ter git" conveys determination.

Dasdy's breakthrough comes through the strong, spiritually inspired, and heartfelt encouragement from her mother to "[t]ry to get through dis week." And it is demonstrated subliminally by her "fine exhibitions of shouting," the vocal sound and the body action. Dasdy demonstrates both: the hollering attention-getting utterance and the more specialized body action, including the stomp—a personal, sacred, emotional expression of praise or a self-determined secular, emotional expression of joy:

> [S]hout'n' as DONE by Black folks is a whole-body act: a foot-stomping, limb-flailing, arm thrashing, sweat-popping, body-hurling, and a soul-freeing good time. Shout'n' signifies the shouter's innermost feelings; feelings too big and spirit-consuming to be reduced to mere words. It expresses joy, sorrow, and maybe even pent-up emotional burdens newly awakened.   (Zeigler 176–77)

Such shout messaging provides multiple means for demonstrating what cannot be expressed verbally, like the desire for answers to questions that go unasked: "Black people tend to shout because nothing has come close to making those of the African diaspora less determined, or less artistic, or less inventive, or less adaptable, or less productive, or less wise, or less creative, or less quite stupendously gorgeous" (Wiley 2). For Dasdy, shouting demonstrates that, as Nelson Mandela said, "a good head and a good heart are always a formidable combination" (131). Shouting, seen in the context of religious expression, is an empowering, spiritual weapon. When her outsider self and insider self come together in accord, Dasdy gains a personal victory.

Step 2: Write It

To show students the linguistic variations in Chesnutt's community language, ask them to write passages that illustrate his language patterning, then to rewrite each passage in standardized English. They should pay attention to the consistency of the patterning and indicate which patterns occur most often. Does a pattern indicate an authentic language difference?

> UNCLE JULIUS'S AUN' PEGGY:
> Dey wuz a conjuh 'oman livin' down 'mongs' de free niggers . . . , en all de darkies fum Rockfish ter Beaver Crick wuz feared er her.
> > Standard American English (SAE): There was a conjure woman living down among the free Negroes . . . and all the darkies from Rockfish to Beaver Creek were afraid of her.
>
> LIZA JANE:
> Is dis yere whar Mistuh Ryduh lib, suh?
> > SAE: Is this here where Mr. Ryder lives, sir?
> Yas, suh, ef I ain't 'sturbin' of you too much.
> > SAE: Yes, sir, if I am not disturbing you too much. . . .
> I'd come roun' an' *ax* you ef you'd ever heered of a merlatter man. . . .
> > SAE: I had come around to ask you if you had ever heard of a mulatto man. . . .
>
> DASDY:
> I feel dat I'm gwine ter git through dis night.
> > SAE: I feel that I'm going to get through this night.
> "Sister Dasdy Williams under conviction," ran round the room.
> > SAE: "Sister Dasdy Williams is under conviction," ran around the room.

Writing Chesnutt's discourse with such contrastive analysis reveals to students many aspects of his attention to language: pronunciation, lexicon, grammar, and syntax. The pronunciation variations involve notable consonants, like *d* for *th*, as in *de, dis, dat,* or *b* for *v,* as in *lib;* consonant cluster reductions or simplifications, including the absence of *-r, -xt, -nt, -nd, -rd* (*nex', Aun', roun', an', vimya'd* for "next," "Aunt," "round," and "vineyard"); and consonant metathesis, like *ax* or *aks* for "ask."

Lexical variations blend with pronunciation differences. Consider Uncle Julius, an insider, as he says *free niggers* and *darkies.* Does *niggers* represent consonant cluster reduction, *Neg'ai? Nigger* is the Anglicized form of the West African names *Niger* ("black") and *Nigeria,* creolized from Portuguese and Spanish ("Nigger").

A verb grammar contrast occurs with *ain't* or *isn't* or *is not* and with *gwine* for "be going to." Notice the absence of *is,* the present tense form of *be,* in the statement "Sister Dasdy Williams under conviction." It demonstrates a focus of the predicate strongly modifying the subject.

This is authentic language difference: the variations are systematic patterns, and their usage is substantiated by Anne H. Charity-Hudley and Christine Mallinson and by many other linguistic scholars (e.g., Fasold; Smitherman; Rickford and Rickford; Green; and Wolfram and Schilling-Estes).

Step 3: Speak It

Examine the strength of verbal interaction with nonverbal accompaniment by acting out a conversational passage. Set up the content from the discourse text as a theatrical performance, using the narrator as a character. Keep the language, especially with the pronunciations, as used in the conversation.

For example, when Liza Jane approaches Mr. Ryder sitting on his porch, there is also a narrator, therefore three characters. The narrator begins the discourse and tells as if in stage directions who is speaking and doing. The presentation should run from five to six minutes, and a written script should be provided for the audience.

> NARRATOR: Mr. Ryder rose from his chair and came over to where Liza Jane stood.
> MR. RYDER: Good-afternoon, madam,
> NARRATOR: Mr. Ryder said.
> LIZA JANE: Good-evenin', suh,
> NARRATOR: Liza Jane answered, ducking suddenly with a quaint curtsy. Her voice was shrill and piping but softened somewhat by age.

The discussion afterward should recognize the verbal as well as the nonverbal practice in addressing these questions: What is the message? Who is delivering it? To whom is it being delivered? How is it delivered?

This performance experience shows students the authenticity of language usage at the same time that Chesnutt's messages are being analyzed. The linguistic rules are accompanied by the reality of the natural human language.

This step-by-step approach to Chesnutt's sociocultural discourse helps teachers and students

> understand variation in oral discourse and its influence on written discourse
>
> analyze grammatical structures in written discourse and relate them to levels of comprehension
>
> read and revise lexical and semantic structures to heighten communication effectiveness
>
> free themselves from the linguistic shackles of Standardized American English

Chesnutt used his literary talents to entertain, even if his audience gave little or no attention to his message. However, he never stopped delivering the message of African American community strength.

Additional Resources for Teachers

After reading Chesnutt's work, teachers and students may wish to research his use of dialect more fully. Before going to critical texts, they should begin with videos and documentary films, which show the language interactions in their social contexts. *Colorless Green Ideas Sleep Furiously* reveals the insider affects and effects in community languages.

If you use this video in class, discuss its responses to true human language and compare some of the forms, functions, and meanings of that language with what Chesnutt does in his writing. Teachers can then turn to "English in America," a documentary that examines the external influences on the internal components of American English.

Black on White examines the influence that African Americans from West Africa had on English when they were brought by force to the American colonies. The Europeans and the Africans, two outsider groups coming together in America, develop into American insiders yet maintain their outsider affects on their new communities. This video provides useful background as it questions the problems of teaching Black English.

Understanding English Language Variation in U.S. Schools argues that language variation is essential to humanity because it allows speakers to be their own unique selves even when they communicate effectively with others in their communities and beyond (Charity-Hudley and Mallinson). "The book is for teachers who ask, 'Do these differences stand in the way of our students learning to read and write?' and, if so, 'What do we do about it?'" (Labov xiii). When teachers demonstrate positive attitudes toward language variation, they will help all students, and themselves, develop an appreciation for the richness of language and become more aware and respectful of language differences (Charity-Hudley and Mallinson 20–21).

Seeing standardized English in this way prepares us to understand the patterned discourse features in Southern American English as a regional and cultural variety and in African American English as an ethnic and cultural variety. When applied to Chesnutt's language usage, such research underlines the value of African American language and culture and reveals how the lack of knowledge of them creates a problem both for its speakers and for educators (Charity-Mallinson and Hudley 73–79).

Possible Writing Topics and Assignments

How does Chesnutt use verbal and nonverbal features together to represent caste, region, time period, or personal and social identity? Select a feature, give examples of it, and explain its function. What do critics and linguists say about this feature in literary texts or in the works of Chesnutt?

When Dasdy is "slamming her iron viciously on the ironing board," what message does that send to her mother? What is the verbal context that accompanies the action? What is the personal situation that prompts it? What effect does it have? If this statement had been written in another way, would the message be the same?

A writing assignment that addresses such questions can be developed into an oral research essay. Focus on one aspect of Chesnutt's use of language and study that use independently with the help of the critical literature and general references.

NOTE

[1]*Tote* ("carry") is a term from Kikongo, the Bantu language that is the lingua franca throughout west central Africa. Kikongo was transported into the American South through Africans in the Gullah Geechee Cultural Heritage Corridor, which runs from coastal North Carolina to Florida.

TEACHING THE SHORTER WORKS

Visualizing the Landscape of Slavery:
Architecture and the Built Environment
in the Conjure Stories

William Gleason

The fictions of Charles W. Chesnutt demonstrate a profound and abiding inter-est in architecture and the built environment. He uses built forms in his novels and short stories not only to concretize their settings but also to carry sym-bolic weight: think, for example, of the partially screened home at the center of his novel of passing, *The House behind the Cedars,* or the looming staircase at whose foot Dr. Miller stands in the final paragraph of *The Marrow of Tradition.* The conjure stories are particularly important in this regard, because they take place in a specific historical and architectural landscape that students often know little about: the built environment of slavery in the antebellum South. While many students may understand slavery as a system of oppression, few have a clear sense of the ways in which slavery's built environment gave physi-cal form not only to the power of the slave owners but also to the strategies of rebellion undertaken by the slaves. In Chesnutt's conjure tales, these spatial dynamics become powerfully visible and are central to his investigation of the history of American race relations. Indeed, in organizing the tales around the spaces of slavery, Chesnutt even takes care to arrange each tale architecturally, using the scaffolding of a frame story to prop up the narrative interior furnished by Uncle Julius, a former slave.[1]

In this essay I describe how teachers can help students understand the im-portance of architecture and the built environment for Chesnutt's storytelling through a close focus on the conjure tales. Using diagrams of the typical layouts of slave plantations like the ones featured in these tales, as well as historical photographs of slavery's actual structures, from the big house and slave cabins to the variety of outbuildings in which slaves labored, students can begin to visualize the physical and symbolic buildingscape imaginatively reconstructed by Julius at the heart of every conjure tale. Such a lesson plan helps students see the relation between space and power in slavery and how Chesnutt uses landscape in his stories to critique the oppressive social and political relations that endured during Reconstruction (the setting of every frame story) and continued to endure in the 1880s and 1890s (when he published all but one of the tales). There are several excellent sources in which teachers may find these diagrams and images, including John Michael Vlach's *Back of the Big House*, which uses photographs and drawings from the Historic American Buildings Survey to recreate the built environment of slavery; Catherine W. Bishir's *North Carolina Architecture*, a photographic history of the private and public buildings of North Carolina; and the National Humanities Center's *The Making of African American Identity, Volume I: 1500–1865*, an online library of primary resources that includes a detailed section on plantation life under slavery ("Plantation Life").[2]

This approach to teaching Chesnutt's conjure tales not only gives students a concrete and contextual sense of the spatial relations described in his work; it also shows them the value of using material culture in the interpretation of literary texts. Chesnutt knew the material history of slavery and wanted to bring its lessons to bear in his fictions and for his audience. By reconstructing the physical landscape described in the tales, teachers can help students visualize the built environment of slavery both as it existed in history and as Chesnutt transformed it imaginatively in his stories.

How you might prepare for this kind of contextualization will vary depending on the type and size of class you are teaching as well as on how many of Chesnutt's conjure tales you have in the syllabus. I have done such contextualization with large classes and small, with graduate students and undergraduates, in survey courses on American literature and in courses on literature and environment (both natural and built). This approach can work with a single Chesnutt story (with "The Goophered Grapevine" and "Po' Sandy" especially), with all seven stories of the 1899 edition of *The Conjure Woman*, or with Chesnutt's full repertoire of fourteen conjure tales.

There are a few ways you might prepare the class for this kind of work. It might be helpful for them to know, for example, that Chesnutt was quite familiar with the region in which he set the conjure tales—Cumberland County, North Carolina, particularly around Fayetteville—having moved there at age eight and lived and worked in the area (with the exception of three years in and around Charlotte) until he was twenty-five. His stories often include real place-names and building names, and their descriptive details bear a "striking fidelity," as Sarah Ingle notes, to "the Fayetteville region's important landmarks and geographical features" (150). Students could be given copies of the two superb maps that preface her essay, which set in context the broad "terrain" of

Chesnutt's conjure tales and provide a closer look at the Cumberland County "neighborhood" described by Julius. These maps also mark the locations of some of the structures (e.g., plantations, mills, houses) that you might ask students to analyze later in the activity.

When you move to the stories themselves, you might choose one of two strategies. The first is inductive: have students generate lists of key structures, buildings, and places mentioned in the story or stories assigned, then consider which structures, buildings, and places appear to carry the most significance and why. (If there is limited time, you can ask them to do this work beforehand.) If you are teaching only one or two stories, you can have each student create a list (or pair students up, for more active learning) and then compare the lists. If you are teaching a large number of stories, you can divide the task up (perhaps assigning several students or student pairs to each story) and ask them to collate their findings. The point of this approach is to avoid lecturing the students on architectural history or the buildingscape of slavery, instead letting them try to map out the built environment themselves using Chesnutt as their guide. As your class assembles and then shares or compares the data, you can ask them more pointed questions. For example, in what kinds of structures or spaces does Chesnutt set the main action of the story? Does the built environment that appears in the story's frame (the opening and closing sections told by John, which are set in the narrative present of Reconstruction) differ from the built environment of the story interior (the tale told by Julius, which is set during the storytelling present of slavery)? How do the differences mark—or fail to mark—the differences between slavery and Reconstruction? This approach asks students to decide, from the evidence in the stories, how the built environment shapes the lives of the characters and the telling of the tales.

The second strategy is deductive: you give students specific historical information about the built environment of slavery and then ask them to read the stories. For example, you might show them some of the reconstructed views and site plans of antebellum plantations depicted in Vlach or Bishir or at *The Making of African American Identity* Web site. (In Vlach, try the aerial view and site plan of Uncle Sam Plantation in St. James Parish, Louisiana [fig. 12.45 and 12.46]; in Bishir, the view of Coolmore Plantation in Edgecombe County, North Carolina [fig. 3.138]; at *The Making of African American Identity*, the map of Green Hill Plantation in Campbell County, Virginia, or the plot plan of Thornhill Plantation in Greene Country, Alabama.)[3] You can also try a general online image search for other antebellum plantation site plan sketches. (One recreated site plan of the Tullie Smith House in Atlanta, Georgia, highlights the placement of a "scuppernong arbor" not far from the main house [T. Jones], a very suggestive detail if you are teaching "The Goophered Grapevine.") The point is not so much to find the perfect plan as it is to have students recognize the spatial and structural divisions inherent to slave plantations: the central position of the big house; the collateral distribution of the slave quarters, which are usually apart from the big house but close enough to be kept under the surveillant eye of the master; and the arrangement of other structures (especially smokehouses, barns, and gardens) that belong to the slave owner but are tended by the slaves. How does Chesnutt use these divisions in his stories? Where on the plantation, whether in the frame tale or the inner tale, does the main action take place? Who appears in those spaces, and how are they used? How closely do Chesnutt's plantation layouts resemble the site maps of actual plantations? For an advanced class, you could also assign short excerpts from a volume like Clifton Ellis and Rebecca Ginsburg's *Cabin, Quarter, Plantation*, an excellent source for analyses of the built environments in Chesnutt's stories.

Whether you ask students to work inductively or deductively, they can draw their own interpretive maps, following the example of Ingle's terrain maps but zooming in more to depict the layout, for instance, of the fictional McAdoo plantation on which Julius was formerly a slave and whose grounds John and Annie purchase at the beginning of "The Goophered Grapevine." (Making maps in class is not only fun but also produces more variety than you might imagine. If you want to get a lively conversation going, have students compare their maps.) Drawing a decent map of the McAdoo plantation will likely require reading several of the stories, but you can have students work with just one story and ask them to make educated guesses about the rest of the details: What other structures are likely there, and where would they be? What other structures are likely to have disappeared and why? Having students defend their choices against those of other students can lead to spirited discussion.

There is great value in letting students draw their own conclusions about the material relations that structure Chesnutt's tales, but there are also specific sites and structures in his stories to which you can draw their attention for more focused work. Here are four:

1. The Patesville Market House Described at the Beginning of "The Goophered Grapevine"

> [A]fter several days of leisurely travel, the last hundred miles of which were up a river on a sidewheel steamer, we reached our destination, a quaint old town, which I shall call Patesville, because, for one reason, that is not its name. There was a red brick market-house in the public square, with a tall tower, which held a four-faced clock that struck the hours, and from which there pealed out a curfew at nine o'clock.   (*Conjure Woman* 32)

Patesville was Chesnutt's invented name for Fayetteville, and the red-brick market house on the town square invokes an actual building that still stands in the center of town. If you have students work inductively, don't tell them about the original structure; instead ask them to tell you about the market house as Chesnutt describes it. What does it mean for it to be in the public square? Why have a market house there—why not a bank, church, or some other kind of structure? What might transpire at a market house? Why emphasize the tall tower or the "four-faced clock that struck the hours" or the nine o'clock curfew? (Whose curfew is this and why?) You might ask them to draw the market house. Then show them a picture of the actual building. (There is a very good image in Bishir [173], and a smaller one in the Norton Critical Edition [*Conjure Stories* 165]. You can also find similar images in an online search.) Is that what they imagined? Why or why not?

The long opening paragraph in which this description appears was among the few substantive additions Chesnutt made to "The Goophered Grapevine" when he revised the original 1887 *Atlantic Monthly* version for inclusion as the lead story in *The Conjure Woman*. He wanted to make sure readers had this picture in mind before they proceeded to the rest of the book. Why begin the book this way? If your students suspect that the market house traded slaves among other commercial products, they're right—traffic in human beings was among the activities that defined the public square in Fayetteville (indeed throughout the antebellum South), and this building did hold slave markets (see Ingle 155). As both artifact and symbol, the market house fittingly marks the entrance to a book in which an ex-slave tells stories about slaves who are traded from one owner to another, who are watched over by their masters (much like the "four-faced clock," an overseer in brick), and who have their movements strictly curtailed (in contrast to the "leisurely travel" John experiences). Your students might well decide that the "deeper currents" lurking beneath the "somnolent exterior" (32) of Patesville are already embodied in the hidden but not-so-hidden history of that central market house.

2. The Kitchen Annie Wants John to Build Her in "Po' Sandy"

> One day my wife requested me to build her a new kitchen. The house erected by us, when we first came to live upon the vineyard, contained a very conveniently arranged kitchen; but for some occult reason my wife wanted a kitchen in the back yard, apart from the dwelling-house, after the usual Southern fashion. Of course I had to build it.
>
> (*Conjure Woman* 44–45)

Unlike the Patesville market house, which does not appear again (at least in physical form) in "The Goophered Grapevine," the kitchen in "Po' Sandy" is central to every section of the story: the opening frame, the interior tale, and the closing frame. In the opening frame, Annie's desire for a new kitchen—which John decides to construct by tearing down and repurposing the old schoolhouse on his new property—leads John, Annie, and Julius to the local sawmill, where John plans to place an order for the additional lumber he'll need. In the inner tale, the "moanin', en groanin', en sweekin'" (45) of the saw at the mill prompts Julius's reminiscence of the story of Sandy, the slave protectively conjured by his wife, Tenie, into a tree that is then gruesomely milled for lumber to build "a noo kitchen" (50), which itself is torn down and repurposed into a schoolhouse when Sandy's restless spirit frightens everyone away. In the closing frame, Annie's

decision to forgo using the lumber from the old schoolhouse, which Julius inti-
mates is still haunted by Sandy's ghost, makes John feel that he has been duped,
particularly when he learns that Julius asked permission to use the old schoolhouse for church meetings.

Architecture and the built environment play such a prominent role in this
story that students will find a good deal to talk about without much prompting: the analogy between Sandy's mutilated body and the structural violence of
slavery; the ways that violence haunts the built environment of the plantation,
where every building is a crime; the irony of Annie's "occult" desire to replace a
perfectly convenient kitchen with one separated from the main house, "after the
usual Southern fashion." Ask students why Southern plantation kitchens were
typically detached from the main house. They will likely answer that the exces-
sive heat of the region necessitates a backyard arrangement, yet they would be
only partly correct. As Vlach notes, there were "other important if less immediately evident reasons for planters to detach the kitchens from their residences,"
which was already common in the early eighteenth century:

> Moving such an essential homemaking function as cooking out of one's
> house established a clearer separation between those who served and
> those who were served. Until the last decades of the seventeenth cen-
> tury, slaves and their masters (at least in the Chesapeake region) lived
> and worked in close proximity, often in the same rooms, and sometimes
> shared a common identity as members of a plantation "family." But this
> day-to-day intimacy was progressively replaced by a stricter regimen of
> racial segregation that was expressed by greater physical separation. The
> detached kitchen was an important emblem of hardening social bound-
> aries and the evolving society created by slaveholders that increasingly
> demanded clearer definitions of status, position, and authority.   (43)

As Margaret D. Bauer has suggested, the "occult" reason behind Annie's wish
may be a desire to playact what Annie thinks it means to live in "the usual
Southern fashion," a fantasy that Julius's story quickly sours for her (26). If you
send your students to the *OED*, one of them might discover that an early meaning of *occult*, still operative in the late nineteenth century, was material rather
than metaphorical: "hidden from sight; concealed (by something interposed);
not exposed to view" ("Occult"). The spatial arrangement of a backyard kitchen
could cut two ways at once, screening plantation kitchen workers from the serv-
ing spaces of the main house while also providing a zone of relative privacy and
autonomy for those workers.

3. John and Annie's Piazza

> One Sunday afternoon in early spring,—the balmy spring of North Caro-
> lina, when the air is in that ideal balance between heat and cold where

one wishes it could always remain,—my wife and I were seated on the front piazza, she wearily but conscientiously ploughing through a missionary report, while I followed the impossible career of the blonde heroine of a rudimentary novel. I had thrown the book aside in disgust, when I saw Julius coming through the yard, under the spreading elms, which were already in full leaf. He wore his Sunday clothes, and advanced with a dignity of movement quite different from his week-day slouch.

"Have a seat, Julius," I said, pointing to an empty rocking-chair.

"No, thanky, boss, I'll des set here on de top step."

(*Conjure Woman* 70)

This description in "The Conjurer's Revenge" marks the first appearance of the piazza in the tales and an important stage, Robert B. Stepto has argued, in the development of the physical environment of the first three conjure stories composed by Chesnutt:

The movement from the log of the first story ["The Goophered Grapevine"] to the carriage of the second ["Po' Sandy"] to the piazza of the third ["The Conjurer's Revenge"] communicates that John and Annie are now fully in residence in the South and that a traditional context for storytelling has been constructed. Moreover, it suggests a didactic strategy expressed through the siting of storytelling which plays a major role in the education of John and Annie as listeners. More so than the log or carriage, the "reconstructed" piazza of a southern plantation Big House is a "charged field," full of reference to history and ritualized human behavior. (46)

Part of that history and ritualized behavior is reflected in Julius's hesitation, despite his Sunday "dignity," to accept the invitation to join John and Annie on their front piazza. The piazza, after all, though technically outside the planter's house, is both an extension of the slave owner's authority and a conspicuous marker of his leisure. Piazzas appear in nine of the fourteen conjure tales, including the final four tales of the 1899 *Conjure Woman* volume. In my own work, I have traced some of the hidden racial histories of the Southern plantation piazza. In class, particularly if you are teaching a large set of stories, you might simply encourage students to keep track of the piazza's appearance (or absence) in each story and the encounters it makes possible. How does the space of the piazza help illuminate the developing relationship between Julius, John, and Annie in the frame tales, for example? What role do the piazzas that appear in Julius's inner stories play in Chesnutt's reimagining of slavery?

These three sites and structures—the market house, the detached kitchen, and the piazza—are generally the most productive spaces for analysis in the conjure tales. The final example might work well with more advanced students or in classes devoted primarily to Chesnutt, and it works best when you are able to assign multiple stories.

4. All the Various Outbuildings Mentioned or Described in the Tales

> Dave en Dilsey made up dere min's fer ter git married long 'bout Christmas time, w'en dey'd hab mo' time fer a weddin'. But 'long 'bout two weeks befo' dat time ole mars 'mence' ter lose a heap er bacon. Eve'y night er so somebody 'ud steal a side er bacon, er a ham, er a shoulder, er sump'n, fum one er de smoke-'ouses. De smoke-'ouses wuz lock', but somebody had a key, en manage' ter git in some way er 'nudder. Dey's mo' ways 'n one ter skin a cat, en dey's mo' d'n one way ter git in a smoke-'ouse,—leastways dat's w'at I hearn say.   (*Conjure Woman* 127)

The outbuildings in Chesnutt's tales might be barns ("A Deep Sleeper," "Mars Jeems's Nightmare"), smokehouses ("The Goophered Grapevine," "Dave's Neckliss"), slave quarters ("The Gray Wolf's Ha'nt," "Sis' Becky's Pickaninny"), or off-plantation sites like Aunt Peggy's cabin ("Hot-Foot Hannibal," "Mars Jeems's Nightmare," "A Victim of Heredity"), where specific kinds of transactions—including those that challenge the slave owner's power—take place. Considering them will enable students to fill in the spatial and architectural contours of their maps, physical or mental, of the stories and can complement or complicate the readings of more prominent spaces, like the piazza or the plantation house. As these secondary structures are sometimes sites of resistance to slavery, asking students to think about Chesnutt's use of them can help your class imagine more fully the ways in which slaves at times coopted plantation space for their own purposes. By mapping these outbuildings, students will develop a sense of the larger terrain of the plantation, including the pathways that link one structure to another and that provide the routes of circulation that slaves used every day.

Each of these activities and approaches helps students visualize Chesnutt's imagined plantations as consciously built environments in which architecture is both a sign and source of power—power that nonetheless may be challenged, if not undermined, by its bondsmen and bondswomen.

NOTES

[1] One story, "The Dumb Witness," alters this framework by having John narrate the full tale after having heard it originally from Julius.

[2] Another useful resource is the digital archive of the Historic American Buildings Survey itself, hosted at the Library of Congress (www.loc.gov/pictures/collection/hh/).

[3] The aerial view and site plan of Uncle Sam Plantation, as well as the drawings of the Green Hill and Thornhill plantations, are also available online at the Historic American Buildings Survey.

Teaching Chesnutt's Ghosts

Janaka Lewis

In the light of the racially fraught events that have happened throughout the United States of America since the turn of the twenty-first century, including the 2012 death of Trayvon Martin, a Florida teenager, and the 2014 death of Michael Brown, a teenager in Ferguson, Missouri—both victims of cross-racial gun violence that continues to occur—teachers from elementary and secondary levels and college educators have had to not only interpret the news for themselves but also decide how (and even whether or not) to discuss it with their students. Whether educators have been trained to select and utilize texts that will help shape conversations about race in America in their classrooms is not the only question; in addition, we must ask how they can use tools that are already part of their lessons for this purpose. The study of literature is, of course, an essential part of the curriculum, and teachers are responsible for interpreting current events and society through literary texts.

Literature is an ideal avenue to teach young people about race because it offers a space for them to deal with loaded political, historical, and emotional issues. Charles W. Chesnutt's use of fiction to shape the social consciousness of his reading audience, and specifically his representation of race as literally and figuratively a ghostly incubus, is an especially good example. The ghosts that haunt his fiction can help students understand racial history, particularly the way in which the past demands recognition and reckoning.

An educator turned author who was published in the late nineteenth and early twentieth century, Chesnutt interpreted racial conflict and representation. His short story "Po' Sandy" (1898), his novel *The Marrow of Tradition* (1901), and even his 1899 biography of Frederick Douglass can be used as models in a range of classrooms to depict complex layers of racial interaction. Using the tropes of ghosts and haunting, first with the represented life of Douglass, then with the wisdom of Uncle Julius in "Po' Sandy," and finally with the complex plot of *Marrow of Tradition*, this essay shows how Chesnutt's way of approaching race relations can enlighten American students today.

Lesson 1: The Incubus of Race through Biography

Chesnutt repeatedly attempted to make sense of the racial inequities that pervaded American society during and after slavery. He found the trope of the incubus to be a powerful way to signify how race had always haunted and likely would always haunt his country.

In his biography of Douglass, written for the series Beacon Biographies of Eminent Americans and published by Small, Maynard and Company in Boston, he represents slavery as an incubus that haunted Douglass's life. This notion is antithetical to students' inclination to think of slavery as something in history to be shaken off or forgotten after the Civil War. It also demonstrates how biography can be a creative, imaginative text. Chesnutt relentlessly returns to historical presence lived alongside living presence, not just for Douglass or even for modern African Americans but also for all Americans. Through the trope of the incubus he illustrates the persistent weight of race at the turn of the twentieth century.

Students will probably already have learned in school that Douglass is a figure in both the literary and the historical canons. Chesnutt adds to this awareness by writing that Douglass's *Narrative* is "perhaps the completest indictment of the slave system ever presented at the bar of public opinion" (*Frederick Douglass* 2). He continues, "The real importance of his life to us of another generation lies in what he accomplished toward the world's progress which he only began to influence several years after his escape from slavery" (6). Douglass had written his narrative at least three times by the time Chesnutt wrote the biography, and Chesnutt recounts some of those details: for example, Douglass's life in the Auld house, where Douglass was learning to read before his master, Hugh Auld, prohibited his wife from teaching Douglass, who then learned to write at a shipyard. Chesnutt invokes these episodes as an incubus of slavery that became a ghostly burden Douglass had to overcome. Tracing this trope in class gives students a more nuanced understanding of history and lived experience in, if not Douglass's life, then at least Chesnutt's vision of it.

Chesnutt describes what Douglass and other African Americans faced before and during the early twentieth century:

> The average American of to-day who sees, when his attention is called to it, and deplores, if he be a thoughtful and just man, the deep undertow of race prejudice that retards the progress of the colored people of our own generation, cannot, except by reading the painful records of the past, conceive of the mental and spiritual darkness to which slavery, as the inexorable condition of its existence, condemned its victims, and, in a less measure, their oppressors, or of the blank wall of proscription and scorn by which free people of color were shut up in a moral and social Ghetto, the gates of which have not been entirely torn down.   (viii)

His account was largely shaped by Douglass's success: "But even all this did not entirely crush the indomitable spirit of a man destined to achieve his own freedom and thereafter to help win freedom for a race" (17). This "spirit" helped Douglass fight those who physically oppressed him, escape to New York, then to New Bedford, where he worked on caulking jobs and changed his name. He not only overcomes the baggage that slavery placed on him but works to liberate others as well. Chesnutt writes, "Here, then, in a New England town, Douglass began the life of a freeman, from which, relieved now of the incubus of slavery, he soon emerged into the career for which, in the providence of God, he seemed by his multiform experience to have been especially fitted" (27). Douglass survives and goes on to fulfill the destiny God set forth for him, but tragically many people were not able to do the same thing.

The Douglass biography shows how for Chesnutt a lived experience was shaped by a ghostly presence. Teachers could use his documentation of a life that was already written to discuss how he read not only a text but also a life in order to reread the institution of slavery. The narrative of the biography moves from what haunts Douglass to what he triumphs over. By comparing Douglass's work with what Chesnutt knew and had learned about enslavement, he was able to read and write Douglass in a new American context, while not losing sight of the history that made Douglass's triumph so notable.

Lesson 2: The Incubus of Race through Short Fiction

Many of Chesnutt's tales feature spectral presences, but few are as horrifying and resonant as the one in "Po' Sandy," and the tale works in the classroom to focus students on how both African American and white characters must bear the weight of memory. Told through the eyes of a Northern couple who moved to central North Carolina, "Po' Sandy" is one of Chesnutt's first offerings in *The Conjure Tales* (1898), and it sketches out a reversal of a racial relationship through the ghost of an African American woman, Tenie. Uncle Julius, the coachman, storyteller, and voice of history in the tales, teaches John and his wife, Annie, about the history of the town when they seek to build a new kitchen in a building that was used as a schoolhouse before the Civil War. When the couple wants to purchase lumber for the new kitchen from the sawmill, Julius warns them that the wood is haunted: it came from a tree that Tenie, a "cunjuh 'oman," had turned her husband, Sandy, into in order to keep him from being separated from her. "Ef you'll des say de word, I kin turn you ter w'ateber you wanter be, en you kin stay right whar you wanter, ez long ez you mineter'" (*Conjure Woman* 48). Sandy becomes a "big pine-tree," which dogs track for his scent but can't find him at all.

The story details Sandy's "trials en tribberlations," including a relentless woodpecker that left a scar, but although Tenie is determined to turn Sandy back, she does not reach him before he is chopped up to build a new kitchen for Mars Marrabo. Uncle Julius relates how Sandy was chopped, how he resisted the chain and rolled down the hill as logs, how Tenie wanted to turn him back even though he couldn't lived chopped up "long ernuff fer ter 'splain ter' im dat she hadn' went off a-purpose, en lef' 'im ter be chop' down en sawed up" (51). Tenie was locked in the smokehouse because her "splainin" looked like crazy spells, and she was kept to nurse "nigger chilluns w'en dey mammie wuz ter wuk in de cotton-fiel'" (52).

Julius continues, "De noo kitchen Mars Marrabo buil' wuzn' much use, fer it hadn' be'n put up long befo' de niggers 'mence' ter notice quare thangs erbout it," such as moaning, groaning, and "a-hollerin' en sweekin' lack it wuz in great pain en sufferin'" (52). As Tenie was the only one who could tolerate the noise, Mars Marrabo took the kitchen down and used the lumber for the schoolhouse.

The story within the story concludes with Julius's account of the haunted wood:

> Hit wa'n't long atter dat befo' Mars Marrabo sol' a piece er his track er lan' ter Mars Dugal' McAdoo,—my ole maarster,—en dat's how de ole school'ouse happen to be on you' place. W'en de wah broke out, de school stop', en de ole school'ouse be'n stannin' empty ever sence,—dat is, 'cep'n' fer de ha'nts. En folks sez dat de ole school'ouse, er any yuther house w'at got any er dat lumber in it w'at wuz sawed out'n de tree w'at Sandy wuz turnt inter, is gwine ter be ha'nted tel de las' piece er plank is rotted en crumble' inter dus'.   (53)

Annie and John fear that the wood they purchase will be haunted by the African Americans who used the space before. The ha'nts, or spirits, literally possess the wood; they own it. Because Sandy was turned into a tree, everything that comes from the lumber is "gwine ter be ha'nted" until every piece rots into dust. This fictional reclamation is justified by racial history: Sandy couldn't possess his own body or control his own relationship, but his legacy lives on through the wood.

Although Annie says that the story is "absurd," she and John buy new lumber, and it is not long before half the members of Uncle Julius's church ask to hold their meetings in the schoolhouse, claiming that "ghosts never disturb religious worship" (54). John and Annie may own the space, but Julius assumes the use of it through his manipulation of history.

The haunting that runs throughout this story concerns who controls the knowledge of a place whose history is kept orally and not written down. Students could be led through a dialogue of the history of the land and the relationships on it, especially involving the institution of slavery and the Civil War. They could discuss the forced separation of enslaved couples but also the agency and resistance to endure that separation. Finally, they could discuss the traditions of oral history and how the wood was passed on through storytelling. In Chesnutt's remark in the story's conclusion that the split in the Sandy Run Colored Baptist Church was on the temperance question, African American church histories also haunt the text. It can be productive to tease out from students an acknowledgment that the ironic twist at the end isn't merely funny or indicative of Julius's canniness in dealing with his white employers; it highlights how Julius, the keeper of history, emerges from his tale with greater access to the land. Whether or not the school is actually haunted, he can manage the ghosts of the past.

Lesson 3: Incubi, History, and Memory

Two years after the publication of the Douglass biography and three years after "Po' Sandy," Chesnutt probes, in *The Marrow of Tradition*, the source of American traditions of racial unrest. He goes to the heart of race relations in a town that represents Wilmington, North Carolina, where mob violence exploded in response to fear of a change in the white, male-dominated social hierarchy:

> It remained for Carteret and his friends to discover, with inspiration from whatever supernatural source the discriminating reader may elect, that the darker race, docile by instinct, humble by training, patiently waiting upon its as yet uncertain destiny, was an incubus, a corpse chained to the body politic, and that the negro vote was a source of danger to the state, no matter how cast or by whom directed.   ([ed. Sundquist] 80)

The term *incubus* is here taken in a different direction, the argument being that African Americans are chained despite their will to the body politic and that therefore any change they make for themselves will affect the state and disturb the national status quo. If the Douglass story is one of American triumph through the haunting of a legacy and if in "Po' Sandy" space and subjecthood are reclaimed through haunting, *Marrow* demonstrates for students that despite the gains of the Reconstruction period, it is followed by violence, by attempts to check the presence of African American bodies through codes, riots, and lynching.

Chesnutt suggests through all three texts that the weight of blackness depends in part on the presence of whites in the American body politic. He shows the effects of both the Reconstruction and post-Reconstruction periods on communities at large, by focusing on how African American characters have been victimized or have conquered their circumstances and also on how white characters fared in relationship with blacks. Thus in the reading and teaching of Chesnutt both interaction and integration between white and black histories and present situations are required. Students should reflect on the moments of conflict and conversation between white and black characters in each of these texts and on the reasons that Chesnutt positions blacks as either incubi or fleeting ghosts.

 In each text, Chesnutt uses characters who experience racial trauma. He engages in complex racial histories to show both the weight of blackness through haunting and the need for the removal of this weight.

Teaching Chesnutt's *Conjure Woman* through Its Publication History

Kathryn S. Koo

The publication history of Charles W. Chesnutt's *The Conjure Woman* (1899) offers students a rare opportunity to examine firsthand the politics of publishing at the turn of the twentieth century. Anyone intent on becoming an author must learn to navigate the complexities of the publishing industry, but for African American writers of the late nineteenth and early twentieth centuries the way to authorship was particularly precarious, given that their work had to earn the approval of an industry that was reluctant to offend the sensibilities of the reading public and loath to disturb the racial climate of the times. Chesnutt's own experience is a case in point. While he did manage to realize his lifelong dream of becoming an author, the road was not an easy one, and the publication history of *The Conjure Woman* bears testimony to the considerable challenges facing him as a writer of color.

The story of how *The Conjure Woman* came to be also provides a strategy for reading—and teaching—the work itself. A collection of seven interrelated stories that return to and yet radically revise the black dialect folktale, which was first popularized by Joel Chandler Harris's Uncle Remus tales, *The Conjure Woman* was the product of a series of exchanges between Chesnutt and Walter Hines Page, editor of the *Atlantic*. Chesnutt wrote his earliest conjure tales as works that could stand on their own and managed to place three of them in the *Atlantic* and two more in other journals. In a letter dated 30 March 1898, Page, who also represented the interests of Houghton Mifflin (then the publisher of the *Atlantic*), advised Chesnutt that a collection of such stories might profitably be turned into a book.[1] Encouraged, Chesnutt rapidly composed six new tales and submitted them to Page. Page then selected four of the newly produced tales and combined them with three of the old to create *The Conjure Woman*, published exactly one year after Page first raised the possibility of a book.

The result of this publication history is two very different collections of stories: one shaped and controlled by Page, and the other, a far larger and more diverse collection, created by Chesnutt. Page's version contains seven stories; Chesnutt's spans a total of fourteen, but his was a collection that would never be realized in the author's lifetime as a unified whole. Today, most editions of *The Conjure Woman* do acknowledge the existence of the tales that were rejected by Page, but few reprint all fourteen stories. For the nineteenth-century American literature seminar that I teach at a small liberal arts college, I use *The Conjure Woman and Other Conjure Tales*, edited by Richard H. Brodhead, precisely because it invites students to acknowledge both collections and examine the significant differences between them.[2] It first offers *The Conjure Woman* as it was originally published, then offers as "related tales" the ones that were either passed over by Page or written after the publication of *The Conjure Woman.* The teaching plan provided in this essay owes a great debt to this thoughtfully conceived edition, which includes an illuminating introduction by the editor and publication information for each of Chesnutt's fourteen tales.

The existence of two collections invites a host of questions that I encourage my students to ponder. What led Page to select the seven stories that made up his collection, and what led him to exclude the others? What were his criteria when he decided what the collection should look like? What made certain stories palatable to the buying public and others not? Chesnutt's own unrealized collection raises as many questions. What do his excluded and unpublished stories tell us that Page's collection does not? Should we consider the rejected stories as a chapter of African American literary history that the publishing industry declined to tell? And how should we as readers view *The Conjure Woman,* knowing that the 1899 collection represents only a part of the author's vision for the whole? The above questions are not intended to suggest that the relationship between Chesnutt and Page was a difficult or antagonistic one. The letters exchanged between them indicate that theirs was a respectful and even friendly association. But students should be encouraged to examine the ways in which the two collections diverge.

Most of Chesnutt's conjure tales follow a general formula. John and Annie, a Northern couple who have come to North Carolina with the intention of improving both their economic fortunes and Annie's health, find themselves in conversation with Uncle Julius, a former slave whose deep familiarity with the land makes him an invaluable resource and adviser. Moved by some particular circumstance to tell a tale drawn from his life in slavery, Uncle Julius immerses his Northern listeners in an alternative universe, where blacks and whites alike are subject to the occult power of the conjurer. And he creates in his stories an alternative linguistic universe, where black folk dialect, not the standard English of his Northern interlocutors, dominates. Uncle Julius's stories typically end with a moral, but whether the story is told to exemplify the moral or merely to serve his own interests (which tend to be revealed after the conclusion of his storytelling) is a question that is left to the reader to decide.

In creating the character of Uncle Julius, Chesnutt gave authority to a former slave to name and memorialize the experience of slavery. Far from the one-dimensional Uncle Remus on which his character is loosely based, Uncle Julius shows considerable craft, cunning, and sophistication. He understands that despite the vast social and economic divide between the newcomers and him, he is in a position to compete with them and claim certain rights of ownership based on his long-standing relation to the land and its history. He may lack the worldliness of the Northern couple, but his creator clearly wanted a character who would defy the stereotype of the faithful servant, a common figure in nineteenth-century American fiction, which Chesnutt noted with contempt in his essay "The Negro in Books."[3]

Uncle Julius is no faithful servant, but he is an excellent tour guide. One of the many pleasures of reading Chesnutt's conjure tales is the opportunity to tour the South, just as the Northerners of the story are doing. Not surprisingly, readers tend to identify with the tourists doing the observing rather than with the native who is being observed. Brodhead notes that this narrative strategy, which he terms the "plot of cultural tourism," was by no means new when Chesnutt adopted it. He reminds us that local narratives became the bedrock of American literature just as industrialization and modernization were beginning to create the possibility of a national identity and culture (2–4).

My students like to remind me that the very same plot is alive and well today: reality television shows take viewers to remote parts of the United States not to educate them but rather to provide them with the deep satisfaction of *not* coming from that part of the country. In terms of the tourism that is represented in Chesnutt's conjure tales, readers (as represented by John and Annie) can enjoy the backwardness of their Southern storyteller and the quaintness of his superstitions and all the while rest assured that his world is far different from—and far inferior to—the one that they hail from. John and Annie receive Uncle Julius's tales in ways that suggest the pleasures of cultural tourism: John consumes the tales because they support his criticism of the South as incorrigibly regressive and therefore fair game for his exploitation; Annie consumes them as a way to offer penance for the North's indifference—and contribution—to the problem of slavery.

Since consumption is a key component of cultural tourism, I ask my students to take note of their own consumption of the stories. What are the pleasures of reading Uncle Julius's stories? Which stories go down easily for the reader? Which stories cease at some point to be pleasurable and get stuck on the way down? Consumption itself is an important and recurring theme in many of Chesnutt's stories, as the slaves featured in them are treated as material goods to be bought, sold, and used up by the slaveholder. Chesnutt's conjure woman often transforms a slave into some other form (into a tree, in "Po' Sandy," for example) precisely to keep him from being consumed by his owner. Such transformations indulge the fantasy of escape that slaves no doubt entertained in their hopeless situation. But the result is rarely a happy one. The transformed slave might enjoy a momentary reprieve, but he typically suffers some unintended and unforeseen consequence of his transformation and is later consumed anyway. *The Conjure Woman*'s "The Goophered Grapevine," "Po' Sandy," "Mars Jeems's Nightmare," and "Sis' Becky's Pickaninny" are just such tales.

In "The Goophered Grapevine," Mars Dugal' McAdoo, Uncle Julius's former master, asks Aunt Peggy, the local conjurer, for help when his slaves cannot be kept from eating the grapes in his vineyard. Her "goopher" for McAdoo works, and he enjoys a spectacular wine-making season. When Henry, a newly arrived slave, unwittingly eats the conjured grapes, he seeks a cure from Aunt Peggy. His life is saved, but her cure comes with a curious consequence: when the vines come to life in the spring, so too does Henry, and when they decline in the fall, he follows suit. McAdoo takes advantage of his slave's seasonal changes by selling him in the spring, when Henry is in full bloom, and buying him back in the winter, when he begins to wither. The exploitation ends only with the arrival of a Northerner who persuades McAdoo to treat the vineyard to a deadly mixture of lime and ashes. Both vineyard and Henry die, and McAdoo suffers a double loss of property.

In "Mars Jeems's Nightmare," Aunt Peggy is again asked to employ her talents, but this time it is a slaveholder, not a slave, who undergoes the transformation. In response to his master's refusal to tolerate romance among his slaves, one hopeful slave asks Aunt Peggy to cast a goopher on his master. After ingesting Aunt Peggy's concoction, Mars Jeems is transformed into a slave and given a taste of what his own slaves suffer at the hands of his ruthless overseer. Once returned to his original form, Mars Jeems dismisses the overseer and changes his slaveholding ways. He is richly rewarded: his slaves are happier, his plantation experiences better returns, and his former sweetheart returns to marry him.

Similarly, "Sis' Becky's Pickaninny" offers the optimistic possibility that the inherent brutality of slavery may be tempered by the conjurer's powers. Becky, having suffered the loss of her husband, who was sold to pay off his master's debts, is herself bartered off in exchange for a horse. But her new master has no interest in her infant, and the child is left behind. When little Mose begins to fail, Aunt Peggy transforms him into a hummingbird, then into a mockingbird, which is able to fly away to see his mother. But this arrangement cannot be sustained, and Aunt Peggy comes up with a better solution. Making both Becky and the horse seem far less desirable than they first appeared, she orchestrates the return of both to their original owners, and Becky and her child are happily reunited.

The separation of family members is also the subject of "Po' Sandy." Sandy's master generously loans Sandy out, first to one family member and then another, to the point that the slave has "no home, ner no marster, ner no mistiss, ner no nuffin" (*Conjure Woman* 47). His wife, Tenie, reveals to her husband that she is a conjure woman, and together they devise a plan to turn Sandy into a tree. But the plan is flawed, as the tree becomes the victim of attacks, first by an industrious woodpecker, then by a slave sent to extract turpentine from the tree's bark. Before she can extricate Sandy from his predicament, Tenie herself is lent out to another family. In the meantime, Sandy, still a tree, is chopped down and sawed into boards. Arriving just in time to witness the destruction of the tree, Tenie goes mad with grief and eventually dies in a simple wooden structure built of the boards from Sandy's tree.

Of the four stories, "Po' Sandy" is perhaps the most sobering and startling, as the transformation of the slave into a tree leads to a gruesome image—a man sawed into many pieces in order to satisfy the appetite of many masters. But all four stories, even "Po' Sandy," do little to challenge the institution of slavery. Mars Dugal' McAdoo laments the loss of his vineyard and his slave but does not change his view that blacks are nothing more than a form of property. At the end of the story, he becomes an even more ardent advocate of the South's way of life and embraces the Civil War as a chance to punish the Yankee that ruined his vineyard. Like McAdoo, Mars Jeems fails to grasp the fundamental problem of slavery. After his "nightmare," he does become a more compassionate slaveholder, but, as Eric J. Sundquist has pointed out, he does not adopt the other choice that stands before him: the emancipation of his slaves.[4] "Sis' Becky's Pickaninny" highlights the horrific separation of mother and child, but the institution that permits such inhumanity is not threatened by the end of the story. One might even argue that the story helps perpetuate slavery as a form of benevolent paternalism: mother and child, although still in chains, are allowed to remain together. "Po' Sandy" does little to overturn the system that permits Sandy's division and eventual destruction.

"Dave's Neckliss" and "Lonesome Ben" are also tales of transformation, but my students find that they are far more difficult to consume than the collected conjure stories. Published in the *Atlantic* in 1889, "Dave's Neckliss" was later rejected by Page as a candidate for *The Conjure Woman*. When Dave, a devout and hardworking slave, is framed for a spate of thefts from the smokehouse, his master devises a troubling form of punishment: he attaches one end of a chain to a stolen ham and encircles the other end of the chain around Dave's neck. This necklace isolates Dave from the other slaves, but its eventual removal does not put an end to his sorrows: he now shows signs of madness, lamenting the loss of his necklace and attempting to replace it with another. He is eventually exonerated, but the news comes too late: he has hanged himself in the smokehouse "fer ter kyo" (*Conjure Woman* 134).

"Lonesome Ben" is equally unpalatable to my students. Page rejected the tale when Chesnutt first submitted it for publication in the *Atlantic*, so it is not surprising that he later chose not to include it in *The Conjure Woman*. Ben is a field slave whose attempt to escape to the North literally leads him nowhere: cloudy weather hides the North Star from him, and he ends up exactly where he began. His food long gone, he eats the only thing that is available to him: the clay on the banks of the river. After more than a month of that diet, he seeks out the family that he left behind. But his wife and child fail to recognize him, and even his former master cannot identify his runaway slave. Ben finally discovers the reason: the clay he ate has turned his color from a deep black to "a light yaller" (155). Utterly bereft, he expires, dries out, and eventually turns into powdered clay.

Both stories defy my students' conventional understanding of slavery and its legacy. In "Dave's Neckliss," Dave does not reject his association with the ham; he embraces it. While a story like "Mars Jeems's Nightmare" offers the fantasy that a quick walk in a slave's shoes can suffice to illuminate the experience of slavery, "Dave's Neckliss" presents a more troubling possibility: that slavery's effect on the human mind is far more complex and powerful than has been imagined. In "Lonesome Ben," Chesnutt combines two highly controversial figures in the character of Ben, the clay eater and the mulatto. Both figures confound logic: the clay eater seeks out and consumes that which is not food; the mulatto confounds the black-white divide on which the logic of slavery rests. Both are shamed and shameful figures, belonging to no group and having no certain identity. My students discover that their discomfort as readers is not unlike the ambivalence of the Northern couple at the end of the two stories. After hearing Dave's tragic history, Annie refuses to eat the ham that she had previously enjoyed. In "Lonesome Ben," John decides that the clay that he hoped to turn into bricks is not fit for that purpose. Both husband and wife arrived in North Carolina precisely in order to consume the South but find that its gifts are not always consumable.

The three remaining *Conjure Woman* stories—"The Conjurer's Revenge," "The Gray Wolf's Ha'nt," and "Hot-Foot Hannibal"—are primarily about revenge, although they do feature conjurers and transformations. Here again, the contrast between *The Conjure Woman* tales and their uncollected counterparts is striking. In "The Conjurer's Revenge," Uncle Julius tells the story of Primus, whose clubfoot is the trace of a punishment for his stealing from an unnamed conjurer. Primus was turned into a mule, the quintessential beast of burden and the object of so many tall tales in the African American folk tradition. The conjurer, reconsidering what he did to the hapless thief, turns the beast back into a man, but the restoration is incomplete: Primus is left with the foot of a mule.

In "The Gray Wolf's Ha'nt," the revenge is for a graver crime, the death of a child. Dan, a quick-tempered slave that none dare cross, accidentally kills the conjurer's son after the son attempted to seduce Dan's wife, Mahaly. The conjurer, again unnamed, exacts his revenge by tricking Dan into thinking that he must destroy a vindictive witch in the shape of a cat. The conjurer then transforms Dan's wife into a cat and Dan into a wolf and lets the tragedy unfold. After killing Mahaly, Dan cannot find a way to undo the conjurer's magic. He spends the rest of his days as a wolf, howling his lament over his wife's death.

In "Hot-Foot Hannibal," the last story of *The Conjure Woman*, the master decides that Chloe must marry the house slave Hannibal. She visits Aunt Peggy, determined to marry Jeff instead, the man she prefers. Aunt Peggy's conjuring makes Hannibal forgetful and clumsy, and he is eventually kicked out of the house and replaced by Jeff. Resentful, Hannibal deceives Chloe into believing that Jeff has been unfaithful to her. She retaliates by revealing Jeff's involvement in the plot against Hannibal, which provokes her master to sell Jeff to a speculator on his way to the deeper South. When Chloe learns of Hannibal's trick, she tries to undo what she has done but cannot: Jeff has drowned, having either fallen or jumped off the steamboat.

The stories that Uncle Julius tells in "The Conjurer's Revenge" and "The Gray Wolf's Ha'nt" can be viewed as self-serving: he benefits when his employer buys a horse instead of a mule, and the wolf's "haunt" that Julius tells his employer to avoid is actually the site of a bee hive that Julius, the long-time tenant, hopes to preserve for his own private use. "Hot-foot Hannibal" is told not for Julius's benefit but for the benefit of Mabel, Annie's sister, who, like Chloe, rashly refused her lover. The revenge featured in all three tales leads to varying degrees of misfortune for the slaves, but their misfortunes are minimized by the possibility that Uncle Julius is telling these tales to gain some advantage over John or to promote Mabel's interests.

I pair these tales of revenge with two of Chesnutt's most powerful stories: "The Dumb Witness," a tale that Page chose to pass over for the collection and that was never published as a stand-alone story in Chesnutt's lifetime, and "The Marked Tree," a story that Chesnutt published some twenty-five years after the publication of *The Conjure Woman*. "The Dumb Witness" is remarkable for a number of reasons, not the least of which is that it is John, not Uncle Julius, who narrates the story of the long battle between Roger Murchison, who at the time of John's storytelling is an old man, and the family slave, Viney. When John meets the pair, Murchison is pleading with his slave to tell him the location of his uncle's long-lost will, which can legitimize Murchison's claim to the family fortune. But Viney, the sole possessor of that knowledge, cannot: she is mute as a result of the violence Murchison inflicted on her years ago when she caused his fiancée to break off their engagement. Murchison had attempted to nurse Viney back to health, but none of his efforts succeed, and the two, much like an old married couple, remain at an impasse until the death of the old man. After Murchison's death, John makes a remarkable discovery: Viney could speak all along. More, the will that Murchison spent much of his life trying to discover was hidden in the old oak chair that he had been sitting on for so many years.

"The Marked Tree" begins with the birth of two infants—one white, one black—whose parallel lives are clearly meant to suggest their status as twins. Each grows up, falls in love, and plans to marry. But their similarities end there. When the black man is sold to pay for the marriage of his white twin, tragedy ensues. In an altercation with his new master, the slave commits the most egregious of crimes: he strikes his master. In his attempt to escape, he suffers severe injury but manages to return to his mother's cabin, only to die in her arms. In response, the mother marks the tree under which her owner's family celebrates its most significant occasions. The family henceforth knows nothing but sorrow. One family member after another dies as a result of the cursed tree, until at last the patriarch, determined to remove the tree, is crushed when it falls in an unexpected way.

My students are quick to note that the desire for revenge in both these tales far outstrips the desire for revenge in the collected ones. Both "The Dumb Witness" and "The Marked Tree" offer the uncomfortable possibility that this desire can never be satisfied, given the nature of the grievances suffered under slavery. Murchison suffers endless torment at the hands of his dumb slave, a torment that ends only with his death. And the slaveholding family in "The Marked Tree" suffers tragedy after tragedy until their entire line is wiped out. The revenge that we see in *The Conjure Woman* tales is largely contained, but these two uncollected tales tell us that reparation for the harms and ills of slavery will not be so easily made.

It is impossible to know Page's exact reasons for selecting certain stories and rejecting others for his collection, but the stories themselves provide an index to the appetites and mores of the times. Chesnutt's conjure tales are some of the most accessible and widely taught of his works, but their popularity and appeal should not lead us into readerly complacency. Even today, the tales—all fourteen of them—have much to teach us.

NOTES

[1] For the letter that raised the possibility of a collection of conjure tales, see H. Chesnutt 91–92.

[2] Brodhead's introduction offers a discussion of the Chesnutt-Page correspondence and a speculative reading of why Page chose certain stories and excluded others (15–21).

[3] For the full text of Chesnutt's "The Negro in Books," see C. Chesnutt, *Charles W. Chesnutt: Essays* 426–41. Chesnutt discusses the popularity of the faithful servant on p. 434.

[4] Sundquist argues that Mars Jeems recreates his plantation after the image of the extended "family" that was promoted by George Fitzhugh (*To Wake* 329).

The Gothic Grapevine:
Chesnutt's Conjure Tales as Gothic Fiction

Sarah Ingle

The opening lines of Edgar Allan Poe's 1844 story "The Premature Burial" aptly characterize the domain of gothic literature: "There are certain themes of which the interest is all-absorbing, but which are too entirely horrible for the purposes of legitimate fiction. These the mere romanticist must eschew, if he do not wish to offend, or to disgust" (57). Because of its preoccupation with themes that are simultaneously "all-absorbing" and "entirely horrible," gothic literature is often outrageously popular, but it also always threatens to violate the boundaries of good taste and "legitimate fiction" by giving offense and provoking its readers' terror and disgust. Although the gothic preoccupation with supernatural events and extreme emotions may prompt some readers to dismiss it as mere escapism, I try to show my students how studying the American gothic can yield important insights into the construction of American national identity by dramatizing both the terrors and the buried secrets of American culture.

One author who has become central to my vision of how to teach the American gothic is Charles W. Chesnutt, who, like gothic fiction itself, has staged a remarkable comeback in academic circles in recent decades. Long ignored by teachers and scholars alike, Chesnutt is now widely recognized for his contributions to African American literature and to American realism and regionalism. However, even though the conjure tales are among his most frequently taught works of fiction, his connection to the gothic tradition is easy to overlook. Rooted in African American folklore, the supernatural elements of his fiction seem far removed from the haunted castles of Horace Walpole and the psychological terrors of Poe, in part because they fail to inspire the terror of Chesnutt's white narrator, who dismisses conjure as a form of childish superstition. Although texts such as "The Raven," "The Tell-Tale Heart," and "The Fall of the House of Usher" are frequently taught in high schools, giving most students at least some familiarity with the gothic sensibilities of Poe, few students encounter Chesnutt before coming to college. That is why I have developed a two-part lesson plan that uses Poe as an entry point for thinking about the gothic elements of Chesnutt's conjure tales.

My first class on the conjure tales compares "The Goophered Grapevine" with Poe's "The Oval Portrait" to show students how Chesnutt's story draws both its formal structure and its sense of the haunting influence of the past from the gothic tradition. Once students understand how to read Julius's dialect and how to think about the implicit conflicts over narrative and economic power that are embedded in the frame structure, they can extend their analysis to some of Chesnutt's subsequent conjure tales. For the second class, I assign Poe's "The Gold-Bug" as well as two more conjure tales to focus the class discussion on a more detailed examination of how the stories use dialect and how they represent the gothic motifs of transformation and the "return of the repressed" (Freud 154). By evoking the psychological horrors of slavery, Chesnutt's conjure tales illustrate how gothic fiction provides writers with a set of literary conventions that they can use to explore ideas deemed too controversial for mainstream American literature.

With the 1887 publication of "The Goophered Grapevine" in the *Atlantic Monthly*, Chesnutt established the structure that would characterize all his conjure tales: a frame story narrated by a white man named John—a Northerner who has moved to North Carolina after the Civil War—and a story within a story narrated by Uncle Julius, a former slave who blends folklore with his memories of slavery to produce tales about the haunted countryside of the postbellum South. To emphasize the idea that the American gothic is a complex but cohesive literary tradition with formal as well as thematic conventions, I ask my students to compare "The Goophered Grapevine" with "The Oval Portrait," a story that is more conventionally gothic in its tone and setting. At first, the differences will seem obvious. While Chesnutt's story, narrated by the unfailingly sober and rational John, takes place outside and in the daytime, "The Oval Portrait" is set in an abandoned Italian chateau, which Poe's narrator describes as "one of those piles of commingled gloom and grandeur which have so long frowned among the Appenines, not less in fact than in the fancy of Mrs. Radcliffe" (151). But when students take a closer look at the descriptions of the landscape in "The Goophered Grapevine," they see that the "ruined chimneys" and "decayed gateposts" of what was "evidently a spacious mansion" give a feeling of gothic "gloom and grandeur" to Chesnutt's setting as well as Poe's (*Conjure Woman* 33).

Students soon notice that "The Oval Portrait" has a strong structural resemblance to "The Goophered Grapevine." Both stories contain frame narratives told by narrators who enter an unfamiliar space and then encounter something that triggers their curiosity about the history of the place where they are staying. In "The Oval Portrait," the narrator uncovers the unsettling story behind the painting in his bedroom by reading the "vague and quaint words" of a book that he finds nearby (153). The only living character in the story aside from the narrator is a nonspeaking servant who disappears after the first paragraph, leaving the narrator to explore his surroundings and his feelings about the painting in solitude. In Chesnutt's tale, the narrator learns from Uncle Julius, a black ex-slave who narrates in dialect and has his own personal and economic interests in the property, the supernatural history of the North Carolina vineyard that the narrator intends to buy.

The discussion questions that I pose to my students focus on the structural similarities between the two stories and on the thematization of storytelling itself. How, I ask, does the frame reinforce the stories' gothic theme of the present's being haunted by the past? How would Chesnutt's story be different if the tale of the conjured vineyard had been written in a book discovered by the white narrator, or if the storyteller were a white neighbor rather than a former slave? Through our analysis of the frames, students can see how both authors embed the past in the present, thereby directing their readers' attention not on the past acts of violence themselves but on the lingering, haunting effects that they continue to have on the following generation. The class can discuss the difference between written narrative and oral storytelling and the class-based and race-based tensions that shape the relationship between John and Julius. Poe's frame narrative adds to the suspense of his story and suggests art's ability to resist the confines of the literal frame that separates the portrait from the narrator's reality. In Chesnutt's story, art, in the form of Uncle Julius's storytelling, becomes a form of real-world power to be wielded by the socially and economically powerless. The dual narration of John and Julius reflects the story's theme of contested property ownership; the story of "The Goophered Grapevine," like the vineyard, belongs to both John and Julius.

"The Oval Portrait" and "The Goophered Grapevine" are alike not only in the frame but also in the interior narrative: both depict a figurative vampirism that leads to the gradual wasting away and eventual death of characters who occupy a position subordinate to that of the white male protagonists. In Poe's story, a husband drains away his wife's vitality for the sake of his art; in Chesnutt's, a slave owner places a curse on his property, causing his slave to sicken and eventually die for the crime of stealing a few of his master's grapes. In both stories, a material object is valued more highly than a human life, and, as a result, the object becomes haunted by the spirit of a dead person. Both stories derive a gothic thrill from the breakdown of the boundary between the human and the nonhuman, but only Chesnutt's story does so in order to expose the dehumanization that lies at the heart of the institution of slavery. The curse that falls on Henry, the slave who eats from the goophered grapevine, transforms him into an extension of the vineyard, forcing him to wither and ultimately die along with the plantation's crops. The magic goopher is a metaphor for the brutal economic order that slavery imposes on human life by transforming people into property. Chesnutt's white narrator may scoff at the notion that the land he is purchasing is cursed, but his refusal to take the conjure stories seriously suggests his failure to understand the continuing effects of slavery on the place that he wishes to call his home.

I end my first class on Poe and Chesnutt by asking my students to think about the ethical questions that the two stories pose about the artist's role in society. Poe's depiction in "The Oval Portrait" of a woman who is sacrificed for the sake of art directly raises the issue of an artist's moral responsibility. This topic can lead to a discussion of Chesnutt's mixed feelings about achieving commercial and literary success by writing stories that (at least superficially) reinforce negative stereotypes about African Americans. Asking students to consider his ambivalence about the popularity of his conjure tales with white readers sets up the discussion of Julius's dialect that will begin my second class on the gothic fiction of Poe and Chesnutt.

While my first class on Poe and Chesnutt focuses on issues of narrative structure, the second class uses two additional conjure tales and Poe's "The Gold-Bug" to probe the ethics and politics of the stories. Two Chesnutt stories that work particularly well for this second class are "Po' Sandy" and "The Gray Wolf's Ha'nt." Set in South Carolina, "The Gold-Bug" features both a white narrator and Jupiter, a black slave who speaks in an exaggerated dialect and whose mistakes, such as a malapropism confusing the word "cipher" with the word "siphon" and a failure to distinguish between left and right, are used by Poe for comic effect (276). "The Gold-Bug" is therefore pertinent to an understanding of Chesnutt's conjure tales as an example of the stereotypes associated with African American characters who speak in dialect. Comparing Jupiter and Julius can help students understand and articulate the differences between Poe's use of dialect and racial stereotypes to demean his black character and Chesnutt's subtle suggestions that Uncle Julius is aware and in control of the stereotypical behaviors that he must assume when talking to a white person in the postbellum South.

The opening paragraphs of "The Gray Wolf's Ha'nt" are a wonderful entry point for a discussion of Chesnutt's complex use of dialect and folklore. When Annie asks her husband to help pass the time on a dull, rainy day by reading aloud from the book that he has been silently perusing, the following dialogue between them ensues:

> "I'll read to you with pleasure," I replied, and began at the point where I had found my bookmark:
>
> > The difficulty of dealing with transformations so many-sided as those which all existences have undergone, or are undergoing, is such as to make a complete and deductive interpretation almost hopeless. So to grasp the total process of redistribution of matter and motion as to see simultaneously its several necessary results in their actual interdependence is scarcely possible. There is, however, a mode of rendering the process as a whole tolerably comprehensible. Though the genesis of the rearrangement of every evolving aggregate is in itself one, it presents to our intelligence—
>
> "John," interrupted my wife, "I wish you would stop reading that nonsense and see who that is coming up the lane."
>
> I closed my book with a sigh. I had never been able to interest my wife in the study of philosophy, even when presented in the simplest and most lucid form.
>
> Someone was coming up the lane; at least, a huge faded cotton umbrella was making progress toward the house, and beneath it a pair of nether extremities in trousers was discernible. Any doubt in my mind as to whose they were was soon resolved when Julius reached the steps and, putting the umbrella down, got a good dash of the rain as he stepped up on the porch. (94–95)

Reading John and Annie's exchange aloud in class may produce a few giggles, but the passage does much more than satirize the stodginess of John's taste in reading material. Annie's dismissal of his philosophy book as "nonsense" echoes the dismissive attitude that John displays toward Julius's conjure stories, which he deems little more than childish superstitions. Moreover, as students are quick to point out, the dense, academic prose of John's philosophy text is just as incomprehensible at first glance as Julius's dialect.

After a second reading of the philosophy passage in "The Gray Wolf's Ha'nt," students begin to notice a second element linking the passage to Julius's stories: the idea of transformation. Chesnutt implies that the magical transformations that occur in Julius's stories should also be understood on a philosophical and metaphorical level. I encourage students to take a closer look at the magical transformations in the stories. By depicting slaves who become trees and animals, Julius metaphorically represents the legal and psychological power of slavery to transform people into property. The metaphors of the haunted schoolhouse and the haunted tract of land on John's property hint at a horror that is rooted in the past but also threatens the stories' characters in the present.

"The Gold-Bug" has much in common with Poe's other gothic stories, yet it is also sometimes classified with his detective stories because it features a brilliant but eccentric character who uses his powers of ratiocination to unravel a mystery and find a buried treasure. However, a closer look at the ending can lead not only to a better appreciation of "The Gold-Bug" as a gothic story but also to a more nuanced discussion of the racial politics and gothic elements of Chesnutt's tales. After Poe's characters have found the hidden treasure, Legrand, the story's detective, has one last mystery to solve. Asked why skeletons were found buried with the treasure, he explains to his two companions that the pirate who buried the treasure probably killed his two fellow pirates to keep them from revealing the secret location. The story ends with Legrand's eerily morbid speculation about the number of blows that it took for the pirate to kill his coconspirators. Legrand muses, "[P]erhaps it required a dozen—who shall tell?" (305). As one of my students pointed out, this unusual ending could mean that the seemingly rational detective might be on the verge of killing his own coconspirators, Jupiter and the story's narrator, to keep them from demanding a share of the treasure. With this ambiguous ending, Poe's "The Gold-Bug" suggests that there is a fine line between the calm rationality of the detective and the disorder of the murderer. The final words of the story—"who shall tell?"—chillingly allude to the power imbued in the act of storytelling and the violence of those who seek to control that power. This theme is central to an understanding of the violent struggle at the heart of Chesnutt's conjure tales.

After discussing how Poe crafts an ending to his story that simultaneously ties up all loose ends and hints at a horror that lies just beyond the limits of his narrative, I ask my students to consider the possibility that the endings of Chesnutt's conjure stories are also less tidy than they first appear. John, the white narrator, is like Legrand a character who prides himself on his rationality but also misses no opportunity to prove his intelligence by comparing himself with African American characters such as Uncle Julius, whom he associates with ignorance and superstition. When John concludes each story by dismissing Julius as either a superstitious fool or a con artist trying to keep the vineyard's resources for himself, he offers readers a safe and rational interpretation of the stories. However, the truth of Uncle Julius's stories about the cursed land and people of the American South is that there is no clear opposition between order and reason, on the one hand, and violence and horror, on the other. This horror is what characterizes both Poe's stories and Chesnutt's conjure tales as works of gothic fiction. To read "The Goophered Grapevine" solely as a work of realism is to understand it only as John's story; understanding the story from Julius's perspective means reading it as a gothic text.

Women in Chesnutt's Short Fiction: Canons, Connections, Classrooms

Jennifer Riddle Harding

Short stories can be challenging to teach because of their density; covering just two complementary stories is a fitting goal for a single day in an undergraduate classroom. To represent Charles W. Chesnutt, instructors may find themselves turning to his two frequently anthologized stories "The Goophered Grapevine" and "The Wife of His Youth," particularly if they spend just a day on his fiction in the context of a survey course. These are excellent stories representing his two dominant short forms—the conjure stories and the color line stories—but they do not reflect one of Chesnutt's strengths as a writer, the portrayal of black women. To better engage students with Chesnutt's portrayal of women and with his short fiction, I argue for the pedagogical payoffs of a different pairing: "Sis' Becky's Pickaninny" and "Her Virginia Mammy." [1]

These stories are not just good examples of what makes Chesnutt Chesnutt—wit, linguistic creativity, satire, framing—they are an excellent pair of stories about black women written during an era when black women characters were not plentiful. Instructors may find that "Sis' Becky's Pickaninny" and "Her Virginia Mammy" fit into syllabi for a variety of courses—for example, on American literature, African American literature, American short fiction, and even women's literature. Both stories use satire and emotional ambivalence to present sympathetic and nuanced black women characters in historically determined situations, such as family separation, legally restricted marriage, and structural powerlessness. They echo the themes central to the two most significant books by black women in the nineteenth century, Harriet Jacobs's *Incidents in the Life of a Slave Girl* and Frances Harper's *Iola Leroy*, and prefigure later black women's writing. Published in 1899, they gracefully bridge the gap between nineteenth- and twentieth-century American literature.

The outer story of "Sis' Becky's Pickaninny" frames an inner tale told to two white listeners by Julius, who describes the plight of a slave woman separated from her baby until two women work to reunite them. In this tale, a buffoonish master offers to swap one of his slaves for a racehorse, and the horse trader selects Becky but doesn't want her child. After they are separated, Becky and the baby both become physically ill. To help the baby recover, the baby's caregiver and a conjure woman conspire to reunite mother and son; the conjure woman turns the baby into a hummingbird and then a mockingbird so he can visit his mother. Eventually, by conjuring hornets to sting the racehorse and manipulating the two avaricious white men, the conjure woman arranges the baby's return. Mother and son are reunited, and when the child grows up, he buys freedom for both of them (82–93). The emphasis on women's power to conjure anticipates later texts such as *Their Eyes Were Watching God* and *The Color Purple.*

In the classroom, connections can be made between this story and earlier texts that dramatize the separation of slave mothers and their children, especially *Incidents in the Life of a Slave Girl.* Like *Incidents,* the story brings to light forms of resistance exercised by women, as well as power found in women's collaboration. Like Linda in *Incidents,* Becky is a slave mother who is strong and focused, who suffers acutely when separated from her child, but who manages a limited triumph over the slave system. Like Aunt Martha in *Incidents,* the story's conjure woman is a doyenne who can influence events, but her power is also maddeningly limited compared to the white masters, who are oblivious to the suffering they cause. The story shows that women can find power in conjure, determination, and teamwork but achieve goals only when they muster every source of power to direct events that are easily changed by a white man's whim.

The story presents another female character reminiscent of those in earlier texts—the sympathetic white woman who lends an ear to the slave mother's tale of woe, like Mrs. Bruce in *Incidents.* In "Sis' Becky," the frame is set a generation after the inner tale, and it is Julius who connects with his white listeners, John and Annie, through the conduit of Becky's story. Annie is affected by the tale and chastises her husband when he mocks the fantastic moments in which the baby is turned into a hummingbird and mockingbird; she tells him, "[T]he story is true to nature, and might have happened half a hundred times, and no doubt did happen, in those horrid days before the war" (92). This statement can be read as proof of Annie's appreciation of the symbolic intent of Julius's stories; it also shows her sympathetic connection to the slaves and their experiences, a sympathy her husband rarely displays in any of the conjure stories.[2]

Students may note that a happy ending closes both parts of the story. In the inner tale, baby and mother are reunited and gain their freedom; in the frame, the former slave Julius and the white Northerner Annie become connected by their shared sympathy for Becky—at the conclusion of the story, Annie, who has been ill, recovers her health when Julius gives her his lucky rabbit's foot (93). But students should be made aware of the signs of rupture beneath both happy endings. The slave women's ability to influence events in this one case highlights the vulnerability of their situations in general, and if the fantastic elements of the story give it a mythical and symbolic richness, they also make it seem too idealistic to be real.

In this light, Annie's appreciation for the inner tale becomes suspect. Annie believes in the basic veracity of the tale, and the story makes her feel better after a protracted illness. Yet how can her belief in the depiction of cruel family separations make her feel better? Her emotional response is based on the fact that the characters achieve reunion and eventual freedom, yet that ending is perhaps even more fantastic than the baby's turning into a hummingbird and mockingbird. Students may find the story sweet and not initially recognize its complexity, so it is helpful to remind them that the story represents the separation and powerlessness that were typical of slavery, and a happy ending that was not. The final reunion in the story casts into tragic relief the true history of unrelieved separation, as told in black women's memoirs and narratives. As portrayed in *Incidents*, longed-for family reunions were often delayed, incomplete, or nonexistent. As Sojourner Truth attested in her speech at a women's rights convention in 1851, "I have borne thirteen chilern, and seen 'em mos' all sold off into slavery, and when I cried out with a mother's grief, none but Jesus heard . . ." (248).

"Sis' Becky's Pickaninny" provides an entrance into Chesnutt's use of dialect and framed narratives, and its female characters offer easily spotted connections to previous American texts, especially *Incidents in the Life of a Slave Girl*.[3] Focusing on the issue of female power and powerlessness, students may be led to see that despite the triumphs of the women in the story, Chesnutt may have intended to shine a light on the heartrending plights of actual black women while simultaneously criticizing the need of many postbellum readers to anesthetize themselves from a true understanding of "those horrid days before the war."

From *"The Wife of His Youth" and Other Stories of the Color Line*, "Her Virginia Mammy" presents a tale of family reunion that is emotionally complex because it is only partially fulfilled. The reunion is ambivalent and incomplete—a notable contrast to *Iola Leroy*, in which several euphoric family reunions demonstrate an unequivocal loyalty to mothers who represent family and race. The biracial daughter in Chesnutt's story, the dance teacher Clara, ultimately rejects her mother to enter the white world, prefiguring the themes of passing and independence that would prove so important to later female authors, like Nella Larsen.

The story follows a familiar plot that students may recognize in other literary works:[4] an orphaned daughter, who was raised to adulthood by adoptive parents, remains ignorant of her parentage, though the narrative hints that she may be of African American descent.[5] The mystery of her background complicates her desire to marry. When her visibly biracial mother, Mrs. Harper, finds her and describes her background, the daughter's long-held desire to know her own identity is satisfied. Yet Mrs. Harper deceives Clara by telling her a misleading story that she was born to white parents and that Mrs. Harper was her mammy. Though the plot shares elements with other stories about orphans reunited with family members and with other stories of passing,[6] the unusual outcome of this reunion makes this story distinct.

As with "Sis' Becky," this story's complex use of female character types may serve as a starting point for discussion. A slave mother who has lost her child responds to that loss by denying her own identity so that her daughter can marry a white man.[7] Instead of revealing her identity, the mother turns herself into a female stereotype: the plantation mammy. The daughter may likewise be discussed as a version of the tragic mulatta, in that she has lost her mother and her identity, even though she remains unaware of this loss and at the end of the story says unequivocally, "I am happy" (131). Clara has failed to hear or see the truth that her mother's words and body reveal; she has gained a mammy but lost a mother.

Chesnutt is witty and understated in conveying emotional ambivalence, employing double meanings, hints, and elisions to create irony that undercuts Clara's confirmed identity and happiness. Students may note points when the narrative hints at Clara's true family history, as when Mrs. Harper fails to affirm that Clara's parents were married. Students may also find puns, such as when the daughter's boyfriend urges her to "enjoy the *passing* moment" or when the daughter learns that her mother "*belonged* to one of the first families of Virginia" (122, 128; emphasis mine). "Her Virginia Mammy" uses hints and puns to suggest possible meanings that are hidden or unrecognized, just as Clara hovers in a space of multiple and hidden identities. The uncertainty and multiplicity of surface meanings mirrors the instability in identity and family relations.

To many students, the mother's embedded tale may seem confusing—yet this confusion can be a productive point of discussion. The tale does not really hold together well; the veil of whiteness it provides for her daughter is thin. The mother, not wanting to lie outright, tells a story filled with ambiguities and omissions, but the daughter eagerly helps construct the story by completing unfinished sentences, and she doesn't question the tale's overall coherence. What does her eagerness say about her? Her obliviousness to her mother's true emotions, fueled by her desire to marry a white doctor, contrasts sharply with the steadfast loyalty and sensitivity of Iola Leroy, who rejects a marriage proposal from a white doctor to stay with her mother.[8] The emotionally ambivalent ending to Chesnutt's story, the reunion of mother and daughter that is never realized, contrasts sharply with the many euphoric reunions in *Iola*. "Her Virginia Mammy" deftly demonstrates the emotional costs of passing to both individuals and families. Chesnutt satirizes a culture that segregated families and identities along racial lines and emphasizes the secrecy and omission necessary to maintain the fiction that the races were not intermingled.

"Sis' Becky's Pickaninny" and "Her Virginia Mammy," especially when read together, can enrich classroom discussion by increasing the number and type of female characters that students encounter. Brevity and online accessibility make these stories easy to include in many types of syllabi, and connections may be drawn from them to many literary traditions. Chesnutt's sensitivity to women's issues is remarkably parallel to black women's writing of the nineteenth century, to which these stories can be helpfully compared and contrasted. These two stories, because of their characterization of women and their distinctive and sophisticated style, can provide students with a foundation for provocative, exciting discussions of gender and race while also providing a meaningful introduction to the writing of Charles W. Chesnutt.

NOTES

¹Chesnutt's short fiction collections are available online through the University of North Carolina's *Documenting the American South* online digital publishing initiative.

²See Gilligan for a reading of how Annie functions as "a model reader who demonstrates . . . sentimental engagement" (204).

³Other texts that thematize slave mothers and separations are Stowe's *Uncle Tom's Cabin*, Harper's *Iola Leroy* and poem "The Slave Mother," Lydia Maria Child's story "The Quadroons," Williams Wells Brown's *Clotel*, Twain's story "A True Story Repeated Word for Word as I Heard It," as well as slave narratives like *Narrative of the Life of Frederick Douglass* and Annie Burton's *Memories of Childhood's Slavery Days*.

⁴Dannenberg offers more examples of what she labels the kinship reunion coincidence plot (2).

⁵These narrative and linguistic hints are described more fully in my "Narrating the Family."

⁶The story may be fruitfully compared with earlier and later narratives of passing, including Frank Webb's *The Garies and Their Friends*, Twain's *Pudd'nhead Wilson*, James Weldon Johnson's *The Autobiography of an Ex-Colored Man*, Chopin's "Desiree's Baby," Chesnutt's *The House behind the Cedars*, Pauline Hopkins's "Talma Gordon," and Larsen's *Passing*.

⁷For interpretations of the story in relation to maternal sacrifice, see Chandler; Render.

⁸Henry Wonham first noted that "Her Virginia Mammy" can be read as a "playful rejoinder" to *Iola Leroy* (63).

Dumb Witnesses: Teaching Speech and Silence in the Short Fiction

Sarah Wagner-McCoy

The first major African American fiction author, Charles Chesnutt, was born in Cleveland, Ohio, in 1858, a generation too late, he would later reflect, for the slave narrative and a generation too early for the Harlem Renaissance (*Charles W. Chesnutt: Essays* 543). When I introduce students to his short fiction, I begin not with a political or literary movement but with an educational one: the debates about who could go to school and what students should study defined African American intellectual life throughout Reconstruction and its violent aftermath.

A graduate of a Freedmen's Bureau school, Charles Chesnutt longed to become a member of the African American elite, which W. E. B. Du Bois later dubbed the "talented tenth" (*Souls* 435). However, Chesnutt could not afford to go to college. Instead, he became a teacher, sending his earnings home to support his younger brothers and sisters and buying books with what was left. He used his books to give himself the education he wished he could have had in college, engaging in the kind of critical reading practices I encourage my students to develop over the course of a semester: interpreting passages, finding moments of intertextuality, composing essays, and spotting analogies. As we read the remarkable record of Chesnutt's solitary efforts to read and understand books, to do what we are doing together in the classroom today, I ask my students, Why was literature important to Chesnutt, and why is it important to us?

In asking this question, I have three goals. The first is to grasp what the liberal arts meant in Chesnutt's historical context by examining the education debates of the late nineteenth and early twentieth centuries. The second is to analyze his representations of literary sophistication in his short stories, from illiteracy to misquotation, from calculated use of dialect to vapid book collecting. Chesnutt is fascinated by partial knowledge, by what happens between "reading, 'riting, 'rithmetic" and true understanding of a text. The third goal is to encourage my students to reflect on their college experience, connecting their study of literature with a long cultural history of educational access. In each unit, we revisit these goals, discussing the politics of education then and now as we analyze the language Chesnutt uses to represent learning. His determination to teach himself the liberal arts reveals not only the role humanities played in the fight for racial equality but also the value he placed on literature more generally.

Even as I hope to inspire my students to recognize the importance of the humanities, I also encourage them to question its value and explore its limitations as a tool of social justice. In fact, I preface Chesnutt with the white supremacist fictions that corroded commitment to Reconstruction with nostalgia for the Old South: George Bagby's "The Old Virginia Gentleman," Thomas Nelson Page's

"Marse Chan," and Joel Chandler Harris's Uncle Remus tales. I invite my students to think about how these fantasies of the antebellum plantation offer a chilling example of literature's power as propaganda, shaping the attitudes and in turn the politics of Northern readers. What ushered in the age of lynching was not only the absence of legal authorities preventing mob violence but also the willful obliviousness of the nation's cultural and political elite. Was it coincidence that Harris published his first Uncle Remus stories the year after the last federal troops pulled out of the South? Can stories affect us more than politics, economics, even war? How did the nostalgia and racist stereotypes of the plantation school triumph over the ideals of Reconstruction?

Unit 1: Chesnutt's Journals

I assign Chesnutt's *Journals* because they exemplify both the importance and the impracticality of a liberal arts education. When Chesnutt was eight years old, his family returned to Fayetteville, North Carolina, a community committed to education. His father, a grocer, joined six other prominent African Americans to purchase land for a school site and, with additional funds from the Freedman's Bureau, built the Howard School. When the family's grocery business failed, Charles stayed on as a teacher, studying French, German, Latin, history, algebra, literary composition, and the organ in his spare time. The journals record his ambition to succeed through hard work, and he compares himself with self-made men like Benjamin Franklin and Horace Greeley. I ask my students to read these records, however, with the time line of Reconstruction in mind. The Freedmen's Bureau was abolished in 1872, the year Chesnutt began the journals. Two years later, Democrats gained control of Congress. Instead of attending college, as he had hoped, he taught students with diminishing opportunities as federal troops withdrew and the rise of Jim Crow exposed the falseness of the promises of a meritocratic future.

A passage in the first journal sets up the conflict between his optimism and the historical conditions of the 1870s. In it, he records a conversation he had with a family of sharecroppers in South Carolina about the role of education:

> "We all of [us] work on other people's, white people's, land, and sometimes get cheated out of all we make; we can't get the money."
> "Well, you certainly make something?"
> "Yes."
> "Now, I'll tell you. You say you are all renters, and get cheated out of your labor, why don't you send your children to school, and qualify them to look out for themselves, to own property, to figure and think about what they are doing, so that they may do better than you?"
> "We can't do it," was all I could get out of them . . . they are a very trifling shiftless set of people up there, and their children are following in their footsteps.   (*Journals* 62)

Passages like this one have led many to avoid assigning Chesnutt's journals. The victim-blaming contempt is hard to read, let alone teach, and hindsight makes his blindness to the injustice of the economic system seem even stranger. Yet his inadequate response to the argument against investing in education offers a fascinating provocation for students and ultimately, I'd suggest, for Chesnutt himself, who revisits versions of this conversation throughout his work. How does learning Latin or playing the organ qualify someone to own property? For that matter, how does a United States literature class qualify a student to do anything other than teach literature? What is the point of studying the humanities?

In the nineteenth-century debates over racial uplift and African American education, the college curriculum was a flashpoint. Reassuring skittish white supporters, Booker T. Washington rejected the need for educational equality, instead promoting practical industrial and agricultural training for African Americans at the Tuskegee Institute. Economic advance, he argued, paved the way to racial uplift, and he scorned the shallow "craze for Greek and Latin learning"—then synonymous with the liberal arts—as an affectation with prestige but no clear purpose (40). Angered by this mockery of educational aspiration, Du Bois argued that African Americans should have the same educational opportunities as privileged whites. Indeed, studying the humanities functioned as a retort to John C. Calhoun's famous defense of slavery when he declared, "If a Negro could be found who could parse Greek or explain Euclid, I should be constrained to think that he has human possibilities" (qtd. in Logan, *Howard University* 4). For many African American intellectuals, the need to parse Greek and explain Euclid was a given even though the utility of these skills was not.

Chesnutt's relation to the liberal arts goes beyond mere cultural capital, but, given the significance of his classical learning and the obstacles he faced to obtain it, there's really nothing mere about that capital. He integrates subtle allusions to canonical texts into tales of African American experience, defying cultural hierarchy in favor of a conception of universality. Yet his short stories reveal his growing recognition of meritocracy's failure in America. As he wrote in a letter to Washington on 27 June 1903, no amount of education or money could guarantee equality if African Americans lost the vote:

> I appreciate all you say and have written about education and property; but they are not everything. There is no good reason why we should not acquire them all the more readily because of our equality of rights. I have no confidence in that friendship of the whites which is to take the place of rights, and no expectation of justice at their hands unless it is founded on law.   (*"To Be"* 182)

As we turn to his short fiction, I ask students to analyze how Chesnutt represents both the power and the limits of education in a society ordered by racial injustice.

Unit 2: Allusions in "The Wife of His Youth"

Allusions can show how learned a person is, but they can also expose that learning as partial or flawed. Chesnutt's fascination with this latter possibility—the veneer of education without real understanding—emerges in various forms throughout his mature writings. "Baxter's Procrustes" mocks the members of the Bodleian Club, a literary society that publishes and promotes a gorgeously bound, limited edition of what turns out to be a blank book by the Harvard-educated Baxter; eager to preserve the book's value, no one cuts the pages to read it. In the conjure stories, John peppers his frame narration with ostentatiously learned vocabulary and references, but he repeatedly fails to comprehend the stakes of Julius's tales. The most poignant example of an allusion's double valence comes at the end of "The Wife of his Youth," when incomplete understanding results not from pretension or greed but from the legacy of slavery. On the day that Charles Ryder, a "recognized adviser and head" of the exclusive "Blue Vein" society in Groveland, plans a ball to offer his hand in marriage to Mrs. Dixon, a young widow "whiter than he and better educated," 'Liza Jane, the woman he married before the war, arrives (*Charles W. Chesnutt: Stories* 103, 105). A former slave, 'Liza Jane has been looking for her husband for twenty-five years, certain that he has been looking for her. Slipping into "soft dialect," Mr. Ryder tells 'Liza Jane's story to his guests and ends with the quandary he faces, posed as a hypothetical question: Supposing that her husband, a younger, lighter-skinned, man, had worked his way up in society and now loves another woman, should he reveal himself and acknowledge his slave marriage? The advice Mr. Ryder imagines that he would give this hypothetical husband, "in such a crisis of a lifetime," if they were old friends, takes the form of Shakespearean quotation (113):

> This above all: to thine own self be true,
> And it must follow, as the night the day,
> Thou canst not then be false to any man.

True to himself, Mr. Ryder ends by introducing 'Liza Jane as "the wife of my youth" (114). However, the story undercuts his allusion in two ways. First of all, the multiple narrative frames pose a series of challenges to the unity of the self and the notion of truth expressed in the quotation. Until the last line of the story, Mr. Ryder's disclosure takes place in the third person, and Mrs. Dixon gives him permission to renounce their imminent engagement by responding, still in the third person, to the hypothetical question (113). Second, although the speech is often misremembered as Hamlet's or quoted out of context as the unmediated wisdom of the Bard himself, in the play it is spoken by Polonius, "a foolish, prating knave" ridiculed for sententious advice like the lines Mr. Ryder quotes (*Hamlet* 3.4.189). Why, when Mr. Ryder takes such care to select the appropriate Tennyson poem for his toast, does he inadvertently speak the part of the aging, officious windbag instead of the intellectual bridegroom he hopes to be? These lines, he tells his accomplished audience, are "words that we all know" (114). Knowing lines from Shakespeare delineates the insider status and cultivation of the "we," the Blue Veins, and the parody of collective cultural pretension may remind students of the vapid Bodleian club members who collect but do not read the books. However, Mr. Ryder is well read, has a passion for poetry and literary tastes, and is hindered not by arrogance but by his "lack of early training." His pronunciation (a source of particular anxiety for Chesnutt, we learn reading the journals) is "sometimes faulty" (104). Having been denied educational opportunities, he risks seeming a foolish, prating knave.

When students discuss the story, some blame Mr. Ryder and the Blue Veins for borrowing from European culture, a claim several critics make as well.[1] Although Chesnutt certainly parodies the Blue Veins for emulating white hierarchies based on skin color, he also parodies the ideal of authenticity expressed in Polonius's lines. There is no single self or true racial identity. Chesnutt values literature not for its origins but for its power to move across cultural lines and provoke these very questions. I ask my students to think about how languages are always, to some extent, borrowed. Mr. Ryder borrows 'Liza Jane's dialect as readily as Tennyson's poetry. Moreover, the potential to sound pedantic is a universal phenomenon, mocked in *Hamlet* through Polonius's tedious and often unsolicited counsel. Instead of sustaining the contrasts between white literary culture and black dialect and the racial and cultural binaries they suggest, Chesnutt shifts his focus to the tensions in a literary text. Ryder uses Shakespeare's language as another voice (or mask) to represent a dialogue between two halves of the self, inadvertently performing the profound paradoxes contained in Polonius's banalities. Trying to stage his acknowledgment of 'Liza Jane, Mr. Ryder becomes an actor in a layered drama; his shallow quotation works as a deep allusion for Chesnutt. Shakespeare functions simultaneously as a mark of cultural capital and claptrap, as aspiration and humiliation, as education and limitation.

Unit 3: Silence in *The Conjure Tales*

"The Wife of his Youth" shares a chronological structure with Chesnutt's most famous short stories: the conjure tales. It begins and ends with a cultured, Northern narrator describing postwar life and tells a story of slave days in the middle. There are three important differences, however. The first is ratio: the conjure fiction uses the frames—narrated by John—as brief occasions for the long dialect tale of Uncle Julius, whereas 'Liza Jane barely speaks, and Mr. Ryder takes over her tale in the end. The second is gender: 'Liza Jane is a woman, and Uncle Julius is a man. The third is race: instead of representing divisions in the African American community, Chesnutt's conjure fiction uses an educated, Northern, white narrator to frame the tales of an elderly man of mixed race. Julius and John seem to represent simplistic dichotomies between oral and literary culture, conjure and rationality, dialect and standard speech, past and present, South and North, and black and white. I ask my students, however, to find passages that collapse the binaries suggested by the frame structure. How does Julius's knowledge of antebellum lore and contemporaneous local life refute the nostalgia implied by the format of the frame tale? How does literary logic—metaphor, allegory, metamorphosis—complicate John's denigration of conjure as superstition? Why include Annie, John's wife, as a listener, and what significance does her illness—improved by Julius's stories but not by John's interventions—have? What do John's and Annie's different interpretations of the tales tell us about the ethics of reading?

The rupture of the frame tale structure comes, most strikingly, in the conjure tale that omits Julius's narration altogether: "The Dumb Witness." Instead of framing a dialect tale, John relates a story he first hears from Julius in its entirety, silencing Julius's speech. "The Dumb Witness" describes a transformation wrought not by magic but by horrific violence: a master tries to silence a slave by mutilating her tongue. Chesnutt adapts the brutal rape of Philomel, told most famously in Ovid's *Metamorphoses*. Queen Procne, married to the Thracian ruler Tereus, asks to see her sister, Philomel. Instead, the tyrant abducts his sister-in-law, keeping her in a remote cabin, where he rapes her and cuts out her tongue to prevent her from telling of his crime. Unable to speak, Philomel weaves her story into a cloth and sends it to Procne, who rescues her. Procne takes revenge by killing her own son and cooking his flesh for Tereus to eat unwittingly. As they flee, Procne turns into a swallow, Philomela turns into a nightingale, and Tereus, pursuing, becomes a bird of prey. Chesnutt's story reprises Philomel's fate in the story of Viney. The "hawk-like" master, Murchison, keeps Viney, "a tall, comely young quadroon" related by blood to the family, as a mistress for many years (*Conjure Woman* 159, 163). Worried that she might speak of their relationship, he cuts out her tongue and banishes her from the house to a cabin in the yard. Instead of infanticide and cannibalism, however, "The Dumb Witness" ends with the seriocomic surrogate of a financial loss, as befits an economy in which slave masters father children who are literally metamorphosed into fungible assets. Viney alone knows the location of Murchison's inheritance, but because she (supposedly) cannot speak and was never taught to write, he never finds the money. Ironically, we learn after Murchison goes mad and dies that Viney could speak all along. She tells his nephew where the papers are, and young Murchison begins restoring the plantation.

Chesnutt uses the allusion to Philomel to protest the silencing of an entire race. In his 1905 novel *The Colonel's Dream*, he reprises Viney's story but adds that her name is "a Negro corruption of Lavinia" (240). Is the nickname, like dialect, a mutilation of Chesnutt's tongue that turns out to be a subtly woven form of resistance? The full name suggests yet another source: in Shakespeare's *Titus Andronicus*, Lavinia is the victim of an even more brutal rape by a "craftier Tereus" (2.4.41). Her two rapists cut off her tongue and her hands to prevent her from speaking or weaving the story. In Shakespeare's most overt enactment of textual allusion, Lavinia communicates instead by pointing to the story of

Philomel in her young nephew's copy of Ovid's *Metamorphoses* and then writes her attackers' names with her father's staff. Elementary education—from Ancient Rome to Renaissance England—is literally brought on stage. Like Procne, Titus avenges his daughter with a human feast, feeding the rapists to their mother. Chesnutt's allusion highlights the horror of Viney's biological inheritance. Instead of aiming to protect or avenge her, Viney's male relatives are the white men who perpetrate the twin crimes of incest and slavery.

Shakespeare's staging of literary allusion offers a compelling source for Chesnutt's reflection on the educational spectrum between basic literacy and the liberal arts. For Chesnutt, institutionalized slavery outdoes even Shakespeare's villains. Prevented from learning to read or write by law, he writes, Viney "might as well have been without hands" (*Conjure Woman* 168). I ask my students why Chesnutt draws an analogy between Lavinia, who has no tongue or hands, and Viney, who turns out to have both? Cleverly, Viney feigns dumbness to avenge herself on Murchison and uses the illiteracy enforced by her master to punish him. Yet again, I invite students to consider the full spectrum of educational access in contemplating Chesnutt's analogy. Shakepeare's Lavinia does more than just name her attackers; she uses a book, a literary allusion, to tell her own story. She is able to communicate because she knows the same myth as her brothers and fathers. Common texts are not merely cultural capital, in Shakespeare's play, but the myths that allow us to understand each other across time and place. Fiction, not just fact, gives Lavinia justice.

In 1888, the year after Chesnutt published "The Goophered Grapevine" in the *Atlantic Monthly*, becoming the first African American author with a national readership, Frederick Douglass warned the United States not to forget the atrocities of slavery: "[T]he nation may forget . . . but the colored people of this country are bound to keep the past in lively memory till justice shall be done to them" (qtd. in Blight 97). In his fiction, Chesnutt uses myth to keep memory alive, reminding his readers then and now of the injustice of educational inequality.

NOTE

[1] In *To Wake the Nations*, for example, Eric Sundquist suggests that "the gulf between Ryder's elevated language, laden with idealized notions borrowed from European culture, and Liza Jane's thick dialect must be bridged by his (and Chesnutt's) telling of her story, his virtual authentication of her existence" (301).

Teaching Chesnutt's "The Bouquet":
Combining History and Fiction

Ernestine Pickens Glass

"The Bouquet," one of Chesnutt's most important short stories from his collection *"The Wife of His Youth" and Other Stories of the Color Line*, interrogates race relations and segregation in the South during the aftermath of the Civil War. It is a work given little attention, although it reflects one of the best examples of the author's thinking about segregation, thinking that has roots in his early life in the South. Born in 1858, in Cleveland, Ohio, Chesnutt was the son of Ann Maria and Andrew Jackson Chesnutt, both free blacks who moved back to Fayetteville, North Carolina, in 1866. As a youth during Radical Reconstruction, Chesnutt heard discussions about the passing of the Fourteenth and Fifteenth Amendments, allowing African Americans the privilege of citizenship and the right to vote, respectively. With the removal of the Freedmen's Bureau in 1877 and after the *Plessy v. Ferguson* case in 1896, which institutionalized segregation, Chesnutt, troubled by racial proscription and limited employment opportunities, decided to return to Cleveland and pursue his dream of becoming a writer with a "high holy purpose." He believed that the unjust spirit of "caste" that subjected an entire race to "scorn and ostracism" was "a barrier to the moral progress of the American people" (*Journals* 139–40).

First published in the *Atlantic Monthly* in 1898, and included later in *"The Wife of His Youth"* (1899), "The Bouquet" highlights racial segregation and discrimination and the absurdities of Jim Crow laws in a Southern community. Mainly through the interactions of the three principal characters in the story—a young black student, Sophy Tucker; her white teacher, Miss Mary Myrover; and the teacher's mother, Mrs. Myrover—Chesnutt depicts aspects of both the Old and the New South. My purpose in teaching "The Bouquet" (at the freshman or sophomore level) is to help students understand the restrictions, limitations, and inhumanity of the Jim Crow era and discover, in that era, examples of kindness, civility, courage, and humane behavior. These positive qualities are displayed in the story by characters that represent the kinds of people Chesnutt hoped would become champions for justice in the South. I focus my lessons on his engagement with history and his use of specific literary techniques (such as narrative perspective, symbolic language, irony, and satire) to change negative attitudes.

To interpret the "The Bouquet," teacher and students need to be familiar with the Jim Crow laws that were prevalent in America during the era in which Chesnutt wrote. *From Slavery to Freedom* (especially chapters 12 through 15), by the historians John Hope Franklin and Alfred A. Moss, Jr., and *Trouble in Mind: Black Southerners in the Age of Jim Crow* (chapter 5), by Leon F.

Litwack, provide excellent treatment of the period. I assign these chapters to my students alongside "The Bouquet." This pairing of the historical and the literary

> places the story in its historical context, so that students can identify
> examples of the segregation and discrimination that result from *Plessy
> v. Ferguson*
> helps students recognize the inhumanity caused by racial discrimination
> helps students see the humanity of and resistance to segregation by cer-
> tain characters in the story

I recommend beginning the lesson by letting students share their opinions about "The Bouquet." I ask them to respond to the story orally, by making comments and asking questions. The instructor may add to the discussion by asking how the the story is constructed and if the title fits the plot and how. Responses, of course, will often center on Sophy's yellow bouquet and on the white flowers at Miss Myrover's funeral. Typically, at least one student will say that the title could be a metaphor for the array of colors among the students in Miss Myrover's class, an interpretation supported by some textual evidence: "She had never been brought in personal contact with so many of them at once as when she confronted the fifty or sixty faces—of colors ranging from a white almost as clear as her own to the darkest livery of the sun—which were gathered in the schoolroom on the morning when she began her duties" ("Bouquet" 241). But the bouquet is one color only, yellow, and students will need to discover why it is associated with one character only.

At this point, it is useful to provide an explanation of how the setting of the story is connected with Chesnutt personally. The incidents take place in a small town in North Carolina, which is probably based on Fayetteville. A discussion of the author's life in the South in the late nineteenth century will give students the opportunity to explore the story's commentary on Southern segregation and to offer some thoughts about why he wrote the story. A summary of the Jim Crow laws about segregation and the "separate but equal" dictum, legalized by *Plessy v. Ferguson*, may be introduced here.

The social and institutional segregation is emphasized as soon as Miss Myrover begins her teaching position. Even though blacks of the era were familiar to whites in their roles as servants, they were not considered equal to whites. Miss Myrover feels threatened by a group of "colored children" in the classroom. Her fear is a result of Jim Crow practices, beginning in the 1870s, after the Civil War and Reconstruction. After the Supreme Court rescinded the Civil Rights Laws of 1875, blacks were banned from most public places in the South, such as hotels, barber shops, restaurants, parks, libraries, and theaters. By 1885, most Southern states passed laws that established the color line everywhere, including separate schools for whites and blacks. The Supreme Court upheld these laws in 1896 (Franklin and Moss 242). The inhumanity of these rulings placed such barriers between Southern whites and blacks that it became almost impossible for the two races to interact in a positive way:

> Miss Myrover taught the colored children, but she could not be seen with them in public. If they met her on the street, they did not expect her to speak to them, unless no other white person was in sight. If the children felt slighted, she was unaware of it, for she intended no slight; and though she was a woman of sentiment capable of deep feeling, her training had been such that she hardly expected to find in those of darker hue than herself the same susceptibility—varying in degree, perhaps, but yet the same in kind—that gave to her own life the alternations of feeling that made it most worth living.   ("Bouquet" 243)

This passage illuminates the destructiveness of segregation, as it reveals Miss Myrover's mind-set, her acceptance that normal communication between a white teacher and her black students is forbidden outside the classroom: "[S]he had not been brought up to speak to negroes on the street, and she could not act differently from other people" (243). I often emphasize Chesnutt's use of irony here, as Miss Myrover has not given a thought to the fact that her students may have felt slighted, though she is supposed to be a woman "capable of deep feeling." Readers are sure to conclude that Miss Myrover, at this point in the story, has no feeling for the discomfort of blacks. But there is a deeper problem, of which she is unaware. Before and during the nineteenth century, most white Americans did not believe blacks were fully human. Slave mothers could be torn away from their children with impunity because they were believed not to have the same feelings as whites. Chesnutt shows in "The Bouquet" that Miss Myrover is a product of the old regime and that her upbringing does not allow her to imagine that black people have "deep feeling[s]." He wants his readers to be cognizant of such views and realize that racial attitudes can be passed from generation to generation.

After the historical context is discussed, students will understand that the inhumane practices stemming from the segregation laws prevent Sophy from doing a simple act of human kindness. After her beloved teacher's death, she wants to show her love and respect by placing a bouquet of yellow roses on Miss Myrover's coffin but is prevented, first by Mrs. Myrover and later by the usher at the entry of the church. Sophy views the service through a crack in a stained glass window that depicts Jesus blessing the little children at his feet. The instructor may point out to students that Chesnutt presents Sophy's efforts in a spiritual context: "Suffer the little children to come unto me, and forbid them not," Jesus says (Mark 10.13 [*Holy Bible*; American Standard Version]). The image of Jesus is ironic in view of the white usher's un-Christian act of turning Sophy and the black mourners away from the church and Miss Myrover's funeral.

SallyAnn Ferguson, commenting on Chesnutt's signifying on Christianity, states that the author's black characters often become symbols of "mortal suffering," whose reward "is often death" (8). Sophy does not die but encounters more challenges caused by Jim Crow segregation. When the funeral is over, she faces humiliation and restrictions at the cemetery. At the burial place of her teacher, she reads a sign: "Notice. This cemetery is for white people only. Others, please keep out." Her ability to read the sign is a testament to Miss Myrover's teaching, but her understanding of *other* is grounded in her memory of a black man who was sentenced to a chain gang for disobeying the sign. She hears "thuds of dirt" covering the casket as she leans "sobbing against the iron fence" that separates her from the cemetery ("Bouquet" 248). Clearly, Sophy is an example of "mortal suffering." Instead of eliminating her from the story, though, Chesnutt allows the reader to experience her pain, which represents the pain of all black Americans in the South who suffer racial discrimination. The sign at the cemetery points to the reality of Jim Crow, which forces African Americans to be "outsiders" (Duncan 47). Students now can often see that Chesnutt highlights black peoples' separation from mainstream America by using symbolic language: "barred passage," "locked gate," "keep out," "fence," and "outside" ("Bouquet" 247–48).

My third purpose in teaching this story is to have students recognize its demonstrations of humanity and compassion. One classroom activity might be to ask students to identify the agents and acts of humanity in the story. Sophy and Miss Myrover's relationship is the most prominent example. Sophy is Miss Myrover's favorite student, and her intense devotion to her teacher reminds Miss Myrover of the old regime. Thus the teacher perceives Sophy at first as of a stereotype, and her kindness to the little girl is more condescending than genuine. But students might be asked questions that complicate this initial assessment: Are not Miss Myrover's notions about Sophy clouded by her superficial understanding of blacks? Why does Miss Myrover not recognize the little girl's admiration as coming from innocent, unconditional love? Chesnutt makes Sophy appear, at first, as an ingratiating stereotype from the Old South: the slave who aims to please her mistress. Yet Sophy turns out to be more than a little replica of Uncle Tom.

This meaning beyond the stereotype is made evident through the actions of both teacher and student. From the third-person narrator one learns that Sophy's face is without "envy or regret, nothing but worship for the beautiful white teacher." It is true that Sophy might have been conditioned by her environment to think the teacher is beautiful because she is white, but Miss Myrover is consistently kind to her. She accepts flowers from Sophy and the other children but treats Sophy with special kindness, to the point that the other students grow jealous. Miss Myrover gives Sophy a ribbon from her hair and allows the child to carry her books and follow her home. My students quickly suspect that Miss Myrover appreciates Sophy more than she admits. I help them note that the author changes his point of view from third person to the first, to intensify the personal drama of the wish expressed by Miss Myrover: "When I die, Sophy, I want to be covered with roses . . . I shall rest better . . . if my grave is banked with flowers, and roses are planted at my head and at my feet" (242). This burial instruction suggests a teacher's trust in her pupil that goes beyond a mistress-slave relationship. Miss Myrover also shows genuine affection and respect for Sophy when she accepts the "yellow roses" that come from Sophy's "own bush." She says, "Thank you, Sophy. . . . You are a good girl" (244). This encouragement indicates a change from her previous thoughts about her pupil. The teacher acknowledges Sophy's humanity and personal worth.

As the class discussion develops, students increasingly become convinced that Sophy functions in the story not as stock character but as a person with many fine qualities—determination, perseverance, courage, and intelligence. Chesnutt identifies Sophy with the yellow bouquet, the color of the sun, which symbolizes hope and new beginnings. When the little girl is blocked from delivering the flowers, she gets Miss Myrover's pet dog to do it. Here Chesnutt uses satire to ridicule segregation. The dog, Prince, wanders in and out of the cemetery and among the guests. Unlike Sophy's experience, no one has the heart to bar the dog from the cemetery. By envying the dog's freedom, Sophy shows a new awareness of her own lack of freedom because of her racial status, which is a step in her growing up.

At the end of the lesson, the teacher might pose the question of whether or not Chesnutt kills off Miss Myrover so that her pupil will carry the torch that will bring about better race relations in the town. Remember the image of Sophy at Jesus's feet. Does Sophy act in the story as an agent of harmony and justice? Although the class is sure to have many different responses to these questions, it seems that Chesnutt wants his readers to see a flicker of hope as the yellow bouquet stands out in the sea of white roses.

"The Bouquet" can be taught alone or serve as an introduction to a broader study of Chesnutt's fiction. The story illustrates his efforts to tackle racial problems at the turn of the century through writing fiction that was realistic and did not oversimplify the dynamics of these problems. "The Bouquet" is an excellent introduction to reading his works. Known for his mastery of irony in his short fiction and novels, Chesnutt is considered a major American author.

Chesnutt as Cultural Critic

Mark Sussman

While today Charles Chesnutt is known primarily as a writer of fiction, he made a good living through his legal stenography practice, and he was also a prolific essayist and public speaker. This essay integrates his cultural criticism and professional practice with classroom study of his writing. Although modern readers are impressed by his fiction's critical engagement with the racial politics and attitudes of its day, my purpose is not to argue that his fiction was a transparent vessel for the communication of political positions that were set out more explicitly in his essays, speeches, reviews, and reporting. His cultural criticism can help students understand that his attitudes were always complex, sometimes contradictory, and not necessarily accessible through the fiction. Chesnutt was a Republican but not a doctrinaire one. He was an integrationist but had curiously laissez-faire attitudes about methods of integration. He railed against the disenfranchisement of the average African American but was in no way a populist. He was neither a Du Boisian nor a Washingtonian but saw the virtues in both positions—in fact, he might be thought of as a paradigmatically Du Boisian elite who nevertheless found himself occasionally advocating Washingtonian policies.

To aid teachers in guiding their students through the complex set of critical practices and political positions that characterize Chesnutt's writing and thinking, I have divided this essay into three sections, each reflecting a cultural concern that Chesnutt addressed throughout his career: Education and the Franchise, The Future of the Race, and Morals and Character. These three themes in no way encompass the topics and ideas that he wrote about in his nonfiction and criticism, but they provide a starting point for teachers who want to give students a sense of the political and social discourses that Chesnutt was engaging not only in his criticism but in his fiction as well. While I frequently reference his fiction, I draw primarily on his essays, speeches, reviews, journals, and letters in order to suggest teaching strategies that can illuminate the fraught cultural and political background of his novels and stories. Teachers interested in his cultural criticism and nonfiction are advised to seek out *Charles W. Chesnutt: Essays and Speeches*, edited by Joseph McElrath, Robert Leitz, and Jesse Crisler, which conveniently collects all his known nonfiction, both published and unpublished in his lifetime. Teachers may also find it helpful to consult *The Journals of Charles W. Chesnutt*, edited by Richard Brodhead.

Education and the Franchise

One of the through lines in Chesnutt's criticism is his persistent concern with the problem of disenfranchisement. The denial of voting rights to blacks under

Jim Crow, as Chesnutt saw it, constituted the single greatest obstacle to the normalization of black participation in American culture and society. But this position emerged out of an earlier conviction that education would serve as the primary path to racial uplift. The shift from an emphasis on education to an emphasis on the vote constitutes one of the most important contrasts in Chesnutt's career as a critic.

In his 1882 speech "The Future of the Negro," Chesnutt claimed, "Only by popular education, fostered by a system of well-supported, free, public schools can the state be saved from anarchy" (*Charles W. Chesnutt: Essays* 28). In another 1882 speech, "Methods of Teaching," delivered to the North Carolina Teachers Educational Association, he espoused the ancient Greek view that "[e]ducation is not merely a preparation for life, but an integral part of it; that development is the highest duty and privilege of man, and that whatever promotes development is valuable—indeed is invaluable in a system of education" (42). Contrast this classical notion of education, tellingly stripped of any racial or political context, with his essay of two decades later, "The Disenfranchisement of the Negro" (1903). In it, he writes, "Education has been put forward as the great corrective" to race problems in the United States yet remarks that blacks will be educated only insofar as they are useful to white communities, to which they will remain subordinate. In other words, "it is not quite apparent how education alone, in the ordinary meaning of the word, is to solve, in any appreciable time, the problem of the relations of Southern white and black people" (186). Education, from Chesnutt's perspective, is useless in securing the right of self-determination from Southern states, which implement poll taxes, literacy tests, and other means of circumventing the Fifteenth Amendment and suppressing the black vote.

In the classroom, these essays, alongside speeches on education, like "The Advantages of a Well-Constructed Literary Society" (1881; *Charles W. Chesnutt: Essays* 13–24), and later essays on the franchise, like "Liberty and the Franchise" (1899; 101–08), can help teachers illustrate how Chesnutt's shift from emphasizing educational institutions, like the normal schools, where Chesnutt received his training as a teacher, to political institutions, like the franchise, signals more broadly articulated social and cultural concerns. Teachers could point out that the shift from Chesnutt's first novel, *The House behind the Cedars* (published in 1900 but begun in the mid-1880s), to his second, *The Marrow of Tradition* (1901), reflects what Chesnutt saw as an increasingly dire and dangerous political reality for Southern blacks, one that could be addressed only through the swift reclamation of constitutional rights—in other words, not through the slow and deliberate processes of mass education.

The Future of the Race

Less concerned with the theoretical underpinnings holding his worldview together, Chesnutt was interested in the tangible outcomes of the opinions, policies, and practices he recommended. Yet this emphasis on the practical outcomes of political and sociocultural matters often had a future orientation. In some sense, he was a practitioner of what George Fredrickson has called "racial prognostication." Fredrickson finds that this tendency of white writers, activists, and politicians to forecast the "ultimate destiny of blacks" reveals unspoken assumptions about the nature of white racism (xii). Chesnutt, though, speculated earnestly about the future of race in the United States, and his views hew closer to the anti-essentialist tradition in race thinking than to anything else.[1] In fact, his essays on this subject can help introduce students to the anti-essentialist ideas in *The House behind the Cedars* as well as in critical and scholarly discourses about race more broadly.

Chesnutt explored the political implications of race mixing relatively early in his career as a writer. In his essay "What Is a White Man?" (1889), he argued that the denial of the franchise to African Americans was an increasingly incoherent position, because "where the intermingling of races has made such progress as it has in this country, the line which separates the races must in many instances have been practically obliterated" (*Charles W. Chesnutt: Essays* 68). Given the fact that, as many have noted, Chesnutt could have passed as a white man but chose not to, his concern with the problems inherent to American racial classification has certain unavoidably autobiographical inflections. Teachers may find it useful to teach this essay alongside *The House behind the Cedars*, as the essay demonstrates that, although the novel draws on the tradition of sentimental fiction for many of its emotional cues, it draws equally on a broad, counterintuitive critique of American racial politics. This pairing also shows one of the many ways that Chesnutt uses the conventions of genre fiction to drive home a political point.

The most comprehensive site of Chesnutt's prognostications is the essay series The Future American, written for the *Boston Evening Transcript* in 1900. In these three essays, Chesnutt speculates that, because of intermarriage and "race mixing," a "new type" will emerge naturally through the "amalgamation" of the races (*Charles W. Chesnutt: Essays* 124). Published the same year as *The House behind the Cedars*, the three essays evince the same concern with the social consequences of race mixing as the novel. By the third essay, having argued for the inevitability and desirability of the complete merging of the races, Chesnutt addresses the social and political obstacles to this merging. On the one hand, he finds claims by segregationists that "the Negro ought to develop his own civilization, and has no right to share in that of the white race" untenable insofar as "[t]he white people of the present generation did not make their civilization; they inherited it ready-made, and much of the wealth which is so strong a factor in their power was created by the unpaid labor of the colored people." In other words, the civilizational divide posited by segregationists, if it exists, was made possible only by slavery and the slave trade. On the other hand, he notes that "the low industrial and social efficiency of the colored race" has contributed to the slow pace of "race admixture." If total "amalgamation" seemed to be the future of the race, then the "poverty," "ignorance," and "servile estate" of blacks were the stumbling blocks that would prevent "social fusion" with whites (133).

As a background to Chesnutt's novels, teachers can use these essays as points of comparison and contrast to his color line stories. While commonly taught stories like "The Wife of His Youth," "A Matter of Principle," and "Her Virginia Mammy" see Chesnutt attempting to bridge the divide between an antebellum racial past and a post-Reconstruction racial present, between the separate but interpenetrating social spheres of whites and blacks, his essays on the future of race in America show a thinker much more alive to the social realities and political contradictions of "amalgamation" than his fiction suggests. Teachers may want to use these essays to show that, if these stories advocate political positions we may want to unambiguously endorse, they emerge from analyses of race that are sometimes difficult to square with modern liberal ideas. Reading Chesnutt's stories about race mixing against his essays about the future of the race can help teachers provide a valuable lesson about the historicity of the relation between politics and fiction and the changing ways that we as a culture have learned to speak about race.

Morals and Character

As the editors of *Charles W. Chesnutt: Essays and Speeches* remind us, Chesnutt was, in his morals, ideals, and often tone, "an eminent Victorian" (McElrath et al. xxxiv). The second entry in his journals sees him copying out paragraphs from Samuel Roberts Wells's *A Handbook for Home Improvement* (1857) that concern personal hygiene and etiquette—for Chesnutt these were not superficial concerns but matters of character (*Journals* 40). It is appropriate, then, that he began his career as a speaker and writer with "Etiquette (Good Manners)" (1881; *Charles W. Chesnutt: Essays* 1–12), a speech delivered to the Normal Literary Society of Fayetteville, North Carolina. It frames proper etiquette, polite conduct, fastidious personal appearance and hygiene, and temperance as matters essential to the maintenance of young men's character. At the beginning of the speech, he writes that a teacher ought to be "a Christian gentleman," one who treats his work "as a sacred trust committed to him, for the proper discharge of which he is responsible, not only to school-committees and parents, but to God, who gave him the talent to teach" (1). His writing on character and morals, maybe more than any of his other cultural and political concerns, may help teachers contextualize him as a writer shaped by middle-class values of the last quarter of the nineteenth century. His promotion of bourgeois habits in his essays, along with the more critical perspective taken in many of his color line stories, can illustrate for students what the everyday experience of the sort of social progress Chesnutt sought might have felt and looked like.

From an early-twenty-first-century perspective, his insistence on minute points of etiquette may seem absurd, but for him, as for many late-nineteenth-century writers and thinkers, manners were the most direct way that the internal matter of character made its way into the social sphere. As he says, "According to [a certain theory], the man who wears a dirty shirt for any length of time loses all the finer feelings of humanity, gives way to his baser passions, and is then in a condition to commit almost any crime." Though he finds this view extreme, he sees "a grain of truth to it" (4). Teachers seeking to incorporate this aspect of his cultural criticism into lessons might suggest that his emphasis on manners, morals, and character exemplifies a larger trend in nineteenth-century American culture. As James Salazar has persuasively argued, "character" was "a pervasive and defining keyword across a range of nineteenth-century political, literary, philosophical, scientific, and pedagogical discourses" (1). In the Gilded Age especially, character occupied an essential position in attempts to think about the mutually shaping relation between people and their environments. Amplified in this early speech, then, his insistence on the connection between character, morals, and racial progress was very much in step with his historical moment, and they would remain with him for his entire career.

In "Race Ideals and Examples," a speech delivered to students at Wilberforce University in 1913, for example (*Charles W. Chesnutt: Essays* 331–48), Chesnutt emphasized that personal development would serve as the basis of any advancement for blacks in the United States:

> When a sufficient number of colored men and women have accomplished worthy things in the various fields of human endeavor; when they have attained not only a fair advantage, but enough of them have risen to the top to make the rest of the world sit up and take notice, then prejudice will have lost its chief prop and will have to rest its existence on lower foundations which will not be able to withstand the forces of justice and fair dealing.   (335)

While black suffrage remained at the center of his political concerns, he warned his students that "races are judged by their great men," and so social equality would be attainable only through "adopt[ing] your own personal ideals of character and conduct" (337, 331).

Teachers may find it useful to demonstrate to their students how this concern with Victorian morals and character helped shape Chesnutt's literary historical reception or contributed to the lack of it. By his own analysis, his insistence on the moral imperatives of fiction made him unsuitable for the literary avant-garde of the Harlem Renaissance. In his 1929 speech "The Negro in Present Day Fiction" (*Charles W. Chesnutt: Essays* 516–29), Chesnutt told students at Oberlin College, "The heart of any romantic novel is the heroine," but in "the present day Negro novel . . . precious few of them are given any heroic attributes. With the exception of Mary in [Carl Van Vechten's] *Nigger Heaven*, or the heroine of Walter White's first novel [*Fire in the Flint* (1927)], and the women of Miss [Jessie] Fauset's novels, they are all unchaste" (523). In his last essay published in his lifetime, "Post-Bellum—Pre-Harlem" (1930; 543–49), he again lamented that "the heroine of the [Negro] novel is never chaste, though for the matter of that few post-Victorian heroines are," while adding that "most of the males are likewise weaklings or worse" (547). Teachers may consider using these essays as literary historical signposts suggesting the reasons both for his disappearance (perhaps his criticism of Harlem Renaissance fiction) from the canon and his later reentry to it. In signaling his disdain for the character of contemporary black fiction, he foreshadowed the kind of reading to which his own works would be subjected until his rediscovery in the late 1960s. He proudly laid claim to a set of seemingly antiquated Victorian morals, and it would be several decades before scholars would take the time to notice that his work reflected something much more complex than that.

NOTE

[1] The connection between Fredrickson's "racial prognostication" and Chesnutt's thinking about the future of race was first raised by Friedman.

"[T]o Remove the Disability of Color": Chesnutt in the Context of the American Eugenics Movement

George Gordon-Smith

This essay proposes methods for teaching Charles W. Chesnutt's The Future American essays in the context of the American eugenics movement. My approach introduces critical disability studies as a useful tool for helping students understand how Chesnutt responded to associations of race and disability in the early twentieth century. It also offers methods for examining how his essays directly challenged overwhelmingly popular eugenics arguments for sexual regulation between blacks and whites. Teaching a Future American essay by him in this way helps students see not only the relation between constructions of race and disability in the early twentieth century but also how Chesnutt used biological arguments to criticize eugenic efforts for further African American disenfranchisement.

Teachers unfamiliar with critical disability studies or eugenics may feel uneasy teaching Chesnutt's essays with this approach. My objective here is to introduce a basic understanding of disability studies and demonstrate for teachers how disability theory can transform our basic assumptions about identity, ideology, politics, social justice, race, and the body in Chesnutt's work. My hope is that by putting core issues in disability studies in conversation with Chesnutt studies, teachers will feel comfortable implementing disability theory when teaching his fiction and essays. I begin by offering a brief introduction to disability studies. The sources I cite can be used to familiarize students with this field before they begin an analysis of Chesnutt's essays. I follow with pragmatic teaching suggestions for The Future American essays, which use both disability studies and archival sources from the American eugenics movement.

Critical Race and Disability Studies in the Classroom

For many students the similarities between racial stereotypes and assumptions about people with disabilities are not immediately obvious. Teachers may find it useful to rely on familiar comparative models that demonstrate that critical race and disability studies share scholarly points of contact. In preparation for a discussion on race and disability, I have in the past asked my students to search, before they came to class, for articles that might be useful in beginning a conversation about race, disability, and eugenics. Examples for comparison are articles denying Oscar Pistorius's ability to participate in the 2008 Beijing Olympic games and arguments against Jesse Owens's fitness to compete in the 1936 Olympic games. Students can also turn to newspaper articles about Emmett

Till, the African American teenager lynched in 1955 for allegedly whistling at a white woman; it turns out that he had a speech impediment, a lisp. Teachers can also direct students to statistical records and examine the comparatively high number of African Americans with disabilities, or the shocking fact that African American's limbs are more likely to be amputated than a white's limbs for the same disease. I encourage students to search online for blogs, *YouTube* videos, and scholarly articles that might be useful in beginning a conversation about race, disability, and eugenics. Preparing my students this way allows them to do something they are comfortable with—search the Internet—and sets the stage for teaching them two important similarities between race and disability: that they are both social constructions and both relational concepts.

If you are teaching an undergraduate class, your students may not be familiar with the terms *social construction* and *relationality*. You might use two easily accessible articles to illustrate the first of these points to students: Ian Haney Lopez's "The Social Construction of Race" and Douglas Baynton's "Disability and the Justification of Inequality in American History." When I assign these articles, I like to ask students what race as a social construction might mean. I point out that Haney Lopez argues that "biological race is an illusion," that "social race . . . is not," and that "race has its genesis and maintains its vigorous strength in the realm of social beliefs" (172). Asking students what it means that race is in fact an illusion and has its genesis in social belief shows them how race and disability can become conflated. I draw their attention to Baynton's article, in which various examples are given of ethnicity as disability, and I write the following quotation from his article on the board: "An 'educated negro,' like a 'free negro,' is a social monstrosity, even more unnatural and repulsive than the latter" (21). As a class we discuss what social beliefs this statement portrays and what historical meanings society has constructed of race that might lend credence to this statement.

Similarly, disability is a social construction. This awareness contests the idea that "biology is destiny" (Linton 532) and theorizes the body's place in society and culture. In contrast to clinical, medical, or therapeutic perspectives on disability, which define disability as an individual defect that must be cured or eliminated if the person is to achieve full capacity as a human being, critical disability studies focuses on how disability is defined and represented in society (Siebers 3). From this perspective, disability is not a characteristic that exists in the person or a problem of the person that must be fixed or cured. Instead, it is a construct that acquires meaning in a social and cultural context. In preparation for a discussion on Chesnutt, teachers should point out to students that just as critical race studies helps us understand how *race* acquires meaning in the social and cultural contexts of slavery and Jim Crow, critical disability studies helps us understand how both *race* and *disability* acquire meaning in the social and cultural contexts of the American eugenics movement. Perceptive students will begin to realize that perhaps Chesnutt's claims for complete amalgamation of the races may in fact be a cure for race.

Explaining race and disability as a relational concept can also prepare students for Chesnutt's argument for amalgamation. I often explain relationality to my students by drawing again from Haney Lopez's article and asking them to consider the following quotation: "Races are constructed relationally against one another, rather than in isolation" (168). Once students see that whiteness stands in contradistinction to blackness, we consider the relationality of ability and disability by drawing on work by Rosemarie Garland-Thomson, a disability scholar. I have students read the following excerpt from her *Extraordinary Bodies*: "[W]ithout the monstrous body to demarcate the borders of the generic . . . and without the pathological to give form to the normal, the taxonomies of bodily value that underlie political, social, and economic arrangements would collapse" (20). Such quotations make for a discussion-based class that allows students to ask difficult questions about associating race and disability. Teachers may find it useful to draw students back to the repeated use of the word *monster* and ask, If educated African Americans have been defined as monstrous, and monstrosity sets the boundary by which we define what is normal, what does this tell us about similarities between representations of race and disability? Consider, in Chesnutt's fiction, the "club-footed nigger" from "The Conjurer's Revenge" (47), or Viney, the allegedly mute slave woman from "The Dumb Witness." These two short stories make for excellent readings in race and disability.

It is also important for students to understand that *disability*, like the labels *cripple, handicapped,* and *lame,* traces its origins to a hierarchy of able-bodiedness. In other words, there is no disability without the construction of ablebodiedness. Reminding students of Toni Morrison's claim that "blackness" is not originally connected to black people but is only another's interpretation of a person of African descent makes the point that the denigration of disability depends on a socially and environmentally constructed preference for ablebodiedness (7). I describe for my students the ideology of ability as the invisible center around which contradictory opinions about human ability revolve. In his third Future American essay, Chesnutt writes, "[Black] poverty, [black] ignorance and [a black] servile estate render them as yet largely ineligible for social fusion with a race whose pride is fed . . . by a constant comparison with a less developed and less fortunate race" (*Charles W. Chesnutt: Essays* 133). The invisible center—white, male, educated, and ablebodied—serves as the nucleus around which meanings of nonnormativity—black, female, uneducated, and disabled—are defined. Without uneducated and servile blacks, white achievement would be meaningless.

The Future American

Some of your students may have read a few of Chesnutt's short stories and novels, but few will have read his essays. Moreover, most know little about eugenics. To prepare your class for a discussion of race and eugenics, you might let them know that at the turn of the twentieth century, when Booker T. Washington

proposed a segregationist solution to America's racial problems, Chesnutt explicitly advocated a very different racial theory. In his essays and speeches, he
promoted the revolutionary—and highly unpopular—idea that miscegenation
and intermarriage were the answer to American racial conflict. If racial identity
could be erased, he reasoned, fabricated disabilities attributed to race—such as
physical anomaly, psychological instability, and intellectual inferiority—could
no longer serve as a basis for discrimination, and racial conflict would necessarily disappear. He made his most definitive and comprehensive statements
on racial identity in The Future American, a series of three articles published
by the *Boston Evening Transcript* in the late summer of 1900.[1] The newspaper
generally sympathized with the racial policies of Washington, but its literary
editor, Edgar Chamberlin, solicited the articles from Chesnutt after a conversation with him about eugenics and American fears of miscegenation (Keller 166).
The appearance of these articles coincided with the publication of Chesnutt's
first novel, *The House behind the Cedars*, which makes the same racial argument in fictional form.

By the late nineteenth and early twentieth century, assumptions about race
and racial identity were largely organized around a growing form of intellectual
racism called eugenics. When one moves into a discussion about eugenics, I
recommend relying on an excellent and easily accessible Web site called *Cold
Spring Harbor Laboratory's Image Archive on the American Eugenics Movement* (eugenicsarchive.org) to facilitate in-class exploration of the different resources available. Such a lesson plan will familiarize students with the eugenics
vocabulary they will encounter in The Future American essays. I encourage
them to search this archive in groups and to make a list of key words that they
encounter. As the class begins to share the sources they have read, I ask pointed
questions: How is race represented in the documents you read? How is disability represented? What words or terms are used to describe both race and
disability? What racial stereotypes did you find present in the sources? What
disability stereotypes? Were there overlaps in these constructions? What do
such overlaps tell us about eugenics, twentieth-century views on disability, and
race? Through such questions and group work, I avoid lecturing students about
the history of eugenics.

Another option is to give students specific documents from eugenicsarchive
.org and ask them to view and read them using what they've learned from our
discussions of critical race and disability studies. Most of the documents are
between one and two pages and include newspaper clippings, public service
pamphlets, medical reports, and photographs. I like to begin with image 1243,
Negroid Sane Criminals and Negroid Civil Insane, and image 1244, *Rankings
in Murder*, both of which are dramatic in their absurdity. I encourage students
to consider the social constructions and relationality that shape perceptions of
both race and disability, asking, What strategies do your find eugenicists using
to make their claims about racial incapacity? Images 564, *Difference between
White and Negro Fetuses*, and 568, *Racial Difference in Mental Fatigue*, can

lead to productive conversations about relationality, to observations that resurface in The Future American essays.

In my experience, the most generative Chesnutt essay for discussions of race, disability, and eugenics is the first. I have students examine the subtitle to the essay: "What the Race Is Likely to Become in the Process of Time: A Perfect Type Supposedly to be Evolved." Students should recall the list of terms they came up with while analyzing various archival sources on eugenicsarchive.org. I ask them about the language Chesnutt uses to argue for complete amalgamation. How does he use the word *type* in the essay? Is it similar to the use of the same word in the eugenics documents (e.g., "Nordic type" or "Mongolian type")? What does Chesnutt mean when he calls for a "future ethnic type," one that is mixed (*Charles W. Chesnutt: Essays* 121)? How does he justify the term, and is his justification similar to or dissimilar from the claims of eugenics? I ask, Given what you've read about eugenics, how might proponents of eugenic thought respond to Chesnutt's proposal? Note that Chesnutt defines *race* in his article "in its popular sense—that of a people who look substantially alike, and are molded by the same culture and dominated by the same ideals" (97). What does this definition tell us about social constructions? How is Chesnutt's *race* different from *type*? How is it similar? What is his genetic formula for racial equality, and what does it require? Chesnutt suggests that it should be a "misdemeanor for two white or two colored to marry" (124).

For a more focused discussion of his goals in the article, teachers can have students read the following quotation from his essay "Race Prejudice: Its Causes and Cures," published in a 1905 issue of *Alexander's Magazine*. Here he asserts that physical "antagonisms" are the product of differences of color, form, and feature among black and white Americans (219):

> They [genuine whites and blacks] differ physically, the one being black and the other white. The one constituted for poets and sculptors the ideal of beauty and grace: the other was rude and unpolished in form and feature. The one possessed the arts of civilization and the learning of the schools: the other, at most, the simple speech and rude handicrafts of his native tribe, and no written language at all. The one was Christian, the other heathen. The one was master of the soil; the other frankly alien and himself the object of ownership.   (218)

Students are often struck by how racist this quotation seems. Teachers may want to ask students, What are the characteristics of whites, according to Chesnutt, and of African Americans? He argues that because of black deficiencies—which seem both physical and mental—the race needs to dilute itself through miscegenation with apparently superior whites. How is this reasoning similar to the methodology of the eugenicists who were his contemporaries? How does it differ? Ultimately, the dilution would yield Chesnutt's racial ideal, an ethnic type or raceless hybrid formed from an admixture of the red, white, and black races inhabiting America. It can be useful at this point to make references to this type of thinking in Chesnutt's fiction. Recall that in *The House behind the Cedars*, John Walden calls those who have lightened their restrictive appearance and physical differences through miscegenation a "new people" (57).

I want students to realize that implied in Chesnutt's statement is that associations of race and disability will somehow be eliminated as amalgamation occurs. The distinctions, for example, that Chesnutt highlights in the above quotation are rooted in the assertion of black mental deficiency. African Americans, he seems to suggest, possess simple speech and no written language; they are unpolished in form and feature—what does "unpolished" mean?—and are the object of ownership, and therefore dependent on others. But if amalgamation eliminates these constructions, how are we to respond to his assertion here? Students tend to take one of two sides: Chesnutt is either suggesting that breeding out blackness will in fact lead to a more educated and mentally superior collection of people of African descent as they mix with whites; or he is suggesting that as black physical differences are bred out, associations of blackness and disability will disappear.

Teachers may want to point out to the students who say that Chesnutt is merely using eugenic language in his essays to make a more convincing case that he believed that the future American would look white, that all the racial and ethnic variances that account for physical difference would be erased. By now, students should see that The Future American essays complicate Chesnutt's egalitarian call for amalgamation. In his 1889 essay "What Is a White Man?," Chesnutt writes, "The states vary slightly in regard to what constitutes a mulatto or person of color, and as to what proportion of white blood should be sufficient to remove the disability of color" (*Charles W. Chesnutt: Essays* 69). What are the implications of his suggestion that color is a disability? Is he saying that color can be diagnosed and cured or merely that being black in the early twentieth century is a burden? Can we use disability to describe being black in America this way? What does this equation tell us about the influence of eugenics on his thinking? Is amalgamation a cure for blackness or a solution to racial strife? The purpose of these questions is not necessarily to find an answer, and arguing that Chesnutt advocated an infusion of curative white blood into a socially and physically dysfunctional black race is not the point. Rather, examining the potential alliance between racial uplift and eugenic theory, an alliance not uncommon among his African American contemporaries, offers new and insightful ways of reading his fiction.

For those students who feel that Chesnutt aligned himself with eugenicist thought, teachers should point out the desperate straits in which black Americans found themselves at the turn of the twentieth century. Chesnutt may not have been accepting a eugenics agenda but speculating on the semiotics of skin and the conditions necessary for racial accord. In a 1906 letter to Washington, for example, he expressed skepticism that blacks and whites could coexist without intermingling (199). As eugenicist rhetoric increased, he became more involved with his arguments for the amalgamation of the races. As late as 1928, in "The Negro in Present Day Fiction," an address to the Dunbar Forum in Oberlin, Ohio, he said:

> A better word to describe the modern American Negro would be the "New American." In my opinion, the American Negro, so called, or mis-called, is destined, if his ultimate absorption into the composite American race is long deferred, to develop a type which is widely different from the West African type from which he has descended. (520)

In teaching Chesnutt in the context of the American eugenics movement, teachers might conclude by noting that eugenics was simply the evolution of two hundred years of racism that maintained white hegemony through pseudo-science-based arguments for the superiority of Europeans over Africans. Racial theorists like Samuel Morton, and later Samuel Cartwright, Thomas Drew, and Frederick L. Hoffman, influenced public opinion to such an extent that the American eugenics movement simply became the next stage of scientific racism, assigning the opprobrium of blackness from physiological difference to genetic heritage. Chesnutt's awareness of the power and appeal of eugenic thought among white and even black Americans is obvious in his The Future American essays, which argue that social equity could be achieved only through the corporeal perfection of racial admixture. Disability is a useful lens through which to explore these essays because eugenic arguments for racial purity are similar to arguments that disability is something to be cured or eliminated. Just as constructions of disability depend on built environments that fabricate normativity, Chesnutt claims that black inability is not genetic but situation-based.

NOTES

The title of this essay is drawn from Chesnutt's own words in his 1889 essay, "What Is a White Man?," where he writes, "The states vary slightly in regard to what constitutes a mulatto or person of color, and as to what proportion of white blood should be sufficient to remove the disability of color" (*Charles W. Chesnutt: Essays* 69).

[1] The essays are "The Future American: What the Race Is Likely to Become in the Process of Time," *Boston Evening Transcript*, 18 Aug. 1900, p. 20; "The Future American: A Stream of Dark Blood in the Veins of the Southern Whites," *Boston Evening Transcript*, 25 Aug. 1900, p. 15; "The Future American: A Complete Race-Amalgamation Likely to Occur," 1 Sept. 1900, p. 24.

The Marrow of Allusion:
Ivanhoe and *The House behind the Cedars*

Hollis Robbins

Allusion: (Lat. *alludere*, "to joke, jest" [from *ad-* "to" + *ludere* "to play"]), originally meaning "to mock" and later "to make a fanciful reference to." A brief, indirect, and deliberate reference—in a poem or other medium— to a person, place, event (fictitious or actual), or other work of art, allusion may be used by its author to enhance a work's semantic and cultural density, topicality, or timelessness. Despite its etymology, allusion need not be playful but does require that the audience recognize the borrowed reference. (*Princeton Encyclopedia* 42)

Encountering the references to Walter Scott's medieval romance *Ivanhoe* (1819) in Charles W. Chesnutt's *The House behind the Cedars* (1900), a student might (and perhaps should) ask, What precisely does Chesnutt want the allusions to Scott's novel to accomplish in a post–Civil War tragedy of love across the color line? What work does allusion do generally? More important (to the overtaxed undergraduate), what work is required of the reader to register an allusion? For most of the nineteenth century, the best-selling *Ivanhoe* was as widely read as, say, *Harry Potter* is in the twenty-first. Chesnutt's contemporaries knew Scott's characters by name. But what must be known about *Ivanhoe* today? The answer is that it depends on what a student wants to get out of reading works of literature.

Readers of *The House behind the Cedars* cannot avoid allusions to *Ivanhoe*. The first mention of Scott appears in the first paragraph of chapter 5, "The Tournament":

The influence of Walter Scott was strong upon the old South. The South before the war was essentially feudal, and Scott's novels of chivalry appealed forcefully to the feudal heart. During the month preceding the Clarence tournament, the local bookseller had closed out his entire stock of "Ivanhoe," consisting of five copies, and had taken orders for seven copies more. The tournament scene in this popular novel furnished the model after which these bloodless imitations of the ancient passages-at-arms were conducted.   (31)

One of Chesnutt's main characters is named Rena, lengthened to Rowena, after one of Scott's heroines. (*Ivanhoe*'s other heroine is Rebecca, the "keen-witted" Jewess). Chesnutt's Rowena meets her fiancé at a mock jousting tournament for which the jousting contest at Ashby-de-la-Zouch in Scott's *Ivanhoe* "furnished the model." Both Scott's and Chesnutt's heroines are named Queen of Love and Beauty during the match. Familiarity with Scott among North and South Carolina white townspeople is indicated in chapter 15, "Mine Own People," where Miss Mary, a character described as being "well up in her Scott" (92), suggests that the secretly mixed-race Rowena should have been named Rebecca, after *Ivanhoe*'s sable-haired heroine. As Bill Hardwig sums up, *The House behind the Cedars* "is replete with direct and indirect allusions to Scott's *Ivanhoe*" (37).

Nearly every important literary figure in the nineteenth century, from Lord Byron, Goethe, and Victor Hugo to Mark Twain and Sir Arthur Conan Doyle, had something to say about *Ivanhoe*. Two aspects of Scott's novel often commented on—the long-standing animosity of the vanquished Saxons to their Norman conquerors and the Romantic figure of black-eyed Rebecca, whom everybody loved and nobody could marry—certainly resonate with Chesnutt's *House behind the Cedars*, set in the post–Civil War American South and featuring a mixed-race heroine. Yet today's students, who do not know Scott's characters as well as they know Harry, Hermione, and Dumbledore, can take heart that, at the level of plot, Chesnutt's novel requires no prior knowledge of Scott's. Chesnutt's narrator carefully explains and contextualizes the references to Rebecca, Rowena, chivalry, and jousting. Chesnutt's novel would work, that is, if in a Borgesian sense there were no real-life *Ivanhoe*, if Walter Scott were a figment of Chesnutt's imagination and if the influence of Scott's novels were a fiction entirely contained in the universe of *The House behind the Cedars*. (Chesnutt's 1904 short story "Baxter's Procrustes" directly engages with the question of material influence of a text that nobody inside or outside the tale has read.)

Full knowledge of *Ivanhoe* is not critical to understanding *The House behind the Cedars*. More direct literary influences on Chesnutt are the nineteenth-century American tragic mulatta genre and novels about passing. Chesnutt's plot is simple: an ambitious, well-read, mixed-race young man leaves home, turns his back on his origins, and succeeds financially and socially in a town in a nearby state. He returns home and invites his sister to enter his new sphere. She accompanies her brother to his new town and soon becomes engaged to an acquaintance of her brother. Yet she, less well read than her brother and more attached to her home, cannot completely sever her roots and create a new, fictional existence. When her fiancé learns of her origins, she is ashamed, goes home, turns to teaching, faces further embarrassments, is discovered by her former fiancé, and dies. The brother, still secure in his social standing, carries on with his constructed life, reproached by some readers and not a few literary critics. Scott's novel seems to be incidental rather than central to this story line—an embroidering, as it were, adding surface decoration but not providing structure. In fact, Chesnutt's first version of the story, a short tale entitled "Rena Walden," does not mention Scott or *Ivanhoe* at all; the expansion of Rena's name to Rowena appeared in revised versions of the story years later, as did the plot elements taken from *Ivanhoe* and narrative discussion of Scott's influence in the South (C. Chesnutt, Papers; see also Sedlack).

The rare twenty-first-century student who approaches Chesnutt already familiar with *Ivanhoe* or who decides to read Scott alongside Chesnutt may bring to her or his reading of *House behind the Cedars* Scott's engagement with history: the power relations between conqueror and conquered, the melding together of multiple languages and cultures, and the celebration of the vernacular speech of the oppressed. The student may notice that both Scott's novel and Chesnutt's feature comic loyal servants who speak in the local idiom, dramatic scenes in which the heroine's virtue is imperiled, a learned and articulate protagonist who knows how to win arguments, and a wry narrator who stands apart from the action of the novel, mocking chivalric pretenses and commenting on the relation between past and present.

What of these similarities?, another student may ask. Chesnutt may simply be paying homage to the more famous novelist's liberal view of race, culture, and romance. Certainly literary allusion at some level is a gesture of respect. Scott was beloved and influential in America and the most successful and popular novelist of his generation writing in English, perhaps because of his Romantic nationalism. Chesnutt's statement in the *Boston Evening Transcript* (1900) that "the secret of the progress of Europe has been found in racial heterogeneity" (from "The Future American," qtd. in Schmidt 553) as well as his interest in representing dialect and vernacular speech indicate a literary as well as political kinship of his work with Scott's novels. Are the *Ivanhoe* allusions meant to signal that his mixed-race heroine is as deserving of admiration as Scott's Jewish one?

Familiarity with *Ivanhoe* should provoke discussion of the differences between Scott's novel and Chesnutt's. Beyond the obvious issues of the scope and reach (Scott's historical drama is on a far grander scale than Chesnutt's, two and half times the length, with scores of characters, meticulously choreographed battle scenes, colorful and carefully researched historical digressions), Chesnutt's Rowena is not at all like Scott's or even, beyond coloring, like Scott's Rebecca. Both Scott's heroines are feisty and articulate, while Chesnutt's is timid, self-effacing, and does not exhibit great strength of character. There is little about Chesnutt's Rowena to admire beyond her delicate beauty. There are no mothers in *Ivanhoe*, only controlling fathers; there are no fathers in *The House behind the Cedars*, only controlling mothers. Coincidence plays an out-sized role in Chesnutt's novel; fighting ability plays an outsized role in Scott's. Scott is pedantically concerned with matters of historical dress and costume; Chesnutt describes his characters' dress vaguely if at all.

A brief listing of the differences between the two novels will signal to the reader that analyzing Chesnutt's allusions to *Ivanhoe* on the basis of likeness (or difference) may not yield clear results. What else, then, does allusion accomplish? The *Princeton Encyclopedia* definition is both roomy and vague, itemizing the effect of allusion as potentially "enhanc[ing] a work's semantic and cultural density, topicality, or timelessness." Why spend precious hours reading the work alluded to if allusion's purpose is something as ambiguous as enhancement?

Consider also the notion of "timelessness." Allusions to *Ivanhoe* alter and enlarge the realm of Chesnutt's novel, undermining categories of region and pe-riod. The allusions expand the universe of *The House behind the Cedars* across the Atlantic to include twelfth-century Europe (and perhaps Palestine) as well as early-nineteenth-century Britain, the period of Scott's narrator. A student might rightly argue that by alluding to *Ivanhoe*, Chesnutt is no longer writing a particular story of a biracial family and a broken engagement in the Reconstruc-tion South but instead a timeless tale of cultural dialectics and love across social boundaries.

So far so good. But, a sharp-eyed student might ask, Why do the allusions to Scott matter in different ways to each character in *The House behind the Ce-dars* and perhaps differently also to its reader? For Chesnutt's South Carolina characters, Scott is simply an admired novelist and *Ivanhoe* simply a beloved tale. For John Warwick, however, novels are guidebooks for self-invention. As we are told in chapter 2, "An Evening Visit," John has taken his name from a character in a book: "From Bulwer's novel, he had read the story of Warwick the Kingmaker, and upon leaving home had chosen it for his own" (20). The reference is to Edward Bulwer-Lytton's 1843 *Last of the Barons*. Mary, the well-read daughter of Dr. Green, catches the allusion in reference to Rowena's new last name: "Warwick the Kingmaker!" she exclaims in chapter 15, "Mine Own People" (92).

Students may be assured that they do not have to read Bulwer in addition to Scott, though the novel suggests they might. Chapter 18, "Under the Old Regime," lists the books owned by John and Rena's father—read avidly by John but not by his sister:

> Among the books were a volume of Fielding's complete works, in fine print, set in double columns; a set of Bulwer's novels; a collection of every-thing that Walter Scott—the literary idol of the South—had ever writ-ten; Beaumont and Fletcher's plays, cheek by jowl with the history of the virtuous Clarissa Harlowe; the Spectator and Tristram Shandy, Robinson Crusoe and the Arabian Nights.   (108)

The bookshelf includes volumes by Shakespeare, Milton, Cervantes, Bunyan, Volney, Thomas Paine, and various historians. Again, Scott's importance is emphasized.

Book titles are also, of course, brief allusions. Graduate students will grasp that the gentleman's broad-mindedness about race and romance is indicated by his literary sensibilities. Not a few of the books here are adventure stories featuring wandering, self-made men. Chesnutt makes clear the work of these volumes: in reading, John's horizons are broadened: "When he had read all the books,—indeed, long before he had read them all,—he too had tasted of the fruit of the Tree of Knowledge: contentment took its flight, and happiness lay far beyond the sphere where he was born" (109).

Thus allusions to Scott mean something very different for John Warwick than for anyone else in the novel (except the well-read Miss Mary Green) and perhaps mean something different for him than they did for his gentleman father. Did the father expect his son to draw on these volumes to create a new identity or simply to enjoy them in his leisure hours? In opening *The House behind the Cedars* from the perspective of his most erudite character, Chesnutt signals his indebtedness to the worldly, historical consciousness of novelists such as Scott. We are introduced to a town situated in history and to a man who is both of and not of the town, who returns to the town and notes the marks of the past. John's inner musings, his reference to "Phryne confronting her judges" in the first chapter (6), supported by his confident "South Carolina renaissance" speech in chapter 5 (32), make clear that his personality is shaped by books. Both John Warwick and Chesnutt himself might well chafe at literary critics such as Ross Posnock, who nullify the main character's literary self-fashioning by referring to the adult Warwick as "John Walden," following the "condition" of his mother (346).

So, a student reader might interject, what does Chesnutt expect us to know about Scott (not to mention Bulwer) and when are we expected to know it? Consider, you might respond, that Chesnutt was alluding not simply to Scott but also to what Southern readers and American readers in general thought of him. During the ten years that Chesnutt was writing *The House behind the Cedars*, he was aware that Mark Twain had on many occasions criticized Southern Scott fandom, most notably in his memoir *Life on the Mississippi* (1883). Twain blamed Scott for bewitching Southern readers into looking backward instead of forward:

> Then comes Sir Walter Scott with his enchantments, and by his single might checks this wave of progress, and even turns it back; sets the world in love with dreams and phantoms; with decayed and swinish forms of religion; with decayed and degraded systems of government; with the sillinesses and emptinesses, sham grandeurs, sham gauds, and sham chivalries of a brainless and worthless long-vanished society. . . . There, the genuine and wholesome civilization of the nineteenth century is curiously

confused and commingled with the Walter Scott Middle-Age sham civilization; and so you have practical, common-sense, progressive ideas, and progressive works; mixed up with the duel, the inflated speech, and the jejune romanticism of an absurd past that is dead, and out of charity ought to be buried.   (327–28)

Chesnutt assumed that his readers knew Twain's criticism of Scott; Chesnutt admired Twain and sought to travel in the same literary circles. Chesnutt had been publishing stories in *The Atlantic* since 1887; Twain had published pieces in that magazine from the mid-1870s until 1880 (though not the criticism of Scott). Chesnutt's 1901 novel *The Marrow of Tradition* was seen by critics and readers as indebted to Twain's *Puddn'head Wilson* (1894). Chesnutt attended Twain's seventieth birthday party in New York in 1905.

Chesnutt's literary and social relationship with Scott's greatest American critic complicates the allusions in *The House behind the Cedars* to *Ivanhoe*. Chesnutt may indeed be criticizing the townspeople of Clarence, South Carolina, for their "jejune romanticism" and love of "sham grandeurs." Yet what of Warwick, whose self-fashioning clearly emerges from the Romantic novels that Twain disdained?

Students may rise up in revolt and ask how much Twain they are expected to read on top of Scott (and perhaps Bulwer) in order to understand Chesnutt! We understand, students may argue, that allusion creates cultural density and layers of intertextuality, like a literary lasagna, but do we need more than just a taste of each layer? Can't we simply read *The House behind the Cedars* and be done with it? Does it matter to a twenty-first-century reader what Chesnutt was reading and what the world thought of it when he published his novel at the turn of the twentieth?

Allusion tends to assume an intelligent reader, a shared body of knowledge, and the value of previous works or contexts, but its manifestations in [history] and culture are extremely varied. . . . As Ricks has written in *Allusion to the Poets*, "allusion is one form that inheritance can take."
                                                      (*Princeton Encyclopedia* 43)

Literary criticism has evolved over the last hundred years from a practice concerned with authorial intent to one that also sees a literary text as produced by its era and its political conditions and as produced in concert with an engaged reader who brings his or her own interpretations to the table. Where once an author's allusions were assumed to be reasonable and a reader could with reasonable effort (or knowledge) comprehend them, now a reader must distinguish among aspects of allusion that are in the power of the author from those dictated by history, politics, literary tradition, or the author's (or reader's) subconscious.

Among Chesnutt scholars there is little consensus about how to approach the allusions to *Ivanhoe*. Hardwig argues that *Ivanhoe* is a frame allowing Chesnutt to critique Southern Romanticism, to read Scott ironically, to extend "the mythos of a Scott-based chivalry . . . to expose the fiction of race" (40). *Ivanhoe*, with its mocking narrator, fits Chesnutt's satirical purposes. Peter Schmidt argues that the "ironic allusions" to *Ivanhoe* are a political "deep response" to Scott, asking us to consider Chesnutt's and Scott's shared concerns with romance and cultural synthesis (545). Ignoring Twain and focusing on Chesnutt's grasp of the absurdity of how "the literary legacy of sentimentalism maps onto race," Kerstin Rudolph argues that in transforming Rena to Scott's heroine Rowena, John and Rena are "embodying fictional legends that the South reveres for their symbolic racial purity; that is, for their graceful, old world whiteness" and that Chesnutt is making a powerful joke "on sentimentalism's racial bias, encoded in its obsession with romantic idealism and pure, white womanhood" (31). M. Guilia Fabi argues that "Chesnutt plays with intertextual references to such popular texts as Sir Walter Scott's *Ivanhoe* . . . in order to ridicule the chivalric pretenses of an unregenerate post-Reconstruction South" (45). Discounting the tragedy of Scott's Jewish characters, Maria Orban suggests that Chesnutt "fashions" his "romance of race liberation on the model of Walter Scott's *Ivanhoe*, another narrative about the triumph of the underdog in the face of adversity" (82).

Most Chesnutt scholars do not say so explicitly, but their readings suggest that to apprehend fully Chesnutt's ironic use of Scott (because it must be ironic), a student first needs to understand Scott's influence on the South, the regionalism, nationalism, sentimentalism, and Romanticism that so affected Southern readers. But a deep reading of *Ivanhoe* is less necessary than simply noting the fact that it is being alluded to. While William Andrews (*Literary Career* 173) and Daniel Worden both observe that *The House behind the Cedars* is divided into two halves, halves perhaps termed "Rena in White Society" and "Rena in Black Society," neither notes that apart from the flashback to the bookshelf, there are no literary allusions in the second half of Chesnutt's novel. Rena may make her living by teaching, but she shows little interest in reading or learning. Chesnutt makes Rena's indifference explicit. In chapter 2, John remarks to his mother, "There are the dear old books: have they been read since I went away?" Molly responds, "No, honey, there's be'n nobody to read 'em, excep' Rena, an' she don't take to books quite like you did." Molly adds, "She ain't as quick as you was, an' don't read as many books" (12). Rena has no apprehension of allusion; she is not, as the *Princeton Encyclopedia* puts it, "an intelligent reader." What does it mean that her literary ignorance is linked to her downfall, that she disdains her father's literary inheritance? What does it mean that Chesnutt employs overt allusion (as William Irwin [287] and others call it) for the benefit of some of his readers and some of his characters, while other readers and other characters are left untouched?

> Allusion, while usually featuring an exact iteration of a prior text, can sometime paradoxically derive its power from a misquotation or inexact recollection.   (*Princeton Encyclopedia* 42)

We are left wondering about the essence, the meaning, the *marrow* of Chesnutt's allusions to literary works in general and to *Ivanhoe* in particular. Chesnutt titled his novel *The Marrow of Tradition* (1901), after a line from the opening quatrain of Charles Lamb's poem "To the Editor of the Every-Day Book" (1825), itself an homage to another text, the reformist bookseller William Hone's *Every-Day Book* of 1825:

> I like you, and your book, ingenuous Hone!
> In whose capacious, all-embracing leaves
> The very marrow of tradition's shown;
> And all that history—much that fiction—weaves.

Chesnutt did not elaborate beyond telling the Cleveland *World* in 1901 that the phrase "embodies the theme" of tradition's domination ("Charles W. Chesnutt's Own View"). This quatrain appears after the title page of *The Marrow of Tradition* with a provocative change: Chesnutt substitutes "ingenious Hone" for Lamb's original "ingenuous Hone." (This was a frequent printer's error in early editions of Lamb's works.) *Ingenious* means "innately clever"; *ingenuous* means "noble or frank." The misquotation persists unnoticed by Chesnutt scholars.

Lamb's coinage of "marrow of tradition" evidently piqued Chesnutt's literary sensibilities. *Marrow* can mean essence or center (as in bone marrow) or a "compendium or digest of writings in a subject" ("Marrow," def. 4b). Lamb seems to mean the second (a digest of tradition), but the word circulated in race-conscious America in the physiological sense of "essence." For example, in an 1887 speech entitled "The South and Her Problems," Henry Grady, editor of the Atlanta *Constitution*, said that the truth of "the supremacy of the white race . . . has abided forever in the marrow of our bones" (33).

Chesnutt's choice of the incorrect version of of Lamb's text (if indeed it was chosen knowingly) may be key to the meaning of literary tradition to Chesnutt. Compiling (and devouring) a literary digest is a matter of art, not of artlessness: you make yourself in reading; you are what you have read. Tradition's "capacious, all-embracing leaves" enter your blood. Chesnutt asks readers to apprehend the marrow of tradition—and thus the marrow of allusion—in every sense of the term: the essence, the vital force, the notion of a physiological, biological, cultural, familial, and literary inheritance as well as the combined sum of knowledge circulating in an allusion. John Warwick is indeed what he has read. Rena Walden has no literary marrow.

For Chesnutt, literary allusion is a means of demonstrating the material influence of literary tradition inside and outside a text. Scott may have been a bad influence on the South, but his works (and those of many others) were a productive influence on the bookish John Warwick and no influence at all on the unfortunate Molly and the doomed Rena.

In revising and expanding his failed 1889 short story "Rena Walden" into *The House behind the Cedars*, Chesnutt seems to have seized upon the similarity between "Rena" and "Rowena" as the basis of an allusion crucial to the diverging narrative trajectories of John and Rena (Papers). Tragically, Rena has no active relationship with *Ivanhoe* or other literary works, only a passive one that she cannot control. Rena is, in the words of Richard Watson Gilder, the editor of *Century Magazine*, "amorphous" and lacking "spontaneous, imaginative life" (qtd. in *"To Be"* 67),[1] though her passivity serves a structural purpose. While Worden remarks that "Rena is misplaced in the novel because of her failure to mesh with the social script borrowed from *Ivanhoe* . . . [which] drives her inevitable removal from white southern culture at the end of the novel's first part" (8), it might be simpler to say that Rena fails because she hasn't read *Ivanhoe*. Had she read the books on her father's bookshelf and understood the contours of the role that her brother was asking her to play, the story would have been less tragic. Knowledge is the marrow of allusion. Whether to follow the model of John or Rena is a question that Chesnutt leaves up to the reader.

NOTES

I thank Mariann J. VanDevere for invaluable research assistance in the Fisk University Library Special Collections and Chantel Clark, the Fisk University reference librarian for special collections. Thanks also to Bill Gleason, in whose course at Princeton I first read *The House behind the Cedars*.

[1] For fuller treatment of this rejection, see Andrews, *Literary Career*; Hardwig; or Wonham. *Century Magazine* rejected the story in June 1890 on the grounds that the mixed-race characters were "unnatural" and the short story's sentiment was "amorphous." Wonham argues that "Rena Walden" is Chesnutt's "most important short story" (4).

Teaching *The House behind the Cedars* in an Introductory Literary Theory Course

Ryan Simmons

This essay describes a way of using *The House behind the Cedars* in an introductory literary theory course for undergraduates. Charles W. Chesnutt's first novel is particularly useful in such a course both because of its richness in raising a panoply of issues of interest to literary theorists and because of the relative lack of published scholarship on the novel compared with other texts frequently used in literary theory courses, affording students the opportunity to practice building their own theoretical applications unhindered by the weight of established interpretations. *House* interweaves not only issues of race and history but also problems of gender, of psychology, and of economics and class, showing the meaning of each to be inflected by the way in which the others are understood. A multilens approach to the novel is valuable in revealing both its complexity and the ability of each methodology to produce new insights into a single text.

I typically teach the novel in an introductory course on literary theory alongside three other texts: an introduction to theory, such as Peter Barry's *Beginning Theory*; a compilation, most often *Great Short Stories by American Women* (Ward); and a text drawn from Bedford's Case Studies in Contemporary Criticism series, most recently James Joyce's "The Dead," which presents the story followed by several articles, each drawing primarily from and illustrating a particular methodology (Schwartz). During the first half of the course, we read and discuss the major approaches described by Barry and attempt to utilize the works in *Great Short Stories* to illustrate the methodologies discussed. For example, we might work through a Marxist reading of Louisa May Alcott's "Transcendental Wild Oats," a psychoanalytic reading of Charlotte Perkins Gilman's "The Yellow Wall-paper," a deconstructive interpretation of Zora Neale Hurston's "Sweat," and a queer theory approach to Willa Cather's "Paul's Case." The next move is to interpret a single text using several theoretical approaches, each of which brings to the fore certain themes and features that might be neglected otherwise.

As many instructors do, I spend substantial time with my students exploring varied theoretical approaches to a single work in depth: first, using one of the highly canonical works in Bedford's Case Studies series, in which students encounter professional scholars' theoretically informed readings of, for example, "The Dead"; and second, having students—working together in groups—develop their own reading of an established but relatively new (from a canonical perspective) novel, like *The House behind the Cedars*, each group relying on their emergent understanding of a prevailing methodology. The assignment guidelines presented to the students follow.

Group Project: *The House behind the Cedars*

Unlike Joyce's "The Dead," Charles W. Chesnutt's 1899 novel *The House behind the Cedars* has received relatively little critical attention, although a resurgence in interest in Chesnutt during the past twenty years has led to the consensus that it is a significant novel. This project asks you to identify a critical question concerning *House* and to develop a convincing answer to that question, which you will present to the class and in particular to a defense committee whose job is to evaluate the appropriateness of your question and the strength of your answer.

You have randomly been assigned to a group that is given a particular critical approach or category of approaches. (If you were assigned to the defense committee, your assignment is slightly different but should become clear as you read this handout.)

Developing a Question

Your group's first job is to develop a critical question, which will probably arise from our class discussions of the novel and your group's thoughts about it. The question should be connected to the critical approach you have been assigned. Here are a few examples of questions that have occupied critics of *The House behind the Cedars*:

> [from a Marxist approach:] The author of *House* was a successful businessman. Is it possible to read his novel as anticapitalist?

> [from a new historicist approach:] The depiction of Frank Fowler has been controversial. In what ways does he reflect—and does he in any way counteract—stereotypes of African Americans that would have been familiar to the novel's first readers?

The question you develop should be:

> Specific—not "What does *House* say about psychology?" (too broad) or "What is the psychoanalytic reading of *House*?" (there isn't just one), but perhaps "How do the novel's various discussions of dreams fit, or not, Freud's attempt to map the unconscious?"

> Significant—that is, capable of yielding insight into the meaning of the novel. Be prepared to address the "So what?" question.

> Arguable—both I and the defense committee that evaluates your presentation will determine whether there is a reasonable possibility of disagreement embedded in your answer—there should be.

How you are evaluated on this project depends to a considerable degree on the question you select, so make that selection with care.

Developing an Answer

Use evidence from the text—along with any of the tools available to you from literary theory and your own critical thinking skills—to formulate a detailed yet succinct answer to your question. (*Succinct* means that an answer should be no longer than necessary to make its case.) To present your reasoning, and your evidence, in a way that will be clear and memorable to your audience, prioritize three or four main points in your chain of reasoning—and perhaps one or two points of textual evidence that your reasoning depends on.

HANDOUT

By the night before its presentation, each group should e-mail to me and to its defense committee a handout of no more than one page outlining (1) the question it proposes to address, (2) three or four priority points it will make in pursuing an answer, and (3) an example or two of relevant passages from the text. (The defense committee is responsible for a different type of report—see below.) I will duplicate this handout for the rest of the class.

PRESENTATION

Each group should take 20–25 minutes to identify its critical question and present the answer it has formulated to the rest of the class. Any techniques you wish to use to make your presentation clear, convincing, and memorable to other readers of the book are fair game (e.g., visual aids, activities, discussion). You are welcome, though not required, to augment your presentation with them.

Role of the Defense Committee

Three groups (one for each day of presentation) will assume the role of the defense committee. Its job is to listen carefully to the presentation; then it will have 5–10 minutes to ask questions of the presenters that will allow them to elaborate on any unclear points and to overcome any possible arguments against their findings. The defense committee will be evaluated on its ability to ask questions that yield insight and on its astute and articulate evaluation of each presenting group. (Did the group ask a specific, significant, and arguable question, and did it answer that question persuasively? Explain your answer using specific examples.) Each defense committee will evaluate two groups in a one-page (total) memorandum and all will summarize their findings on the last day of class.

In this project, the instructor is there to provide guidance rather than answers. I do not encourage students to seek out previously published criticism but instead to develop, present, and discuss their own theoretically informed readings of the text.

The following categories are meant to be suggestive, not exhaustive, of directions students may take as they pursue a theoretically informed reading of *The House behind the Cedars*.

New Historicism

It is no overstatement to say that the past is the central preoccupation of *House*. As Hollis Robbins discusses elsewhere in this volume, Scott's *Ivanhoe* and its

Romantic ideal of chivalry are used by the novel's white Southerners to structure their own experience. Chesnutt writes, "The South before the war was essentially feudal, and Scott's novels of chivalry appealed forcefully to the feudal
heart" (*House* 31). Students should consider how constructions of the past make
sense of experience for the novel's characters and which meanings are regu-
lated, or obscured, by notions of history. John's stated desire that he and Rena
become "new people," unencumbered by history (57), is both sympathetically
portrayed and shown to be impossible and even destructive. Students may wish
to investigate how "co-texts" (Barry 172) contemporary to the novel illuminate it,
and, conversely, how the novel illuminates them. As practicing new historicists,
they may wish to seek out artifacts that provide a sense of lived experience at
the turn of the century, using resources such as the American Memory project
of the Library of Congress (memory.loc.gov/). They should note the differences
between the new historicism and cultural materialism, related methodologies,
which Barry lucidly describes—for example, "the new historicist situates the
literary text in the political situation of its own day, while the cultural material-
ist situates it within that of ours" (179). Students should ask themselves which
factors external to the novel shaped the understanding of Chesnutt's original
readers and which factors shape our understanding of the novel today.

Marxist Criticism

In *House*, arbitrary distinctions of race govern the type of life one may lead, as
they did in the South of Chesnutt's day; this limitation is precisely what John
Walden attempts to circumvent by disguising his black heritage. The economic
underpinnings of this state of affairs are easy to overlook, so students must bring
them to light. They will probably begin with this passage, in which John's men-
tor, Judge Straight, explains the basis for the color line:

> "It may all be true," replied the boy, "but it don't apply to me. [The law]
> says 'the negro.' A negro is black; I am white, and not black."
> "Black as ink, my lad" returned the lawyer, shaking his head. . . .
> "Somewhere, sometime, you had a black ancestor. One drop of black
> blood makes the whole man black."
> "Why shouldn't it be the other way, if the white blood is so much supe-
> rior?" inquired the lad.
> "Because it is more convenient as it is—and more profitable."   (113)

In Chesnutt's analysis, racial segregation was at bottom an economic practice,
designed to preserve the authority of the privileged classes at the expense of
those on whose labor they relied. Students pursuing a Marxist reading of the
novel need to enrich and complicate this quotation by finding additional evidence from the novel—that is, to move past a "vulgar Marxist" reading (Barry
154) and toward one that represents the novel's complexity. They should be

encouraged to pay close attention to references to labor: Rena's vocation as a teacher (for which Chesnutt consistently uses the term "labor"); Frank and Peter Fowler's work as coopers; and the respective class status and markers of Rena's suitors, Frank Fowler, Jeff Wain, and George Tryon. Students also may notice that the prospective marriages in the novel, such as George Tryon's contemplated union with Blanche Leary (*House* 47), come across as economic exchanges, belying claims about love.

Feminist Criticism and Gender Studies

More than Chesnutt's other novels, *House* attends to issues of gender. Passing as white has a strikingly different outcome for Rena than for her brother: she is punished for her attempt to escape the confinements of social convention, but her brother blithely escapes. His freedom is made possible by his gender identity, as reflected in the narrative's frequent mention of "manhood" and "fathers" in chapter 18, when John announces his determination to pass. Although she is not willful in her pursuit of a new identity as a white woman, John having worked to overcome her reluctance to pass, she and not he suffers the disastrous consequences of her failure.

It is interesting to analyze how Chesnutt codes femininity. His sympathies clearly are with Rena more than with any other character, and he seems to be aware that the limitations facing her, including her sense of fidelity to their mother (a fidelity that John utterly lacks), are highly gendered. As Rena states, "A man may make a new place for himself—a woman is born and bound to hers." In this statement, and in her renouncing of a second attempt to pass, saying, "I'll not leave mother again. God is against it" (121), readers today will note her adherence to nineteenth-century gender mores. A difficult question is whether the novel criticizes this inequity or reinforces it as natural. In the eyes of the novel's male characters, Rena is an object, a symbolic representation of their preferences and desires. But how does Chesnutt regard her, or how does he incline his readers to regard her? To what degree does the text reveal the constructed nature of Rena's (or John's) gender identity? Students, provided with some contextual information about the literary traditions of sentimentalism and the tragic mulatta narrative, may debate whether Chesnutt adopts or exposes the underlying assumptions embedded in these forms. The susceptibility of the novel's commentary on gender to divergent conclusions is, from the standpoint of this student activity, an advantage.

Psychoanalytic Criticism

If students locate an online text of *House* (available at the University of North Carolina's *Documents of the American South*, the University of Virginia's *Electronic Text Center* database, and elsewhere), they can search for key terms:

dream, imagination, human nature. The results illuminate some of the possibilities for a psychoanalytic reading of the novel. With its frequent discussions of dreams of special significance, *House* seems to demonstrate its author's awareness of Freud's early findings. Science, Chesnutt says, "has shattered many an idol and destroyed many a delusion, [but] has made but slight inroads upon the shadowy world of dreams" (62). When John counsels Rena in chapter 10 to disregard her dream about her mother's illness, the result is to delay Rena's return home, which contributes to the disaster that awaits Rena there. The interruption by "a negro woman" of Tryon's odd lucid dream of Rena (72) suggests that he is dimly aware of a situation that, had he analyzed it more thoughtfully, might have led him to a better result. Chesnutt is not suggesting a supernatural quality to dreams; rather, he implies that people are motivated by forces from their unconscious, about which their dreams may provide some insight. Tryon's feelings for Rena become not only ambivalent but also heightened after the revelation of her racial heritage makes his love forbidden; students should consider the psychological significance of this development. The absence of fathers—most conspicuously that of John and Rena Walden—is also suggestive, as is Frank Fowler's relationship to his castigating (castrating?) father, Peter.

Deconstruction

Students may notice Chesnutt's use of wordplay, such as puns on George Tryon's name ("the prince would never try on the glass slipper" [48]) and the introduction of a character named Mary B., or "Ma'y B." (133). *House* shows an interest in narrative play and in the slipperiness and unreliability of language. We depend on words to make sense of our world, yet the sense they make of it is tenuous, and language can upend our governing assumptions. In other words, the novel suggests Chesnutt's advocacy of what would now be termed a deconstructive critique. Most students will find it easier to interpret Chesnutt as a protodeconstructive critic than, in their own right, to deconstruct his novel. They are likely to begin with observations about the novel's treatment of race. As the quotation above about the color line being "profitable" suggests, *House* explores the indeterminacy of racial categories, showing that the distinction between black and white is a fiction though central to the maintained social order. John Walden sees this hypocrisy, but his simple reversal—"I am white, and not black"—fails to interrogate the nature of the categories themselves. A closer look will reveal that Chesnutt's awareness of linguistic indeterminacy is not restricted to race. Encourage students to generate a list of binary oppositions that propel the story and to notice Chesnutt's analysis of how the possibility of meaning is, paradoxically, both constricted and enabled by the authority of essentially linguistic concepts, such as the "one-drop" rule (87).

Critical Race Theory

Critical race theorists contend that racism and its underlying ideology, white supremacy, are deeply entrenched in American life; that law is not a neutral and objective standard but rather a practice deeply infused with power; and that the important work to be done is to "contest the terrain and terms" of legal and political discourse, which perforce must lead to significant structural changes (Crenshaw et al. xxii). Many students assume that racial and gender discrimination should be analyzed primarily as a moral issue, yet from the perspective of critical race theory (CRT), this approach leads to reforms that do little more than relieve white guilt. For example, Derrick Bell, a founder of CRT, advances such an argument regarding *Brown v. Board of Education* (*"Brown"*). From a CRT perspective, the salient question is not "What ought one to do?" but "Whose interests are served?" Students should know that Chesnutt consistently argued, in both fiction and nonfiction, that the Jim Crow regime harmed both black and white citizens. He wrote, "[T]he brunt of [segregation] falls on the Negro, but the white does not escape" ("White" 140). Students should analyze the novel through this lens, asking how individuals' sense of their own interests inform their behavior in the novel. George Tryon's evolving interpretation of events is worth particular attention: by the end of the novel, he "felt some dim realization of the tyranny of caste, when he found it not merely pressing upon an inferior people who had no right to expect anything better, but barring his own way to something that he desired" (*House* 177). His desperate, romantic conclusion at the end of the novel, "Custom was tyranny. Love was the only law" (194), is, as he seems to understand, ineffectual and naive; both he and Rena operate in a system that ignores such abstractions. The interests of whites as much as of blacks lie in a structural change in society, and Tryon's late-arriving commitment to an egalitarian ideal is, until such change comes about, pointless. Chesnutt's observations pave the way for the yet more pessimistic analysis of Bell, whose own turn to fiction, "The Space Traders," suggests that the commitment of whites to the equality of African Americans is tenuous and ultimately hollow.

The House behind the Cedars is deeply engaged with the sorts of questions that literary theory today considers, and students will benefit from encountering this novel in varied contexts, not exclusively that of an American literature survey. *House* raises significant questions about race and history, gender, psychology, economic interests, power, and language. Richer than one may initially suppose, it has the potential to be a central text in any course that asks what literature is and what kind of work literature can do.

Rebooting Race: Virtuality and Embodiment in *The House behind the Cedars*

Marisa Parham

> Nothing is less real than realism.
>
> —Georgia O'Keeffe

The House behind the Cedars is Charles W. Chesnutt's fin de siècle novel of a brother and sister who move from North Carolina to South Carolina so that they can pass for white. Published in 1900, it exemplifies what many undergraduate students vaguely imagine late-nineteenth-century writing looks, moves, and sounds like, even if this sense comes only by virtue of their imagination of its difference from contemporary writing. Some of this response might also stem from the novel's fidelity to its wayward aesthetic period, as in every way *The House behind the Cedars* is representative of its transitional historical moment, formally oscillating among literary styles, by turns American gothic, sentimental romance, and realist fiction. Its uneven contouring, that readers can sometimes see its discursive seams, is one of the reasons I include it in an undergraduate English course called Ghosts in Shells: Virtuality and Embodiment from Passing to the Posthuman, which is also cross-listed in the Black Studies and Film and Media Studies departments at my institution. As you might imagine, students are quite surprised to read early African American literature in a class on robots, artificial intelligence, and extensible identities and to be asked to take this kind of text as a lens through which to understand emergent futurist concerns.[1]

In this essay I explore how reading *The House behind the Cedars* can introduce students to contemporary critical conversations around *virtuality* and *embodiment*, terms most people associate more with twentieth- and twenty-first-century science fiction texts like *The Matrix* and *Avatar*. But reading Chesnutt alongside contemporary philosophy and media theory helps demonstrate how these kinds of conceptual considerations were present in black intellectual traditions before the twentieth century.[2] In his attempts to make the facts of racism and the mechanisms of social racialization comprehensible, Chesnutt developed a discursively complex body of writing that was as invested in exposing race as an illusion as it was with illustrating the materiality of African Americans' experiences with racism (Andrews, *Literary Career* 140). In discrediting race as a biological category while at the same time attesting to the social, cultural, and physical effects of racism, writers like Chesnutt had to develop sophisticated strategies for producing dialectics out of otherwise incompatible realities.

In Ghosts in Shells, we are especially interested in how contemporary concerns with nature and culture, with the virtual and the real, and with the constitution of the human as a category have always already been present in the American literary tradition, particularly in texts produced by African Americans. Many of the most interesting meditations on these concerns occur in texts about passing, in narratives about individuals who come to be socially recognized in ways different from the legal description or designation of their race or sex at birth. In its extended considerations of how racial identity is produced through various legal, biological, social, and cultural mechanisms, *The House behind the Cedars* is excellent for helping undergraduates learn to navigate complex ideas regarding how the real is continuously produced and reproduced in every moment.

In our close reading of *House* we map Chesnutt's many descriptions of social forces operating in direct contradiction to one another, namely how a racialized and segregated world that extols tradition, ritual, and rigid materiality might also be characterized by racial passing and other kinds of fluid self-representation. As Alan Goodrich notes, what we think of as "virtuality is of a different order than the actual world . . . but it likewise must be loyal enough to a concept of reality that it retains recognizability (thus it functions as an illusion of an exterior reality)." What we refer to as real is that which exists outside the experiential bubble created by whatever device or mechanism is generating the virtual experience, even as its very existence also structures the virtual experience. This is why a virtual experience can make us feel like we are running on a track parallel to something equally relevant and real that must somehow be cognitively processed simultaneously, which is unsettling.[3] Instead of asking us to linger on questions of what should count as authentically black or white in *House*, Chesnutt directs us to the structures that make black and white visible as such. There can be no virtual without the real, which gives the virtual its aesthetic or affective power, even when we have difficulty making the distinction.

In my upper-level virtuality and embodiment seminar, we come to Chesnutt after spending several class hours with progressively longer (but still short) readings designed to attune us to the idea that representation can be split from origin, even while still making a claim on realism. By guiding the students through close readings of primary texts, I am able to introduce them to a variety of concepts around representation, simulation, media, materiality, aesthetics, performance, and intersectionality. The course begins with a Georgia O'Keeffe letter written to accompany her paintings of flowers—"I know I can not paint a flower" (Greenough)—and moves on to Jorge Luis Borges's "On Exactitude in Science" (325) and also Plato's allegory of the cave. The unit ends with W. E. B. Du Bois's groundbreaking essay from *The Souls of Black Folk*, "Of Our Spiritual Strivings" (7–14).

Du Bois's *The Souls of Black Folk* was published soon after *The House behind the Cedars*. In *Souls*, Du Bois sought to convey how it feels to survive the experience of living one's life as split between competing realities, a phenomenon he refers to as "double-consciousness." In giving shape to what it means to constantly shift across psychically divergent but nevertheless simultaneously material realities, to live as one "born with a veil, and gifted with second-sight in this American world" (8), double consciousness is a useful heuristic for conceptualizing virtuality and embodiment.[4] We then turn to William Craft and Ellen Craft's narrative of their escape from enslavement, *Running a Thousand Miles for Freedom*, which helps move students from thinking about representation that splits from its origin as only an art or literature thing to a lens that can be used to examine social or political identity.

Descriptions of virtual experience often conceptualize the mechanisms through which an experience or representation's reference to an original can or cannot manifest its origin's meaning in an authentic way, but postmodern philosophy also takes up the question of how representations supersede their origins and originals. When I teach *House*, I ask students to read Jean Baudrillard's introductory essay to *Simulacra and Simulation*, "The Precession of Simulacra." Baudrillard is useful in the undergraduate classroom because his work is foundational to both scholarly and pop cultural meditations on virtual experience, which helps students connect Chesnutt's insights to other social or cultural contexts:

> By crossing a space whose curvature is no longer that of the real, nor that of truth, the era of simulation is inaugurated by a liquidation of all referentials—worse: with their artificial resurrection in the systems of signs, a material more malleable than meaning, in that it lends itself to all systems of equivalences, to all binary oppositions, to all combinatory algebra. It is no longer a question of imitation, nor duplication, nor even parody. It is a question of substituting the signs of the real for the real . . . a programmatic, metastable, perfectly descriptive machine that offers all the signs of the real and shortcircuits all its vicissitudes. Never again will the real have the chance to produce itself.   (2)

In Baudrillard's description of simulation, the image of the real overtakes reality as people come to accept the imaginative representation of a thing in lieu of the thing itself. It is important to note, however, that Baudrillard is not particularly nostalgic for the sanctity of originals versus copies, which is often how his theory is described.

Rather, what is at stake in our participation in simulation is the loss of our ability to properly read value and difference, which diminishes our ability to imagine meaningful structures beyond the evidential. In a simulation, knowledge is not undergirded by experience outside of the simulation; it is merely the appearance of experience, or relevance, or relation that matters, and each of those are effects validated by the system of appearance itself, what Baudrillard dubs "hyperreality."

In class, I walk students through to an understanding of Baudrillard's sense of "systems of equivalences" and "combinatory algebra" and ask them to put that into play alongside Du Bois's description of double consciousness, in which survival requires the capacity to navigate psychically divergent but materially simultaneous worlds, to work constantly to inhabit one's life while also accounting for and adjusting for how that inhabitation comports with oppressive assumptions about the manner, meaning, or mattering of that life: "It is a peculiar sensation, this double-consciousness, this sense of always looking at one's self through the eyes of others, of measuring one's soul by the tape of a world that looks on in amused contempt and pity" (8).

As homework, students are asked to illustrate as best they can what each theorist describes. Whether they produce equations, lists, network visualizations, maps, or images, they usually discover that meaning for both Baudrillard and Du Bois is tethered to an unnamed or unarticulated something. In Baudrillard's essay, danger lurks in misperceiving a closed system of signification as an open one: we believe we are freely making choices, but these choices are merely versions of choices that have already been made for us. In Du Bois's essay, danger comes to the racialized individual who treats a closed system as an open one: the world is not a place of choices, unless those choices can be remediated to comport with social expectation, what Ralph Ellison famously refers to as "change the joke and slip the yoke."

Many students are quick to connect these ideas with the plot and theme of the popular film *The Matrix*, in which the protagonist, Neo, learns that what he imagines to be the real world is a subtended virtual reality experienced by human beings trapped in a computer simulation. When students return to *The Matrix* after reading Du Bois and *House*, they are struck by how those previous texts clarify the stakes of the human resistance's desire to live in a world outside of a totalizing manufacture, for that world is literally and figuratively fueled by the destruction of enslaved and entrapped persons' lives. And indeed, if we accept that texts like Chesnutt's were often written out of black authors' a priori understanding of racism as the maintenance of a social illusion, even as they themselves lived in a world in which almost every aspect of their being was materially structured by racism, then we can see that *House* also provides insights into how the conceptual reifications of Baudrillard's essay have deeply problematic implications for those seeking to build a new world in the wake or falter of an oppressive regime. Passing, framed in Baudrillard's terms, might in fact allow an individual to short-circuit the machine. If we were to conceptualize this using Du Bois's terms, passing might be understood as the apotheosis of the veil as instrument of agency and control, second sight operationalized and keyed to a real world intuited as possible outside the illusions wrought by white oppression.

But in instrumentalizing this insight, passing also reifies the forces that make it necessary. The world outside of antiblack racism, the world outside of the veil, is no less an effect of black oppression than the world in which the black American lives. To further this sense of virtuality and embodiment in *House*, I encourage close reading of several scenes. Here are four examples of scenes I bring to the classroom to show how Chesnutt uses equivalence, simulation, and difference to illustrate the divergent worlds of racialized experience in *House*.

1. Reading Bodies

Early in *House*, John, the triumphant and newly returned son, comments on the hair of his younger sister, Rena, which is "long and smooth and glossy, with a ripple like the summer breeze upon the surface of still water." Perched with his sister on a now faded haircloth couch, he admires her beauty:

> "What lovely hair! It has just the wave yours lacks, mother."
> "Yes," was the regretful reply, "I've never be'n able to git that wave out. But her hair's be'n took good care of, an' there ain't nary a girl in town that's got any finer."

There is an apology in Molly's voice, a sense of abiding care tinctured with defeat. John, as they talk, strokes Rena's hair with an unbrotherly luxuriation. The hair is her "great pride," and Chesnutt is careful to tell us that it "had been sedulously cared for" (14). *Sedulously* conveys all the work of *assiduously* but with a sense of lingering. It describes the years of work Molly has put into her daughter's hair and resonates throughout the scene and prefigures Molly, moments later, drinking in John's story of his passage into whiteness "with parted lips and glistening eyes" (15). This moment on the couch may not be explicitly sexual, but it is perhaps one of the most erotic in any of Chesnutt's fiction. By emphasizing the erotic quality of Molly's fascination with her son, Chesnutt is able to highlight the depth of her love for a life that she can never have, waiting out the years, trying to brush the wave out of Rena's hair. The fact that John is her biological son is subordinated to the erotic value of the white identity he has acquired. In John's strokes, meanwhile, perhaps we are meant to intuit the social, domestic, and cultural upheaval implicit in his return to his birthplace as a recently minted white man.

Now that John is successfully passing as white, his new embodiment gives his language new power, a power he lacked in his previous life, when his white skin did not conceal his black identity. Readers later learn that when a younger John insisted to Judge Straight, who was white, that John was white because he looked white, the judge replied that John was black, "[b]lack as ink" (113). But now, when John returns as a white man, he tells his mother, "Don't worry about the wave. It's just the fashionable ripple, and becomes her immensely" (14). In their ostensibly innocuous chitchat, the specter of racial evidence, blackness, goes unnamed—even as it drives Molly's apology for what she calls a "wave" and is supposedly exorcised in John's insistence on "ripple." Rena's hair is a metonym for her possible white identity. To Molly, the wave risks betrayal, the revelation of a signifying, underlying kinky texture. And, technically, she is correct, as the difference between "wave" and "ripple" can for this family mean the difference between "being black" or "being white." Indeed, whenever a student comments in class that Rena's hair is "just hair," another will be quick to scold, "no." Or to quote one, delivered without irony, "This hair thing is really real."

Passing narratives like *House* are about how both the biological and intellectual underpinnings of American white supremacy are fragile, suggesting that in some circumstances one's racial identity depends less on the body into which one is born and more on the presentation of that body in support of whichever cultural story the body is desired to tell. As Samira Kawash and numerous other contemporary theorists have pointed out, racialized societies are structured around the notion of race as a self-evident truth, as an epistemological fact that operates with the force of law. According to doctrines of racist pseudobiology, skin color denotes an essential, foundational difference. The skin of a visibly brown person is supposed to reference a cascading series of other "interior" differences; it is a placeholder, a metonym. By removing skin color from the equation yet illustrating how a person without brown skin is still "black as ink," Chesnutt suggests that John's blackness is mainly virtual, and as such carries all the significatory power of the absent brown skin. It does not matter *what* John looks like; what matters is that Judge Straight must continue to see John's blackness, even if this requires a kind of blindness regarding John's white appearance. He literally cannot see straight.

When it comes to Rena's beauty, to her status as a desirable woman, an innocent onlooker would likely find little difference between a "wave" and a "ripple," because they would not be looking for a meaningful distinction between the two as racial markers. Once Rena is installed as white, the curl of her hair becomes a superficial quality, making no reference and having no significance. To evoke Baudrillard, in disallowing visual signs to fit sociolegal imaginations of biological expression, passing short-circuits systems of racial difference. Once made equivalent, both wave and ripple are shown to have never signified a difference that can be made to matter on its own. The body's racial meaning is correlative to its signification in a structure of reception—clothing, dialect, and local history. In this reading, the body becomes articulable as a platform or medium, "as a capacity for relationality that literally requires mediation and that, in a sense, cannot be conceptualized without it" (Mitchell and Hansen xiii). Like ink, racialization is an often overlooked technological feat.

2. The Bloodless Virtual

In Chesnutt's text, white identity never just "is"; it is produced. To get at this, I engage the students in a close reading of one of Chesnutt's carefully constructed set pieces, "[t]he annual tournament of the Clarence Social Club" held at the county fair (31). Clarence, South Carolina, is where John has made a new life as John Warwick, and it is where he brings Rena to live as white. The tournament demonstrates how Chesnutt's use of language generates a coherent system of meaning that supports the novel's thematics—how the novel theorizes itself.

The annual tournament is a reenactment from Sir Walter Scott's *Ivanhoe*, which provides "the model after which these bloodless imitations of the ancient passages-at-arms were conducted" (30). Throughout the scene John relent-lessly highlights the absurdity of the community's simulation, pointing out the tournament's ironies. In this simulation, hurt feelings replace physical harm: "Wounded vanity will take the place of wounded limbs, and there will be broken hopes in lieu of broken heads" (32). John, bloodless himself—after all, he is passing because he lacks the proper bloodline to legally present himself as white—describes a world in which everything has become a placeholder for something else. In this battle constituted only by signifiers, the emotional ef-fects of winning and losing can be experienced without any substantial trans-formation of reality.

Baudrillard again proves useful, as he asks us to imagine a world wherein meaning is built without reference to an objective reality that can be located outside of simulation itself, even as the simulation consolidates the meaning of the world in which people live their daily lives:

> Simulation is no longer that of a territory, a referential being, or a sub-stance. It is the generation by models of a real without origin or reality: a hyperreal. The territory no longer precedes the map, nor does it survive it. It is nevertheless the map that precedes the territory—precession of simulacra—that engenders the territory. . . . It is the real, and not the map, whose vestiges persist here and there in the deserts that are no lon-ger those of the Empire, but ours. The desert of the real itself. . . . It is no longer anything but operational. In fact, it is no longer really the real, because no imaginary envelops it anymore.   (2)

To show my students that the town's tournament is more than a kind of harm-less or misguided nostalgia, I turn them from reading *House* as mere illustra-tion of Baudrillard's "desert of the real" to considering how the novel raises the stakes of his theory. The Clarence tournament is not fake: Chesnutt, in his attention to social detail—in the spatial arrangement of society's members, distributed by race and wealth across stands, seats, and bleachers—makes clear that the event's purpose is to produce a shared imagination of an ideal society's history. The tournament itself validates the town's segregationist social, legal, and economic structures; a reiteration of white supremacy. Though the sport is bloodless, the tournament's virtual simulation is a placeholder for material violence.

3. *"The Desert of the Real"*

Refracting *The House behind the Cedars* through contemporary terms helps students independently develop a language for the very real nonreality, the hy-perreality, that underpins American processes of racialization. It gets students to understand how people who are members of different races, genders, and classes may walk the same earth but literally live in different worlds. Chesnutt illustrates this power differential by forcing a black character, Frank, out of the simulation when a horse inadvertently shatters a lance and sends a broken piece flying over the railing opposite the grandstand: "The flying fragment was dodged by those who saw it coming, but brought up with a resounding thwack against the head of a colored man in the second row, who stood watching the grand stand with an eager and curious gaze" (33). Frank does not see the fragment coming because he is looking the wrong way, searching the audience for an actor, Meanwhile, Rena inadvertently drops her white handkerchief from the stand, catching Frank's eye (34).

As Chesnutt has staged it, Frank's fall out of the simulation is simultaneous with another man's further immersion into it. When I ask students to locate the exact moment of Rena's successful passage into whiteness, they often name this scene at the tournament, this long, cinematic moment at the center of which her white handkerchief floats gently to the ground. Off to one side is Frank, the black protector of her past, his still-fresh head wound wrapped in a red bandana; to the other is George Tryon, a white tournament contestant with a swath of crimson tied across his chest. Before the handkerchief hits the dirt—before Frank can call out his recognition—George catches it on the end of his lance, "ere it touched the ground" (34). Because Frank chooses not to call out, Rena successfully earns a place in the town's history and a role in its story. Hidden from George is the fact that the white handkerchief did not fall from the hand of a white woman. As George ties it around his lance, Rena leaves Frank behind, bleeding in the desert of the real.

4. Tinted Windows

Passing as white does not guarantee peace of mind in *House*. Through an intricate series of interlocking events, Chesnutt arranges the plot so that George and Rena both travel to her hometown of Patesville, each unaware of the other. Visiting a doctor's office, George catches a nap, dreaming of Rena, who he assumes is waiting at home for him in Clarence. His arm is around her waist, and he is waiting for her to speak. But, instead of consummation, disruption occurs when a different woman's voice suddenly penetrates his dream from the outside, calling for the doctor from the next room. The convergence is uncanny; Rena's and George's divergent realities cross:

> Tryon was in a state of somnolence in which one may dream and yet be aware that one is dreaming,—the state where one, during a dream, dreams that one pinches one's self to be sure that one is not dreaming. He was therefore aware of a ringing quality about the words he had just heard that did not comport with the shadowy converse of a dream—an incongruity in the remark, too, which marred the harmony of the vision. The

shock was sufficient to disturb Tryon's slumber, and he struggled slowly back to consciousness. When fully awake, he thought he heard a light footfall descending the stairs.   (72)

The material space of the office dissolves his virtual space, as he hears his beloved's voice in the wrong place and presumably from the wrong body, once she is described as "a Negro woman":

> "Was there someone here?" he inquired of the attendant in the outer office, who was visible through the open door.
>
> "Yas, suh," replied the boy, "a young cullud 'oman wuz in jes' now, axin' fer de doctuh."
>
> Tryon felt a momentary touch of annoyance that a Negro woman should have intruded herself into his dream at its most interesting point. Nevertheless, the voice had been so real, his imagination had reproduced with such exactness the dulcet tones so dear to him, that he turned his head involuntarily and looked out the window. He could just see the flutter of a woman's skirt disappearing around the corner.   (72)

George catches only "the flutter of a woman's skirt." As is the case throughout the novel, he only glimpses Rena in facets and fragments.

The conjuration of Rena in the voice of a black woman is experienced as an uncanny glitch in the whiteness machine, foreshadowing George's painful shock of recognition. Indeed, within moments of asserting that "tinted beauty had never appealed to him," he learns that the object of his affection was tinted all along, when he looks into a drugstore: "Between the colored glass bottles in the window he could see a young woman, a tall and slender girl, like a lily on its stem. . . . Her face was partly turned from the window, but as Tryon's eye fell upon her, he gave a great start. Surely, no two women could be so much alike . . ." (94). In 1900, Rena's placement among the colored bottles hints at the unreality of George's earliest apprehensions of her. In the twenty-first century, however, my students often read the window as itself a relevant surface, an important element in the media event that is Rena. Surrounded by glass, she becomes a projection. The screen, lit momentarily from the wrong side, turns from opaque to transparent. George is horrified when she comes from behind the glass, emerging fully into his view as a black woman:

> When Rena's eyes fell upon the young man in the buggy, she saw a face as pale as death, with staring eyes, in which love, which had once reigned there, had now given place to astonishment and horror. She stood a moment as if turned to stone . . . the color faded from her cheek, the light from her eye, and she fell fainting to the ground.   (94)

Bloodless, George rushes away. Bloodless, Rena falls to the ground. If in "The Precession of Simulacra" Baudrillard identifies the forces by which generative origins are swept away, Du Bois and Chesnutt force us to think about where personal agency resides in the social, as women and people without white skin are forced to navigate overlapping yet divergent worlds.

NOTES

[1] African American literature is especially useful for teaching theory at the under-graduate level because it helps students resist the temptation to use critical texts to read a work of literature paradigmatically, as an example of a theory. As well, it encourages them to identify the theoretical dimension available in a wide variety of texts. This ability empowers them as thinkers beyond the boundary of a specific course.

[2] The notion that some texts are fiction, some nonfiction, and some philosophical or theoretical is a recent scholarly invention, and humanities students should be disabused of their assumptions regarding who is allowed to speak on what, and how, and when such speaking should be done—especially because we *also* know all the various ways women and people of color would not have been welcomed in the various historical milieux out of which we imagine theory to have emerged. What does it mean to imagine American political theory without Ida B. Wells or gender theory without Pauline Hopkins?

[3] It is worth noting that the central nervous system trying to process the body in two divergent spaces or experiences at once (for instance, feeling as if you are moving when you are not) is also why virtual reality (VR) simulations literally produce motion sickness. Because such a dual state of being should not be possible, the brain therefore tries to evacuate hallucinogenic toxins from the body.

[4] Indeed, by the time they get to more recent theorists, and before they get to *House*, the students have begun to develop some techniques for reading theoretically. In larger, lecture-and-discussion classes of up to seventy students, I reduce the reading of contemporary theory and instead model close reading through lecture, inviting students to do the same in exam responses that are short, structured, and written or spoken. Versions of the two passing courses in which I teach Chesnutt are archived at mp285 .com/courses.

Fact into Fiction:
Teaching Chesnutt's *The Marrow of Tradition* and the 1898 Wilmington Coup d'État

Margaret D. Bauer

Before I was interviewed to take over the editorship of the *North Carolina Literary Review* (*NCLR*), I was sent back issues of the journal, including one featuring the "Wilmington Race Riot of 1898." This little-known chapter of North Carolina history is the only successful coup d'état in American history, yet I had never heard of it until seeing the 1994 *NCLR*. But neither had a lot of people, I later learned, even many native to the Old North State. The first semester I taught North Carolina literature at East Carolina University, in the spring of 1997, I included Charles W. Chesnutt's 1901 novel, which was inspired by this momentous event. During our discussion of *The Marrow of Tradition*, I was surprised to find that even students who were from Wilmington or New Hanover County had never heard about what had transpired there in the fall of 1898. It was then still relatively recent that *NCLR's* Wilmington race riot issue and Philip Gerard's 1994 novel *Cape Fear Rising* (not to be confused with the movie *Cape Fear*) had reminded the public, particularly in North Carolina, of this history, and although the reception of these publications was not entirely positive (some Wilmington citizens would have preferred to keep this particular skeleton in the closet), by 1998 Wilmington was ready to commemorate the centennial anniversary of what was then still called the Wilmington race riot. I was not the only reader encouraged to learn more and to teach others.

In 1998, the University of North Carolina Press published *Democracy Betrayed: The Wilmington Race Riot of 1898 and Its Legacy*, a collection of essays edited by David S. Cecelski and Timothy B. Tyson, and in November of that year the Raleigh (NC) *News and Observer* published a section of articles and remembrances about what had transpired—as far as people knew (Cecelski). The story, it seems, had been quietly passed down in the African American community of Wilmington but not so much among the white citizens. The city hosted town hall discussions on the matter—which apparently became quite heated at times. Deciding that this dark chapter of the state's history needed to be studied, the North Carolina General Assembly formed the Wilmington Race Riot Commission, which presented its report and recommendations in 2006, prompting another series of articles in the state's newspapers.[1]

The commission's recommendations include incorporating this historical event into the curriculum of the state's Department of Public Instruction, but I teach Chesnutt's *Marrow of Tradition* regularly and have yet to have a class in which more than a few students ever heard of the Wilmington race riot or a successful American coup d'état that occurred in North Carolina. I have also added this novel to my syllabus for Appreciating Literature, a kind of special topics course in which I teach historical fiction set in North Carolina, showing students how history inspires fiction—and how good fiction can come closer than other media to exploring truths that resonate far beyond the local events reported by journalists and historians.

The secondary readings that I assign when teaching *The Marrow of Tradition* include a variety of historical resources that explore the events that inspired Chesnutt's novel, and I divide the readings among the students. The students then present reports to the class, in which they explain the historical context of their assigned text, summarize its content, and analyze the significance of its genre, particularly regarding how the author and medium reflect a particular bias. In this way we put together one chapter of a historiography of the 1898 coup d'état. What follows is an account of these materials and how I guide class discussion of them.

We begin with a speech by Rebecca Latimer Felton and Alexander Manly's editorial prompted by her speech,[2] both of which fanned the flames as the Wilmington political climate heated up in the fall of 1898. In August, Felton, the wife of a United States congressman, gave a speech in Atlanta, which was then published in the *Atlanta Constitution*; a week later, Alex Manly, a black newspaper editor, wrote an editorial in reply in the *Daily Record*, Wilmington's African American newspaper. Felton draws on the brute Negro stereotype in her characterization of black men and employs the usual rhetoric of concern about the threat of these men to the purity of white women. While she chastises white men for not properly protecting white women from black sexual violence, she also advocates lynching, if that is what it takes to stop black men from raping. In his editorial, Manly makes three important points in rebuttal: first, he asserts that not all sex between black men and white women is nonconsensual; second, he suggests that some white women cry rape when their affair with a black man is discovered, in order to protect their reputation; and third, he notes the hypocrisy of advocating the lynching of black men while turning a blind eye to (if not condoning) the rape of black women by white men both during and following the period of slavery. When my students and I discuss these two readings, we consider how they influenced what happened in Wilmington, and we examine how Chesnutt employs (and transforms) these pieces of history in his fiction.

Dolen Perkins's *NCLR* article "'White Heat' in Wilmington: The Dialogue between Journalism and Literature in *The Marrow of Tradition*" is particularly helpful in understanding the significance of the 1898 newspaper coverage of the riot before it became history. Perkins reminds us that in the late nineteenth century, journalism shared some of the elements of literary fiction. (This reminder no longer surprises in the twenty-first century, the time of Fox News, but I tell my students that once people had faith in the veracity of journalism.) Perkins argues that, unlike the newspapers, Chesnutt's novel tells both sides, the white and the black, of the story. Illustrating how it takes a variety of voices to provide a more complete accounting of history, she notes that most of the few sources available to the historians who have tried to figure out what happened in Wilmington were biased.

Perkins begins with Alfred Waddell's *Collier's Weekly* article, long considered the definitive account of events and not contradicted in the historical record until Helen G. Edmonds's 1954 *The Negro and Fusion Politics in North Carolina, 1894–1901* (39–40). Perkins points out that situated between these two sources—the magazine article by a person involved in the event, who became mayor after it, and the book by Edmonds published over fifty years later—one finds Chesnutt's novel, which appeared three years after the event and which was fiction, not masquerading as history. Yet several chapters of the novel (3, 8, 21, 22, 28, and 29) explore what "motivate[ed] the 'literary' riot" and "speak to" the Wilmington journalism that helped motivate the government coup (Perkins 40). The historical Secret Nine are comparable to the three white men plotting in the newspaper office of Chesnutt's novel. By reducing the number to three, Chesnutt "emphasizes how violent historical events could begin within the hands of a few powerful men in combination with a powerful press" (41). Perkins argues that Chesnutt's title reflects the source (or marrow) of the trouble, "the *tradition* on which core assumptions of white supremacy rested," in contrast to the newspaper headlines, which "focus on the violence and accuse African Americans of starting the riot" (43).

That the newspapers report the black men killed and the white wounded gives the message of white empowerment, Perkins believes.[3] She contrasts the newspaper reports with the fatalities given in the novel: the deaths of a woman (Mammy Jane) and a child (the Millers' son) during the violence. And Josh Green, a black man, achieves empowerment through his revenge on Captain McBane, a white man (44). That Chesnutt moves the site of violent altercation from Manly's newspaper office to a hospital, Perkins argues, emphasizes the "helplessness" of these citizens against mob rage (44).

Perkins shows that in both the white mainstream press and the black-owned newspaper accounts of the 1898 riot, the headlines reflect the sympathies of the editors. The journalists reporting the facts had as much of an agenda as the various creative writers who were inspired by the history afterward. The students come to see from Perkins's essay how perspective and politics influence everyone, how the news can be as fictional as a novel, and how Chesnutt's novel comes closer to the truth of what happened in Wilmington than the early history books do.

My class examines the 1898 headlines from the Wilmington *Morning Star,* the Raleigh *News and Observer,* and the *Washington Post* in the days after Colonel Waddell led the coup that replaced the Wilmington city government with himself as mayor and a new, carefully selected board of aldermen: "Bloody Conflict with Negroes," "Negro Rule Ended," "Democratic Regime Strangling Anarchy," "Order Is Restored," "Good Order Rules," "Order Now Reigns." We contrast these headlines with "Horrible Butcheries at Wilmington," which is from a black-owned newspaper published in Richmond. The three headlines referencing the restoration of order are particularly disturbing in their sugges-tion of the restoration of the *old order*, a term often used in reference to the Old South, which of course supported the institution of slavery. From Perkins's essay and the next set of secondary readings, other creative writing about these historical events, students realize that the versions of this story that were ac-cessible and accepted for over fifty years after 1898 were by the white-owned press, the white leader of the coup, and a white (supremacist) novelist (Thomas Dixon). Most of the African Americans who had witnessed and survived the riot barely talked about it, much less published about it, but that they did remember was demonstrated when Wilmington held discussions about the riot before its centennial anniversary.

Just two weeks after the Wilmington coup, *Collier's Weekly*, a nationally read magazine, published Colonel Waddell's version of events, and it is his article and Dixon's description of the rioting in his 1902 novel *The Leopard's Spots* that were the most broadly read accounts of the event in their day. I direct the students to chapters in *The Leopard's Spots* where the "Negroes" are shown instigating the violence. We contrast Dixon's story with Chesnutt's. In their re-search, students discover that Dixon's novels, tedious (and offensive) to many of today's readers, were very popular at the time, while the reviews of *The Mar-row of Tradition*, even by fans of Chesnutt's earlier fiction, were not positive. Reviewers and Chesnutt's own editor were disappointed in the "bitter" tone of this novel (Howells, "Psychological Counter-current"). Such readers had appar-ently missed the depiction of the horrors of slavery in Chesnutt's lighter conjure stories (see Byerman). It is interesting that these readers were less tolerant of Chesnutt's use of the Wilmington events for subject matter than readers were of Dixon's use: Dixon's resentment of Reconstruction was apparently more pal-atable than Chesnutt's bitterness about the continued oppression of African Americans almost a half century after the Civil War.

The students who are assigned to report on another novel about the coup, *Hanover; or, The Persecution of the Lowly* (1901), by David Bryant Fulton, an African American writer, will likely find it uninspiring. Like Dixon's books (though with the opposite ideology about race), *Hanover* is heavy-handed in its agenda, which makes for dull reading. I challenge the students assigned to *Ha-nover* to figure out what exactly the author made up—or was this novel actually the African American side of the story, masked as fiction to protect the author (who published it under the pen name Jack Thorne)? Chesnutt wrote about the Wilmington coup and the violence that led to it, but his novel rises above his politics and the particular place and time of the events that inspired it. Ches-nutt's novel is different from the other novels inspired by the coup in that there is more story in his, less agenda than in Dixon's novel. But Chesnutt makes less effort than Fulton, his contemporary, and Philip Gerard and John Sayles, our contemporaries, to employ details of the actual events. *Marrow* has far fewer characters, which makes it easier for readers to get to know them and keep them straight. The attention to historical detail in the other novels results in a lot of characters to remember and a lot of politics to decipher. A story suffers when it is too burdened by history.

When I ask students to contrast search results on each of these authors using the *MLA International Bibliography*, they see that Chesnutt has received the most scholarly attention. Even so, his popularity waned during his lifetime, significantly so after the publication of *Marrow*. However, like many other African American writers, he was given another chance after the civil rights movement, when people began to revisit the works of early black writers. As we survey the lengthy list of the MLA bibliography results to a search of criticism on *Marrow*, we note that the earliest critical essay is dated 1972, forty years after the author's death, but also that in recent years several books have been published on Chesnutt.

Next we turn to the historical scholarship about the coup. Students learn that the 1898 Wilmington chapter of North Carolina's history is not covered by an in-depth historical study until Edmonds's 1954 book, and then not again for three decades, when H. Leon Prather, Sr., published *We Have Taken a City: Wilmington Racial Massacre and Coup of 1898*. After still another decade, an essay about the coup by Bennett Steelman reached the office of the founding editor of *NCLR*, Alex Albright, a North Carolina native who had never heard of these events. Around this same time, Tyson and Cecelski were putting their collection of essays together in anticipation of the centennial anniversary, and Gerard was finishing his novel.

A Delaware native, Gerard moved to North Carolina to teach creative writing at the University of North Carolina, Wilmington, and became interested in this then obscure chapter of his new home's history. During a talk at East Carolina University in 2007, he credited Albright with starting the conversation about it with the Wilmington race riot *NCLR* issue, which contained an excerpt from Gerard's novel. And the rest, I tell my students, is history. Our knowledge of what happened in 1898 is limited—the sources are all biased—but as much can be learned from the fiction as from the facts. Chesnutt's novel leads us to question our understanding of both fact and fiction as it unveils truths about humanity and society.

Writers continue to be fascinated by the Wilmington race riot or coup détat, as it is now more accurately called. As editor of *NCLR*, I published Michael White's poem "Coup," which my class also reads. This poem was published in 2009, three years after the state's commission report. Also not a North Carolina native, White, like Gerard, teaches creative writing at the University of North Carolina, Wilmington. My class discusses how these historical events have inspired these two emigrant writers who made Wilmington their home. "Does the history of the place you call home matter?" I ask, prompting an interesting discussion of William Faulkner's notion of the presence of the past.

In *The Marrow of Tradition*, Chesnutt illustrates the power of the written word: the editorial that the Big Three hold for an opportune time to stir people up; Olivia's father's will, leaving part of his estate to his mixed-race daughter

Janet, his letter to his lawyer, revealing his marriage to Janet's mother, and the marriage certificate; Mr. Delamere's final will, leaving all to his devoted servant Sandy and to Dr. Miller's hospital and disinheriting his grandson Tom. We note that these documents must be read to exert power. The timeliness of the release of the incendiary editorial (mirroring Manly's editorial) nearly incites a mob to lynch Sandy for a crime he didn't commit. Sandy's reputation as a devoted servant is forgotten, or it is irrelevant to people like Captain McBane, for whom punishing any black man will suffice as retribution for the death of Mrs. Ochiltree. Olivia burns her father's will, and her husband informs her that a mixed-race marriage was not legal in North Carolina. But the documents are her secret; no one will know about them unless she tells them—and she doesn't, until her son's life is at stake, by which point Janet does not want any connection to this sister, whose husband has incited the violence that killed her son. And General Belmont withholds the will that disinherits Tom, allowing Tom to get away with the murder of the woman of whom they were ready to lynch an innocent man to avenge. General Belmont will use the will to control Tom; he prefers to have a murderer go free than to have African Americans inherit such wealth.

Understanding that the written word would have no power unless it was read, Chesnutt wrote to his publisher about his concern about the marketing of his novel. Alas, *Marrow* was not his most successful work, though many argue it is his best. I point out to my class that the writer had a promising start—publishing stories in *The Atlantic Monthly*, then being picked up by a major Boston publishing house, which brought out his first two books in the same year. Yet after *Marrow* Chesnutt published just one more novel in his lifetime, even though he continued to write: several novels by him have been published since 1997 (he died in 1932). Perhaps he knew that his contemporaries were not yet ready for him but that later readers would be.

NOTES

[1] Read the commission report at www.history.ncdcr.gov/1898-wrrc/report/report .htm. For the 2006 press coverage, see Tyson, and for another excellent source, published since the commission report, see Umfleet.

[2] These two brief texts were reprinted, along with biographical information on Felton and Manly, in the Bedford Cultural Edition of *Marrow* (405–11), edited by Bentley and Gunning, and in its Norton Critical Edition (250–57), edited by Sollors. For further discussion of the speech and the editorial, see Whites; Kirshenbaum.

[3] Perkins's essay, published four years before the report from the 1898 Wilmington Race Riot Commission, saw that the number of deaths could not be determined so long after the fact, because no effort was made at the time to record such data.

Chesnutt as Political Theorist: Imagining Democracy and Social Justice in the Literature Classroom

Gregory Laski

Charles W. Chesnutt has long been understood as an author who addresses questions of justice, particularly as they relate to the problems of race, rights, and recognition in Jim Crow America. Given his training as a lawyer, such an approach makes sense. But his oeuvre also contains a powerful meditation on the possibilities and problems of democracy, the crucial political context for his literary campaign for racial justice. In his novels, especially *The Marrow of Tradition* (1901) and *The Colonel's Dream* (1905), and in his nonfiction writings, Chesnutt repeatedly reminds his readers that while both founding texts of American democracy—the Declaration of Independence and the Constitution—claim among their aims the realization of justice, the ability of this political form to secure justice for all is anything but certain. If democracy does not possess a necessary link to just social structures, then how might we imagine configurations of this political system that serve the common good? Approaching Chesnutt as a political theorist working in narrative form, I examine the terms and stakes of this question and offer strategies for encouraging students to explore the possible responses his work holds out.

My method is informed by an upper-level undergraduate English seminar I teach at the United States Air Force Academy, Imagining Democracy and Social Justice in Late-Nineteenth-Century American Literature. Focusing on the socially conscious fiction that appeared at the fin de siècle, the course asks students to consider these two questions: In what ways does democracy promote just social structures, and in what ways does it hinder them? In response, students put novels by Henry Adams, Stephen Crane, Kate Chopin, and Chesnutt into dialogue with contemporaneous historical contexts and with classical and modern works of political theory. The ultimate aim of the course is for students to synthesize these various texts and contexts—literary, philosophical, and historical—to create their own account of democratic justice in a research paper.

Chesnutt's oeuvre—particularly *Marrow*, with which the course concludes—serves as a rich site for exploring the seminar's questions. Depicting the erosion of the black political equality inaugurated during Radical Reconstruction and illuminating the continued violation of liberty after slavery, *Marrow* lays bare the long history of democracy's development at the expense of African Americans. In so doing, Chesnutt reminds us that endeavoring to narrow the gap between democracy and social justice requires the kind of imaginative work that Martha Nussbaum has identified as vital to public life: a style of reading that moves "back and forth between the general and the concrete" (*Poetic Justice* 8), between abstract political values and particular historical realities. Applying this method to *Marrow*, we can approach the novel as a work that is at once informed by its specific historical context—namely, the Wilmington, North Carolina, antiblack riots of 1898—and yet not beholden to it. Situated thus, between historical fact and aesthetic possibility, the text can help us imagine a more just form of democracy. For my students—future military leaders—such an exercise is pressing. But the pedagogical approach to Chesnutt's work that this essay outlines should aid all teachers and students committed to increasing the ability of democracy to secure social justice.

Democracy and Social Justice, Democracy versus Social Justice: Definitions

As the political theorist Ian Shapiro has observed, in the popular mind and the practice of politics, democracy and social justice generally are understood as consonant commitments. That is, we tend to associate political democracy—the sovereignty of the people made material in elections—with the just distribution of rights and opportunities both in political institutions and economic and social structures (Rawls 6). Yet Shapiro also notes that this kinship between democracy and justice is more aspirational than actual (18). In fact, far from securing the ends of social justice—minority rights, religious toleration, or equal opportunity, for example—democracy often subverts them. Chesnutt gave voice to this disjunction in a 1913 lecture when he remarked that in the segregated South there was at best "a hybrid sort of democracy, which, under the forms of free government conducts an oligarchy, which governs with small regard for the rights of those who differ in complexion from the majority" (*Charles W. Chesnutt: Essays* 309). For Shapiro, the asymmetry to which Chesnutt here points presents a choice: theoretically speaking, we could decide to "sever the link between democracy and expectations about justice" or we could attempt to make good on our intuitive sense that democracy and social justice ought to go together by working to realize forms of democracy that are "justice-promoting" rather than "justice-undermining" (18).

In his work Chesnutt took the latter path, but getting students to follow him on it can be difficult, not simply because the concepts involved are abstract and thus intimidating but also because *democracy* itself is a term that we often hear invoked but rarely rigorously defined. In geopolitics, this nebulousness helps explain the fact that so many governments claim to be democratic while engaging in practices that violate the most basic principles of democracy (Dahl 100–01). In the classroom and on campus, such definitional flexibility can make *democracy* a cliché—that is, a term so familiar that serious reflection on or engagement with its meanings seems unnecessary.

This state of affairs obtains even in my institution, one of our nation's federal service academies, where students earn their baccalaureate degree while also training to become a military officer. I anticipated that my students, who on graduating from the academy will take an oath to protect and defend the Constitution, would be interested in the topic of democracy and social justice, so I was surprised when one student commented in the end-of-semester course evaluation that the seminar's topic turned out to be "ten times as interesting as I initially thought."

One way to understand this observation is to hear in it an appreciation for the complexities of democracy and social justice that comes from grappling with these terms from the ground up. Indeed, I began this class, as I often begin courses on democracy, with an examination of that word. Deriving from the Greek *demokratia, democracy* is made up of two root words: *demos,* meaning "people," and *kratos,* meaning "rule." Already we can see in this combination the sorts of practical and philosophical problems alluded to in the comments by Shapiro and Chesnutt. Just who are the people? And what does it mean to rule? At issue in the first question is the idea of inclusiveness; at stake in the second is the arrangement of institutional and political structures, of whether the people will administer the government themselves (direct democracy) or elect representatives to do this duty in their name (representative democracy). Cutting across these various dimensions of democracy is a central tension between liberty and equality, two fundamental democratic values that often operate at loggerheads. As Raymond Williams explains, historically this tension gave rise to two traditions of democratic government: social democracy, which seeks to secure "the interests of the majority," and liberal democracy, which emphasizes the protection of individual rights, such as free speech (96).

Because Chesnutt stages both the different facets of the definition of *democracy* and the tensions that exist among them, his oeuvre represents a rich archive for students to mine as they begin to think through the meanings of the word. To facilitate this work, I ask them to imagine that they have been charged with writing the entry on *democracy* for an American encyclopedia and that the only source on which they can draw is a passage from one of Chesnutt's texts. For *Marrow* students will likely (and rightly) want to focus on the way that Wellington's Big Three—General Belmont, Major Carteret, and Captain McBane—seek forcefully to equate *the people* and *white* in their campaign to disenfranchise black Americans, thereby violating the principle of inclusiveness. The near lynching of Sandy Campbell and the riot with which the novel concludes provide powerful examples of how popular sovereignty, a fundamental tenet of democracy, can function as an instrument of injustice when the meaning of *the people* is thus delimited.[1]

But Chesnutt offers more ambiguous accounts of democracy, and students would do well to consider them. For instance, what are we to make of Dr. William Miller's rumination on the "democratic ideal" as he rides in the Jim Crow car of the train that will deliver him to Wellington, North Carolina (61)? With this phrase, Miller seems both to recognize the efficacy of group solidarity for African Americans—"They were his people," he reasons (60)—and to signal discomfort with subsuming himself in this collective, which is to say, with the sense that these black Americans from the lower end of the socioeconomic spectrum somehow represent him. Similarly, in studying *The Colonel's Dream*, students might attend to the reverie of Henry French near the end of the novel, in which he envisions a "regenerated South" where "every man could enter, through the golden gate of hope, the field of opportunity, where lay the prizes of life, which all might have an equal chance to win or lose." As the next paragraph makes clear, however, this vision has important limits: "That all men would ever be equal he did not even dream; there would always be the strong and the weak, the wise and the foolish" (345).

This qualifying comment, like Miller's meditation, lays bare the complexities that attend the democratic value of equality, because *equality* is a term that has political, economic, and social dimensions. As Robert Dahl explains, a desideratum for democracy is a commitment to "treat[ing] all persons as if they possess equal claims" to "life, liberty, and happiness" (65)—in short, to political equality. But just what does it take to secure political equality? What other forms of equality—say, of economic conditions, of institutional access, and of educational opportunity—are needed to make it possible? What would it mean to realize what French refers to as the ability for all to have an "equal chance"? Chesnutt criticized those who, in discussing the case of African Americans, tried to analyze *equality* in such a way that effectively stripped it of its force. "There is but one kind of equality," he proclaimed: "Political equality, civil equality, social equality are all mere forms of words." If in practice equality resists atomization, however, the parsing of its "forms" is in fact necessary to getting "your definitions correct," as Chesnutt put it (*Charles W. Chesnutt: Essays* 316).[2]

Chesnutt's fiction makes clear that getting the definition of *democracy* right—and perhaps even getting democracy itself right—is a process that cannot be accomplished in a historical vacuum. Accordingly, once students have grasped the basic tensions animating *democracy*, they should put the term into dialogue with some of the historical contexts on which Chesnutt draws in *Marrow*. Particularly powerful in this regard is the White Declaration of Independence, a document from the "revolution against interracial democracy" that took place in Wilmington in 1898, during which white Democrats wrested control of local government from a "Fusionist" alliance of black Republicans and white Populists, terrorizing and murdering black Wilmingtonians in the process (Tyson and Cecelski 6, 4). Standing in front of a group of white men assembled in the city courthouse on 9 November, a day before the violence broke out, Alfred Waddell, a Confederate officer during the Civil War and the man who would become Wilmington's mayor, read aloud a document composed by the leaders of the coup that asserted in part that the "framers did not anticipate the enfranchisement of an ignorant population of African origin" and that the "men of the State of North Carolina, who joined in forming the Union, did not contemplate for their descendants a subjection to an inferior race." The text continued, "We, the undersigned citizens . . . do hereby declare that we will no longer be ruled, and will never again be ruled, by men of African origin" (Wilmington Race Riot Commission 115).

At first students might understand this document as a perversion of one with which they are more familiar, the Declaration of Independence, drafted by Thomas Jefferson in 1776. Such a response is correct in a way. But it is important to alert students to the textual history of this more famous declaration. The vision of democracy in its original form—a version that the Committee of Five, made up of Jefferson, John Adams, Roger Sherman, Robert Livingston, and Benjamin Franklin, submitted to the Continental Congress on 28 June 1776— differed considerably from that of the declaration approved by Congress on 4 July. Because students usually do not know these details, I devote a session to examining those pieces of the initial submission that Congress cut, specifically a long passage in which Jefferson, the draft's author, imputed the crime of African slavery to King George III, asserting, "He has waged cruel war against human nature itself, violating [its] most sacred rights of life and liberty in the persons of a distant people who never offended him, captivating & carrying them into slavery in another hemisphere" (22). When students respond to this passage, they tend to comment on Jefferson's own complicity with slavery. But in this draft Jefferson condemns bondage "as a violation of the universal laws of justice and right inscribed within human nature and shared equally by blacks as well as whites" (Erkkila 282). That is, although the final version of the document excised this passage, the first incorporated the slaves into a more inclusive vision of the promises of liberty and equality.

Read against this historical backdrop, the political disenfranchisement and racial violence on display in *Marrow* become at once easier to understand and more difficult to evaluate as a violation of democracy. If it is an important first step for students to acknowledge that the coup incited by the Big Three compromises the liberty and equality of black Americans, barring them from the pledges of the Declaration of Independence, then the textual history of this founding document alerts students to the fact that the uprising in Wilmington is not the first time that those of African descent have been so excluded. Accordingly, when McBane states, "This is a white man's country" (252), he not only expresses a normative claim that he and his associates seek to translate by violence into empirical fact; he also makes a historical assertion about the meaning of America that is at once supported (and not supported) by the different versions of the Declaration of Independence.

What I hope to underscore for students through this pairing of text and context is that considering democracy's relation to social justice requires thinking that accounts for the historical weight of the problem that racial marginalization presents for realizing black liberty and equality. In *Marrow*, Miller gives voice to this idea when, reflecting on the aggrieved Josh Green, who is haunted by a history of racial violence even before the riot commences, he realizes "how inseparably the present is woven with the past, how certainly the future will be but the outcome of the present" (112). This line suggests the importance of the past, including the wrongs of slavery, but the novel itself—much less Chesnutt as author—does not believe that this history will completely determine the future of democracy. Rather, Chesnutt suggests a double move: an appreciation for the presence of the past but also a sense of the possibilities (and, to be sure, the difficulties) of imagining other futures.

Indeed, Chesnutt understood the function of literature as this kind of imagining, as a potential force for social justice. In his lecture "Literature in Its Relation to Life" (1899), he noted that literature has two sides: the historical and the dynamic. In its historical dimension, it "is instructive, and may warn or admonish." But it also holds the "faculty of persuasion, by which men's hearts are reached, the springs of action touched, and the currents of life directed." Understood through these two poles, literature works as both "an expression of life, past and present, and as a force directly affecting the conduct of life, present and future" (*Charles W. Chesnutt: Essays* 114). I would suggest that Chesnutt's comment in this lecture offers a guide not just for reading *Marrow* but also for conceiving "justice-promoting" forms of democracy, a task that, as Shapiro notes, represents a "creative challenge" (19).

Imagining Democratic Justice: Practices

To show how Chesnutt's novel might be used as a resource to meet this creative challenge, I have composed interpretive templates that help students engage literary works both from the perspective of historical contexts, such as the White Declaration of Independence, and from conceptual vantage points. Posing a series of statements that students must complete, the templates suggest different ways of putting a literary work—in this case, *Marrow*—into dialogue with historical documents and philosophical studies.

When we are reading the novel in relation to the period of its publication, I ask students to identify specific passages from *Marrow* that interact in interesting ways with the historical texts we are examining and then to complete some of these statements:

> The description of "the people" in the White Declaration of Independence illuminates (i.e., helps us understand) the representation of popular sovereignty in the novel by . . .
> A definition of "citizenship" that is similar to or different from Chesnutt's emerges in this document when . . .

When considering *Marrow* in conversation with conceptual sources, I ask students to draw on the following:

> The idea of democracy and social justice or democracy versus social justice is exemplified by this passage in Chesnutt . . .
> The idea of democracy and social justice or democracy versus social justice is complicated by this passage in Chesnutt . . .
> This passage in Chesnutt would respond to this theory by saying . . .

The thinking that *Marrow* demands ultimately cannot be schematized in this way, but the process provides a good tool for class discussion and also serves as a guide as students formulate their own visions of democratic justice.

For example, near the end of the seminar, we considered *Marrow* in relation to John Rawls's seminal work of twentieth-century political philosophy, *A Theory of Justice*. We focused on his claim that the meaning of social justice in a democratic society ought to emerge from deliberations conducted under a "veil of ignorance" that allows citizens knowledge of "general facts about human society" (e.g., economic principles, fundamentals of human psychology) but denies them knowledge about their specific identities and the history and shape of their particular society (17, 119). According to Rawls, as people come to determine the principles of justice in what he calls the "original position," "no one should be advantaged or disadvantaged by natural fortune or social circumstance," and "it should be impossible to tailor principles to the circumstances of one's own case" (16). For example, if in the original position someone understood the difference between being wealthy and being poor, Rawls explains, this person might be influenced by such information in debating the meaning of justice as it intersects with economics.[3]

Using the templates above, students can consider whether *Marrow* endorses the "veil of ignorance" as a way of achieving social justice. What in Rawls does Chesnutt's novel accept and what does it reject? In response to this question, many of my students discuss the scene late in *Marrow* when Major Carteret abandons his attempt to entreat Dr. Miller to save Dodie, his ailing son. As the narrator remarks of Carteret, "for a moment the veil of race prejudice was rent in twain, and he saw things as they were, in their correct proportions and relations" (321). For some students, this passage confirms Rawls's emphasis on the need to abandon the peculiarities of race, tradition, and history in assessing matters of justice. In lifting the "veil of race prejudice," that is, Carteret comes to understand what justice really is and begins to see Miller as an equal—someone like him—rather than from his white supremacist perspective. Of course, as my students also appreciate, in its attention to the history of racial exclusion in the United States *Marrow* also complicates the Rawlsian veil of ignorance, anticipating the insights of race theorists like Charles W. Mills, who insists that justice for black Americans can be realized only by introducing the long history of white supremacy into the "veil" ("Contract" 112–32).

Negotiating between these readings, one student argued in his final paper that in Chesnutt's novel the project of imagining a just democracy requires the exercise of "selective memory": even as Chesnutt focuses on the historical, and often intergenerational, injustices that his black characters have experienced, he also suggests that too much attention to these wrongs will make it difficult, and perhaps impossible, to achieve another democratic good—namely, future interracial cooperation. For this student, the causes of racial redress and social concord collide in the novel.

A good deal remains to be explored with respect to this line of inquiry. Ideas of temporality, redress and reparation, intergenerational relationships, and many other issues demand consideration.[4] As Chesnutt himself once said, the "race problem" is "not unsolvable, but it is difficult" (*Charles W. Chesnutt: Essays* 239). Insofar as part of this difficulty inheres in the work of imagining forms of democracy that can support social justice, I hope that the strategies outlined here will ease what finally is no easy task. In his writings, Chesnutt has provided us with a rich space in which to conduct this analytic, deliberative, and creative work. He therefore merits the continued attention of teachers and students in the twenty-first century, a moment in which the question of democracy's ability to secure social justice has yet to be resolved.

NOTES

I offer my gratitude to the students in my spring 2014 junior seminar, especially Sam Sloan, whose contributions I cite here. The quotations from *Marrow* in this essay are taken from the Sundquist edition.

[1] These episodes also offer an opening for thinking about the relation between the popular will and the law or, as Chesnutt's narrator puts it, about how the "inherent sovereignty" of the (white) people can be invoked as a "higher law" that can "set aside . . . ordinary judicial procedure" (*Marrow* 186).

[2] For Chesnutt's treatment of perversions of liberty, see "Peonage; or, The New Slavery" (*Charles W. Chesnutt: Essays* 205–08) and *The Colonel's Dream*.

[3] Later in the book, Rawls notes that the veil is gradually lifted to reveal more and more facts about the society in question (171–76).

[4] For more on these matters, see chapter 4 of my *Untimely Democracy*.

Persons in the Balance:
The Scale of Justice in Chesnutt's
The Marrow of Tradition

Trinyan Paulsen Mariano

Charles W. Chesnutt's *The Marrow of Tradition* is a novel of weights and mea-
sures dedicated to gauging the difference between the justice that was prom-
ised and the justice that was delivered to black Americans in the closing decades
of the nineteenth century. In *Marrow*, Chesnutt explores the balance scale as a
figure for defining justice according to a rational system of measurement aimed
at maintaining equality between persons by returning measure for measure,
like for like. I demonstrate how the balance scale can be used as an organizing
idea for reading and teaching *Marrow*. Chesnutt employs the scale to evidence
racial disparity but also to explore the possibility that such a rational framework of measurement can repair the personal and collective injustices of the
Jim Crow South.

   I introduce my students to the balance scale by spending a class period studying the iconography of justice in Western cultures. I ask them first to draw
the image they most associate with justice, reminding them to represent the
concept rather than any particular case where they think justice was or was not
served. Far and away the most common symbol they draw is the scale, by itself
or in the hands of Lady Justice. Known as Maat by ancient Egyptians, Themis
by the Greeks, and Justitia by the Romans, she sometimes wears a blindfold,
sometimes wields a sword, is depicted in a range of dress (and undress), but she
almost always carries a scale. After students' visual responses are discussed, we
explore the ubiquity of the scale in representations of justice in painting, sculp-
ture, and architecture. Judith Resnik, Dennis Curtis, and the Yale Law Library
have gathered hundreds of such images in an online archive entitled *Justitia:
Iconography of Justice*.[1]

   In its simplest form, a balance scale works much like a seesaw. A middle pillar
supports an attached beam that is poised so that the weight of the object at one
end of the beam can be measured in reference to the weight of the object at the
other end. The scale is thought to have been in commercial use since 5000 BC,
and its symbolic significance in cultures throughout the world dates to antiquity
(Schwark 745). It is no understatement to say that the balance scale is the primary figure for conceptualizing justice. It has been evoked in over five hundred
United States legal cases and is omnipresent as a metaphor for justice in literature (746). In her *Residues of Justice*, Wai Chee Dimock identified the scale as
the central motif of nineteenth-century literature, and in Resnik and Curtis's
collection a scale appears in nearly every image. Aristotle famously theorized
the balance scale in his philosophy of justice as equality. Injustice, he writes,
disturbs the equality between the doer and the sufferer of a wrong. Where "one

has received and the other has inflicted a wound . . . , the suffering and the action have been unequally distributed" (469). The role of corrective justice, then, is to reestablish balance by restoring the intermediate between them. The scale rests on the twin notions of commensurability and correlativity. Commensurability means that suffering and rectification must both be rendered using a common currency, otherwise no calculation or adjustment can take place, and correlativity defines the relationship between the doer and the sufferer. As Ernest Weinrib explains, loss and gain "are correlatives because each is constituted by the other. . . . The sufferer loses by virtue of the doer's gain, and vice versa" (280). Similarly, justice is not executed by "two independent operations, one of which removes the gain and the other of which repairs the loss," but the "doer is directly liable to the sufferer," so that a single transaction repairs the loss by disgorging the gain (281). Because the wrongdoer bears the cost of restoring the loss to the sufferer, the scale connects them in the action that upsets the balance as well as in the action that restores it.

The principle of reciprocity underlying the scale exerts a powerful influence on policy and popular consciousness, even though, in practice, restoring balance is largely impossible. Many losses cannot be literally restored, distinguishing wrongdoers from victims can be complicated, and our formal systems of justice are ill equipped to implement the literal dictates of the scale. We strain to locate correlativity in the punishments doled out by the criminal courts, and there is much lost in the translation of injury into the money damages assessed by the civil justice system. By contrast, fiction provides readers with satisfying calculations of commensurability and relationships of correlativity. Investigating the mysterious lines of cause and effect that constitute poetic justice frees students to ponder whether characters have or have not received what they deserved. In this way, the opportunity for comeuppance, revenge, and psychological closure, so elusive in everyday life, are accessible imaginatively in literature.

I suggest here three ways that the balance scale can be used to teach *The Marrow of Tradition*.[2] First, the conflict between Captain McBane and Josh Green illustrates the depth with which Chesnutt stages the ideas of corrective justice. Second, *Marrow*'s lynching plot dramatizes the implications of the color line for addressing racial injustice utilizing a scale. Third, *Marrow*'s conclusion is Chesnutt's attempt to examine mercy as a means of reconciling the demands of justice.

The ideas outlined here can facilitate a sustained approach to *Marrow*, but they are also severable. In upper-division and graduate courses that are oriented thematically (a course on the segregation narrative, for example, or on the idea of justice), or in courses where *Marrow* serves as a foundational text (I don't begrudge time spent on the iconography of justice or the history of lynching if those topics are going to be relevant throughout the course), I will cover all the material in five or six class periods. In survey courses, I will spend one or two class periods on the scale, to leave room for addressing other aspects of *Marrow*.

I ask my students to use the concepts associated with the scale to analyze the conflict between Green and McBane. McBane's murder of Green's father creates a correlative relationship between the men and sets them on a collision course that culminates during the riot, when McBane's bloodthirsty white mob is met by Green's armed black resisters. Green's long-awaited justice is portrayed with highly romanticized language that invites readers to see his actions as heroic. "Lit by a rapt expression," he lunges into the white mob, who "instinctively" part before him. He cannot be stopped, even by bullets, until he has "buried his knife to the hilt in the heart of his enemy" (309). The two men die together. Their double death marks the gratifying pinnacle of Green's existence and seemingly rebalances the scale as Green dies accomplishing "jus' w'at [he was] livin' fer" (111).

Many students find the death of McBane satisfying. He sowed violence and death; thus he reaped violence and death (304). I challenge their initial response by confronting them with the closing paragraphs of chapter 35, where the narrator comments, "[O]ne of the two died as the fool dieth. Which was it, or was it both? 'Vengeance is mine,' saith the Lord, and it had not been left to Him" (309). Although this line seems to criticize Green for taking matters into his own hands, the narrator also remarks, "But they that do violence must expect to suffer violence," and points out that "McBane's death was merciful" compared with the "horrors" he had inflicted on others (309–10). Students can see how the narrator's disquiet centers on the balance scale, here haunted by the torture chamber as readers imagine what amount of suffering would make the agony McBane should experience equal to the agony he has caused. Ultimately, Green's heroism is swallowed up in the wreckage of Wellington as the chapter closes with the city in ruins.

Heroic vengeance juxtaposed with community devastation raises problems for correlativity. What changes when groups rather than individuals are placed on either side of the scale? To address this question, I ask my students to consider chapter 12, in which Dr. Miller and Josh Green debate about justice. The two characters are traditionally seen as embodying alternate approaches to justice, the dark-skinned Green representing "righteous male violence" and the mulatto Miller representing pragmatic appeasement (Gunning 72), but a closer look reveals that the balance scale orients both their mind-sets. The difference between them is not how they define justice but how they configure correlativity. Green rests his right to kill McBane on the "Mosaic law" of an eye for an eye (*Marrow* 110), a famously literal scale, while Miller registers injuries and restitution on a group rather than on an individual level. Miller's worry, one the narrative bears out, is over the collateral consequences that follow in the wake of Green's individually calibrated justice, because the color line ensures that the black race "answer as a whole for the offenses of each separate individual" (114). Understanding that racial class has been made the measure of commensurability in the South, Miller urges that group justice take precedence over personal justice.

The scale also structures both Miller's and Green's versions of forgiveness. Green rejects unbalanced, nonreciprocal forgiveness. He won't forgive so long as "de w'ite folks don' fergive" (113). Similarly, Miller's endorsement of forgiveness is bedded on corrective justice in that Miller relies on "the Lord" to "repay" injustice with vengeance (114). He spurns Green's imperfect here-and-now justice for the promise of God's perfect but deferred justice. His advice to "forgive" and "endure a little injustice" (110) should be understood in this context. For Miller, human forgiveness is backed by divine retribution: God, or simply the natural moral order, can be counted on to restore equilibrium.

There is irony in Miller's concern for group over individual justice, given that Miller bristles under the system of racial categorization that places him in the same group as Green. I direct students to this issue by considering Miller's articulation of group justice together with the train scene from chapter 5, "A Journey Southward," where Miller challenges the "vulgar[ity]" of a color line that groups him with black laborers, who are "as offensive to him as to the whites" (39), instead of with his white friend and colleague, with whom he feels deep affinity. Although *Marrow* predates W. E .B. Du Bois's "Talented Tenth" (1903), Chesnutt anticipates the figure of the educated, elite mulatto who holds himself apart from the lower classes of darker-skinned blacks and at the same time assumes a burden of responsibility for them.

Throughout the novel, Chesnutt dramatizes the erasure of individuality and the flattening of difference attending Jim Crow laws that made access to rights contingent on racial status. The implications of correlativity defined by race affiliation come to a dramatic head in *Marrow*'s lynching plot, where the color line functions as a literal fault line. Miller's logic of group-level correlativity, it turns out, parallels the logic underlying segregation and lynching in a way that aligns Miller, on this point, with Wellington's white supremacists.

The lynching of innocent Sandy is barely averted by the actions of Mr. Delamere, a white man who crosses racial lines to surrender his own nephew as the guilty party. Students are quick to note the disparity in how the law treats Tom and Sandy, but the analysis prescribed by the balance scale does not measure Tom and Sandy directly against each other; it weighs each one in turn against Polly Ochiltree. Polly's weight, when measured against Sandy's, is immense. Polly's suffering triggers outrage and frenzied rhetoric about "the swift and terrible punishment" awaiting "anyone who laid sacrilegious hands upon white womanhood" (186). A change in the race of the perpetrator, however, causes a drastic shift in the value of the victim. Polly, measured against Tom, barely merits notice. White womanhood doesn't weigh heavily enough for Tom to be tried or even publicly named. The shift in correlativity helps students see that beneath the loudly professed concern with protecting white womanhood there is a deeper drive to protect white patriarchy and power.

That the scale serves as the dominant symbol mobilized by white supremacists in the lynching campaign signals Chesnutt's uneasiness with it as a model for racial justice. Before exploring the lynching rhetoric in *Marrow*, I spend a class period introducing some of the arguments about lynching that circulated in the late nineteenth century. To provide factual background, I show to the class the short movie *Without Sanctuary* and photographs of lynchings from James Allen's online archive. Consider that some of your students might be encountering America's history of lynching for the first time and will therefore need an opportunity to express discomfort, sadness, and outrage. I assign excerpts from the first chapter of Hubert Howe Bancroft's *Popular Tribunals*. Bancroft views the Western practice of lynching as a legitimate form of communal justice imposed in the absence of formal legal and political institutions. I also assign two antilynching treatises: "Lynch Law in the South," by Frederick Douglass (whose biography Chesnutt wrote), and "Lynch Law in America," by Ida B. Wells (an outspoken critic of lynching). These short texts are fascinating because, while condemning lynching in the South, they both sanction the Western practice. Douglass writes that when "lawful remedies" have failed and government does not exist or is corrupt, there is "an apology for the application of lynch law." Wells romanticizes the "rough, rugged, and determined" men of the West who "naturally" did not tolerate criminals and had no choice but to "ma[k]e laws to meet their varying emergencies."

Echoing Bancroft, in *Marrow*, Carteret defends lynching as the people's right to "inherent sovereignty" (186). By this reasoning, setting aside "ordinary judicial procedure" is not illegal but done *"in obedience to the higher law"* (186). Judge Everton underscores the argument, claiming that "in an emergency the sovereign people might assert itself and take the law into its own hands" (193). I want students to see how, when communal justice is executed alongside a color line, the balance scale eliminates the need for particularity of guilt and renders crime and punishment as generalized cases of black against white. Carteret demonstrates this aggregation of correlativity when he argues that Sandy's crime was a "fatal assault upon a woman of our race,—upon our race in the person of its womanhood" (182).

Positing a communal victim absolves the white community of the need to find the particular (black) man responsible. As McBane puts it, "It is an assault upon the white race, in the person of old Mrs. Ochiltree, committed by the black race, in the person of some nigger. It would justify the white people in burning *any* nigger" (182). Once the color line has instituted universal black criminality, punishing any black man becomes rational. Dr. Price, who is white, explains, "If [Sandy] is innocent, his people can console themselves with the reflection that Mrs. Ochiltree was also innocent, and balance one crime against the other, the white against the black" (194). Lynching in *Marrow* is presented as the logical outgrowth of a system of racial categorization that makes white and black legally significant and oppositional categories. This logic also explains why there is no need to prosecute Tom. As whites, Tom and Polly are subsumed in the same collective person and thus imbalance between them is a matter of purely internal adjustment. Intraracial crime does nothing to upset the equilibrium and so does not even register as injustice.

The Marrow of Tradition, a novel obsessed with justice, ends with mercy—a fact that has puzzled critics and spawned wildly contradictory readings of the concluding chapters. The range of these interpretations makes for excellent class discussion and provides students with starting points for further research. I provide students with a few of the many critical claims about *Marrow's* ending and have them work in small groups to analyze and respond to them (for a model, see the appendix to this essay). As a class, we then consider what *Marrow's* conclusion means in terms of the balance scale. I build this consideration around a reconstruction of the conflict between Olivia Carteret and Janet Miller, a study of the often overlooked penultimate chapter, in which Chesnutt explicitly maps out the relation between correlativity and commensurability and introduces the idea of mercy.

Olivia confronts the correlative demands of the scale when she discovers that some of her inheritance rightly belongs to Janet, who was not, as she once believed, an illegitimate child, but her legal sister. In a passage I call "Olivia's Calculus," Olivia reasons through the costs that attend recognition of a black woman as a person:

> If the woman had been white,—but the woman had *not* been white, and the same rule of moral conduct did not, *could* not, in the very nature of things, apply, as between white people! For, if this were not so, slavery had been, not merely an economic mistake, but a great crime against humanity. If it had been such a crime, as for a moment she dimly perceived it might have been, then through the long centuries there had been piled up a catalogue of wrong and outrage which, if the law of compensation be a law of nature, must some time, somewhere, in some way, be atoned for. She herself had not escaped the penalty, of which, she realized, this burden placed on her conscience was but another installment.   (266)

I ask students to parse this passage to draw out three insights (among others). First, Olivia accepts the dictates of the scale but concludes that correlativity and commensurability can be maintained only between whites. Second, she arrives at this conclusion because the enormity of the wrongs to be compensated for threatens her social and economic position. Third, her reasoning lacks conviction. Her glimpse of slavery as a "crime against humanity" implicitly recognizes the moral equality of persons, as does the penalty of guilt she shoulders. Her guilt, however, cannot be paid to Janet and so circumvents correlativity by leaving the victim out altogether.

While Olivia rejects cross-racial correlativity, Chesnutt uses Dodie's repeated inability to breathe to insist on it. Dodie chokes on a rattle while his father opines on white supremacy (44), he drowns in Olivia's foreshadowing dream (269), and he struggles to breathe during the riots (312). His breath is a symbol of dependency between the two families and establishes a link between justice for the black community and the future of the white South. Nonetheless,

Chesnutt does not narrate Dodie's fate because the Millers' decision is the proper focus of *Marrow*'s conclusion. The negotiations leading up to their actions reverse the outcome of Olivia's calculus and establish commensurability between the black son of the Millers and the white son of the Carterets. Carteret himself acquiesces to this equivalence. When "the veil of race prejudice" is lifted "for a moment," he is able to accurately weigh "proportions and relations" and sees that Miller's refusal to save Dodie is "pure, elemental justice": "Miller had spoken the truth,—as he had sown, so must he reap!" (321). In Miller and Carteret's negotiations, reciprocity is given literal embodiment, an exchange of like for like that balances the scales. Miller's son is dead. Carteret is responsible. Carteret's son is demanded in return.

The cogency of this verdict contributes to the dismay some students express when they are denied the catharsis of poetic justice. The price of justice is set in chapter 36, "Fiat Justitia," only to be relinquished in chapter 37, "The Sisters,"[3] but only after Janet wrings from Olivia an acknowledgment that the "forfeit" of Dodie's life "is but just" (328). Janet's act of mercy, I suggest to my students, is not a complete abdication of justice. Mercy is importantly distinct from forgiveness. Mercy means to "treat a person less harshly than . . . one has a right to" (Murphy and Hampton 20). Forgiveness, when used in reference to a person, is a matter of changing how one feels about that person (21). Janet's mercy (it is not forgiveness) affirms the logic of the scale by demanding a reckoning that rests on a foundation of commensurable personhood. Olivia's "obscene" bargain (*Marrow* 326) attempts to make correlativity and commensurability a matter of contractual exchange, which ironically renders them impossible. Olivia cannot confer equal personhood in exchange for mercy, since the very bestowing of it would negate it. Janet is not given but assumes her position on the scale equal and opposite Olivia, and Olivia is forced to a new calculus that recognizes these "correct proportions and relations" (321). Mercy depends on this reckoning and recognition. Without an assessment and acknowledgment of the cost of expiation, there is no standard by which leniency can be measured.

The inherent equality acknowledged in the conclusion to *Marrow* is the reason for Janet's mercy, not the outcome of it. Justice in *Marrow* is neither found in nor vitiated by mercy; justice happens in the reciprocal recognition that Dodie's life is not worth more than the life of the Miller's son. This act of accounting requires the framework of correlativity and commensurability, the logic of the scale if not the actual operation of it.

NOTES

In this essay, quotations from *Marrow* are taken from the Sundquist edition.

[1] The Web site address is www.flickr.com/photos/yalelawlibrary/sets/7215762196257 2618/. For more on Lady Justice, see Burnett, who pays special attention to Themis.

[2]I develop many of these arguments in greater depth in "The Law of Torts."

[3]The connection between womanhood and mercy has its own critical tradition. For two classic texts, see Samuels; Nussbaum, "Equity". In the context of *Marrow*, see Najmi; McFatter.

APPENDIX
Some Critical Approaches to *Marrow*'s Conclusion

Samini Namji: The novel uses motherhood as a trope for racial reconciliation.

> "Chesnutt's final appeal is to the maternal instinct in his white female audience—that instinct which he, and Stowe before him, believed to be a powerful, life-affirming force, resonating across the color line" (7). Her "mother's heart . . . hurls [Olivia] across the racial divide," casting off white supremacy, acknowledging Janet as her sister, and admitting her own culpability, and Janet, refusing all other appeals, "responds to Olivia's desperate motherhood" (14).

Christopher De Santis: The novel advocates a color-blind society.

> The "benevolent actions" of the Millers offer "the most socially and politically viable alternative for blacks." They signal hope for a "transition from a racist social order to a color-blind society" in which the "concept of 'race'" is eradicated (92, 93).

James Giles and Thomas Lally: The novel advocates black separatism.

> When the decision to save Dodie is put in Janet's hands, Janet "symbolically establish[es] her position as spokeswoman for the new separatist attitude of the black community toward the white. . . . 'Listen!'" Janet cries, 'I have but one word for you,—one last word,—and then I hope never to see your face again!'" (267).

Michelle J. Wolkomir: The novel advocates racial amalgamation.

> The women's ability to transcend racial barriers (255) leads in the direction of an "amalgamated society" (252). The ending brings the two families and the two races together for the first time. "Consider: Carteret invites a black doctor into his home; Olivia offers sisterhood and a share of her fortune with her mulatto sister; Janet overcomes her fawning subservience to the image of her white half-sister; and Dr. Miller finds himself inside a home from which he had previously been shut out, at the bottom of a staircase, invited by a white man to 'come on up'" (255).

Susan McFatter: The novel stages a conflict between paternal law and maternal forgiveness.

> The paternal "spirit of *lex talionis*" animating the novel becomes untenable, resolving in the actions of Janet Miller, who embodies a contrasting ethic of Christ-like forgiveness (207). Where maternalism "reflects an attitude of 'holding,'" paternal justice is concerned with "acquiring," and so is "instrument[al] of capitalism" (207). Accordingly, Olivia's offer of social recognition, family name, and shared inheritance is paternalistic. But to Janet, Olivia's offer is an "obscene" trade "for the life of her child" (208). By offering mercy and rejecting the exchange, Janet constructs maternal forgiveness as an alternative to strict justice.

Teaching "The Sheriff's Children," "The Wife of His Youth," and *The Marrow of Tradition* in the United States–Mexico Borderlands

Brian Yothers

In Charles W. Chesnutt's fiction, the family motif—particularly the interracial family divided by racism and discriminatory legal and cultural codes—that informs midcentury slave narratives and abolitionist novels of the late antebellum and early Reconstruction periods provides an important thread by which to connect Chesnutt with the wider tradition of writing about slavery, race, and gender in nineteenth-century American literature. This motif also connects him with the contemporary experience of students who are both uniquely situated on the border between two nations and increasingly representative of the future directions of United States higher education. I teach "The Sheriff's Children" and *The Marrow of Tradition*, with their wrenching and violent portrayals of biological families across the color line, in nineteenth-century American literature classes at the advanced undergraduate and graduate levels, when the courses are either centered on slavery, abolitionism, emancipation, and Reconstruction or have substantial thematic strands related to these issues.

My own location as I teach this material matters a great deal: if families arbitrarily divided by legal fictions can seem like a relic of the distant past to some students and perhaps even faculty members in the twenty-first century, it is distinctly otherwise for many who live on the United States–Mexico border, where people often have family members (even parents or siblings) whose citizenship status differs from their own, and that status obviously has profound implications for their lives and legal standing. This analogy between Chesnutt's work and my students' own geographic setting has become crucial in the classroom, because my students have made it so: they have consistently noted the connection, and over time I've come to incorporate it more substantially into our discussions. For example, I ask students to consider Henry Louis Gates's massive African American Lives project as additional historical framing for the familial dimensions of Chesnutt's work and to think about how these stories relate to their own region and experience. What makes the project, which consists of a series of videos in which family oral histories are supplemented by the documentary history that Gates unearths, so valuable is that it displays real-life counterparts to the family histories that Chesnutt recounts, and it carries them through to the present day.

The divided interracial family appears insistently in antebellum slave narratives and abolitionist novels and post–Civil War novels supportive of racial equality alike. When I teach Chesnutt, usually I have already discussed at least some of these representations of interracial families and their problems. Reading him in the context of the late nineteenth century in American literature and culture and in the broader context of debates over race, slavery, and the meaning of the interracial family for both policy and art allows my students at the University of Texas, El Paso, to engage with the troubled American past and to reflect on its relevance to the troubled present of divided families across the Americas.

The context in which I teach is unique in certain ways and in others typical of higher education in the United States. The student population at my university is roughly eighty percent Mexican American and includes many students who are nontraditional in terms of their age and life experience. Our proximity to the United States–Mexico border means that some of our students are Mexican citizens who commute across the border, many are first- or second-generation immigrants, and most have some personal or professional connection to issues associated with immigration and citizenship. The ways in which Chesnutt dealt with matters of citizenship and legal standing at the turn of the twentieth century are resonant here in the early years of the twenty-first. Obviously, the students who live in sight of the large Mexican city of Ciudad Juarez have a different set of experiences from those who live farther from the border region, but increasingly, and for all, the immigrant experience has become a major part of attending a big university in the United States. During my doctoral work at Purdue University in Indiana, I taught students from Mexico, El Salvador, Venezuela, China, India, Pakistan, Bangladesh, Russia, Syria, and Kuwait, and they too were affected by immigration policy, which applies everywhere in the country, not only to the border.

In the sophomore-level introduction to fiction, the Chesnutt text I teach most frequently is "The Wife of His Youth." When I first began to teach this story in El Paso, ten years ago, I was struck by the resonance the story seemed to have with many of my students. When, for example, the Blue Vein Society, which aspired to "absorption into the white race," came up in class discussion (60–61), several students compared it with the social stratification that they had experienced in their hometowns. Most strikingly, the discussion of a later story, "Miss Clairol," by Helena Maria Viramontes, a full month later, led one of my students to recall Chesnutt's Blue Vein Society in a discussion about whether Viramontes was doing a disservice to Mexican Americans by portraying a working-class woman as the sole representative of the community in the story. The student argued that Blue Vein Societies find analogues in divisions by class and legal status today. How solidarity can be achieved and how class barriers in a community should be negotiated were important questions for my students in El Paso in the mid-2000s, and Chesnutt provided us with a context for considering recent work that also dealt with class, pigment, and privilege.

When I teach Chesnutt in the second half of the American literature survey (from 1865 to the present), I do so after students have read works that are engaged with race, like Mark Twain's *The Adventures of Huckleberry Finn*, and alongside later nineteenth-century African American writers, like W. E. B. Du Bois and Paul Laurence Dunbar. I find that *The Marrow of Tradition* works especially well when paired with *Huckleberry Finn*. Twain's representation of Huck and Jim's interracial friendship and Huck's decision to *"go* to hell" and help Jim escape (223), thus rejecting the malformed conscience that had developed from his youth, intersects with Du Bois's and Dunbar's concern with the particularities of the African American experience. We begin by discussing how Chesnutt incorporates the idea of a conscience that can overcome, at least to some degree, its conditioning in order to make independent moral judgments, and we proceed to discuss the special role that questions of family and of legal status play in his novel.

When I teach Chesnutt in an upper-division or graduate class dealing with the literature of slavery and freedom or with war and Reconstruction, the context shifts. In these classes, students have already read such works as Harriet Beecher Stowe's *Uncle Tom's Cabin*, Lydia Maria Child's *The Romance of the Republic*, William Wells Brown's *Clotel; or, The President's Daughter*, Frances E. W. Harper's *Iola Leroy*, and the nonfictional works of Frederick Douglass and of Harriet Jacobs. The texts that they have already encountered thus prepare them for Chesnutt's use of the divided interracial family, and they are struck not so much by his use of this motif as by how he uses it. In "The Sheriff's Children," for example, the motif is invested with new life by Chesnutt's portrayal of a family reunion that is defined not by the joyous overcoming of obstacles, as in so many antebellum narratives and even some postbellum narratives, but by the unhealed wounds of racial division and prejudice. As in *Marrow*, the division of a family by the law, in this case racial, leads the sheriff of the title to a moral epiphany:

> An hour or two before, standing face to face with death, he had experienced a sensation similar to what drowning men are said to feel—a kind of clarifying of the moral faculty, in which the veil of flesh, with its obscuring passions and prejudices, is pushed aside for a moment, and all the acts of one's life stand out, in the clear light of truth.   (86–87)

The tension between the sheriff's relationship to a son legally defined as mulatto and to a daughter legally defined as white is the cause of this epiphany, and it makes "The Sheriff's Children" a powerful story to teach in a borderlands context.

The discussions that my students have regarding *Marrow* grow in part out of the intersections between what is given in the novel and the concrete particulars of our United States–Mexico border. In several classes, students have pointed out parallels between the separation of families on racial lines and the separation created by a border. *Marrow* is all about the legal implications of family relationships and of actions from the past that affect the present, and the uncomfortable but necessary connection between abstract questions of justice and practical questions of law. The entire structure of the novel is built around the idea that African American labor and wealth have been unjustly expropriated and that reparation of this wrong is warranted. The novel plays itself out, however, on a stage where the questions that are most relevant to justice's actually being done revolve around technicalities that seem to mock the moral seriousness of the issues at stake. In moral terms, Janet is owed much by the Merkell family that she never receives. She is the rightful heir to the family fortune, which is being perversely used to foment hatred against the African American middle class in the city (to which she, through her marriage to Dr. Miller, belongs). But the legal technicalities rather than the broad moral principles of this case make Olivia Carteret feel the injustice of her position: she discovers that Julia Merkell's marriage to Sam was legal in the context of the military occupation of North Carolina, and this discovery leads to her epiphany that slavery itself was a crime rather than a mistake. This negotiation of the borderline between the abstract justice and specific legal legwork should be familiar to anyone who has experienced the labyrinth of immigration law in the twentieth-century United States.

Marrow moves adroitly among the registers of philosophical justice, legal difficulties, and personal moral choices. When Mr. Delamere chooses to violate his ancestral code of honor by lying to protect Sandy, he is exploiting his standing in the community and choosing a morality of empathy over one of integrity. This choice is mirrored at the end of the novel, when Janet Miller can take the path of vengeance or reconciliation. My students typically are divided in their response to her decision to allow her husband to save her half sister's child: some admire her act of charity and forgiveness, but others are frustrated that *Marrow*, following the pattern of antislavery novels, demands a higher ethical code for those who have been enslaved than for those who have enslaved.

Brook Thomas provides a useful frame for considering the legal issues and larger questions of justice in *Marrow*, and I assign his essay "The Legal Argument of Chesnutt's Novels" to undergraduate and graduate students alike. Thomas elegantly outlines the layers of legal discourse that obtain in Chesnutt's novel, and this essay is particularly useful in its discussion of Chesnutt's treatment of Chinese immigration. My students discuss how someone who disputes so many of the racial conventions and classifications of late-nineteenth- and early-twentieth-century American life can nonetheless reinforce others. That Chesnutt emphasizes African American belonging and citizenship but does not advocate human rights for all—for recent immigrants, for example—shows the weakness of an essentialist narrative.

I frequently supplement Thomas with Eric Sundquist's "Charles Chesnutt's Cakewalk." Sundquist shows how Chesnutt reveals precisely the places of division, trauma, and exploitation that many turn-of-the-twentieth-century writers wished to obscure. A cultural masquerade by white Southerners is used in *Marrow* to create a vision of blackness that ignores the facts of discrimination in late-nineteenth- and early-twentieth-century North Carolina.

In "The Sherriff's Children" as well, the confluence of legal and familial issues is of interest to my students. This story narrates the encounters of a white Southern sheriff with his black son, and it examines the growing tension between the son and the father who has declined to acknowledge him, concluding with the suicide of the son and the father's recognition of his own culpability. Having read so many stories where a family reunion provides redemption (there is a variation on this theme in *Marrow*), students find the tragic conclusion of "The Sheriff's Children" to be bracing. In this story, Chesnutt writes about an unresolved conflict, about a matter of justice that cannot be solved by the reuniting of a family.

Gates, in his PBS series *African American Lives,* provides a useful context for the way that legal questions and family history connect. I either assign students selections from the series out of class or screen brief excerpts in class. (A good example of the intersection of justice and the American legal system is the story of the flawed trial of 1915 leading to the execution of Tom Joyner's great-uncles in "The Road Home.") What is particularly noteworthy about the oral histories that Gates collects in this series is how they reconstruct family histories that were erased, in a manner similar to Chesnutt's imaginative reconstructions in "The Sheriff's Children" and *Marrow*. I find that the segments that deal with the judicial system and the family histories that are repressed in the wake of legal injustices are especially helpful in framing Chesnutt. Reconstruction of family history often parallels projects that some of my students are pursuing in classes that they take in history or anthropology.

A significant parallel between these novels and the present situation on the United States–Mexico border that my students have observed is the DREAM Act, a piece of legislation that applies to people who were brought to the United States as children and whose status remains in a legal limbo because they possess neither citizenship nor a straightforward means of obtaining it. Neither can they claim any country other than the United States as a homeland. These young undocumented residents are like Janet Miller, who is denied her inheritance and the recognition of her sister on the basis of withheld documentation.

Recent events have broadened the range of connections that students make with Chesnutt's stories. It is hard to consider, for example, the question of Janet's exclusion from her inheritance without thinking of the present debates about marriage equality. Violence against minorities and concerns over the impunity of law enforcement officials make *Marrow* more relevant than ever. What becomes increasingly evident in my students' classroom and written discussions of Chesnutt's work is that the legal, ethical, and moral questions they raise remind us that neither moral breadth and depth nor legal precision is dispensable.

NOTE

In this essay, quotations of "The Wife of His Youth" are taken from *The Portable Charles W. Chesnutt.*

Teaching Whiteness, Folklore, and the Discourses of Race in *The Colonel's Dream*

Shirley Moody-Turner

When I teach my Introduction to Folklore Studies course, I always begin by asking the students, "What is folklore?" When I pose this question, I am careful to specify that I am not asking them to tell me what they think I want to hear; rather, I want to know what their perceptions of folklore are when they enter the classroom. I will often prompt them further by asking, "Who has folklore?" and "Where does folklore reside?" In response, they will identify folklore as songs, stories, sayings, or even lies and as consisting of things made up or make-believe. They will identify it as belonging to African Americans or Native Americans and say that it exists in out-of-the-way places, like mountain or rural communities. What stands out most about these answers is that the students perceive folklore as belonging to some other people in some other place. Usually they are unaware how their own traditions, stories, family practices, values, and belief systems constitute a folklore and unaware of what's at stake in identifying folklore as someone else's.

Teaching Charles W. Chesnutt's last published novel, *The Colonel's Dream*, encourages students to think about folklore in ways that complicate traditional notions that tether it to only certain racial-ethnic groups or regional locations.[1] Chesnutt is best known for incorporating African American folklore in his collection of short stories, *The Conjure Woman*, but in *The Colonel's Dream* he uncovers the ideologies that construct white perceptions of black folklore, showing what is at stake in those perceptions, while bringing attention to white forms of folklore. In this novel he identifies the fictions that have asserted black inferiority and dictated racial separation as a kind of white folklore of race, and he exposes the interrelations among constructions of race, the formation of folklore studies, plantation tradition mythology, and the turn-of-the-century revival of medieval romance in creating and sustaining this white folklore. Attention to this aspect of his work allows us to see how white folklore was integral to creating the customs and practices that defined race relations in the New South.

In teaching *The Colonel's Dream*, I first provide students with historical context that can be used to locate Chesnutt's representations of folklore—specifically, conversations about folklore and race that took place in the late nineteenth and early twentieth centuries. I ask students to consider important questions, such as, "What was at stake in Chesnutt's decision to treat folklore, and especially white forms of folklore, in his fiction?" We can then identify the cultural and literary traditions—specifically, medieval romance and plantation tradition mythology—in which Chesnutt situates white folklore. Articulating the features of these traditions will help students identify and interrogate the ideologies embodied in and represented by the various folk practices. By turning his literary lens on forms of white folklore and the discourses that have constructed whiteness, Chesnutt makes his white readers aware first of their own folklore, then of the ways in which it has played a key role in the larger discourses and practices of race.

Historical and Cultural Context

The Emergence of Folklore Studies

Teachers might begin by explaining that folklore was an emerging discipline of study at the end of the nineteenth century. The field was part of an increasing effort to create new ways of organizing and analyzing cultural materials and racial-ethnic groups. In defining the parameters of American folklore studies, William Wells Newell was a significant figure. A cofounder of the American Folklore Society and the editor of the *Journal of American Folk-lore*, he was influential in determining how folklore studies would come to be institutionalized in the United States. In articulating his agenda for the 235 members of his organization, Newell identified the following four areas that required the immediate attention of the folklore society:

(a) Relics of Old English Folk-lore . . .
(b) Lore of the Negroes in the Southern States of the Union
(c) Lore of the Indian Tribes of North America . . .
(d) Lore of French Canada, Mexico, etc. ("On the Field" 3)

John Roberts points out that Newell's shift from discussing the "lore" of Native Americans and African Americans to collecting the "relics" of the earlier stages of English folklore "made clear [Newell's] view that British descendants represented a contemporary and enlightened element in American society" (48). This shift in terminology, and Newell's larger theories and practices, suggests that Newell did not consider Euro-Americans, especially those of English descent, to be folk in the way that African Americans and Native Americans were folk. In an 1894 speech, he notes that although he is of English ancestry, he truly can claim no racial affiliation other than that of the "human race" ("Importance" 132). He defines *folk* as synonymous with race, maintaining that folklore belongs to the primitive stage and that, as races moved through the stages of culture en route to civilization, folklore provides a record of their evolution (131). His comments suggest that white Western middle-class values are the universal, unquestioned norm. His notion that African Americans would eventually shed their distinctive folklore and become part of the human race indicates that folklore marked racial difference and inferiority, an inferiority that could be overcome with proper training and education.

Plantation Tradition

Newell's approach to folklore, and to late-nineteenth-century folklore studies more broadly, must be located in a larger cultural milieu. The association of folklore with African Americans was part of a process of marking them as distinct from and inferior to white Americans. In two of the nation's most popular cultural forms, minstrelsy and plantation tradition literature, black folklore was parodied, infantilized, and stereotyped in a way that made blacks childlike, primitive, less evolved, and intellectually and socially inferior. The plantation tradition in particular romanticized the antebellum South as a simpler time and place, an idealized past valorizing white Southern patriarchy and supporting the notions that blacks had been happy and faithful under the master-slave system and that authority for addressing the Negro problem in the post–Reconstruction Era should therefore be entrusted to Southern whites. This elaborate fiction allowed Northern whites to avoid the contemporary crisis precipitated by the presence of free blacks by returning responsibility for the Negro problem to the benevolent rulers of the former slaveocracy. This tradition gained popularity in the 1880s and 1890s and is evidenced most explicitly in works by authors such as Joel Chandler Harris, Irwin Russell, and Thomas Nelson Page.

Revival of Medieval Romance

Put simply, *medieval romance* refers to a literary genre featuring the deeds of a heroic figure who is often on a quest to save a lady, liberate a besieged land, or fight for a noble cause. Chivalry, honor, adherence to codes of conduct, and refined manners figure prominently in medieval romance. Interest in the genre reemerged as a cultural influence in the second half of the nineteenth century. White male writers, such as John Pendleton Kennedy and William A. Caruthers, drew on the conventions of the medieval romance and stressed the heroic deeds of noble aristocrats. These works too idealized a past in which a select group of honorable (i.e., white and wealthy) men ruled the land and received the unquestioned service of their grateful subjects. Revitalized interest in the medieval romance can be understood in part as a response to the post-Reconstruction crisis faced by Southern whites who perceived that their former way of life was challenged by their defeat in the Civil War, the abolition of slavery, and Northern intervention in Southern political and social life. In folklore studies, this same interest was shown in the collecting and documenting of examples of Arthurian legends and medieval literature. Roger Abrahams finds that the attention of folklore studies to medieval romance was part of an antimodern turn, representing a quest to recover the symbols and artifacts of an earlier time freed from the concerns of a rapidly modernizing world (62).

In *The Colonel's Dream*, Chesnutt enters this cultural fray by criticizing the racial biases of folklore studies, which identified African Americans as a folk relegated to a slave past; by challenging the nostalgia inherent in the plantation tradition, exposing the brutal realities that characterized both the antebellum and postbellum South; and by uncovering the patriarchal and paternalistic nature of the ideologies represented in the renewed interest in recreating the convention of the medieval romance in postbellum literature.

Close Reading Informed by Historical and Cultural Context

Plot Summary

Henry French, the main character in *The Colonel's Dream*, is a former officer in the Confederate Army who relocated to New York after the Civil War. French and his partner built a bagging firm and after ten years sold it for a sizable profit. Though French is a staunch believer in the principles that enabled his success in New York, a life dictated by reason, hard business sense, disciplined investing, and calculated risk—in other words, a life dictated by the mechanical and unforgiving rhythms of modernity—has taken its toll: when the sale of the firm is consummated, French collapses. At the advice of his physician, he returns with his son, Phil, to their ancestral abode in the South. French must reconcile the progressive, modern, Enlightenment ideas he has acquired in the North with the realities of the antebellum past and postbellum present. By evoking the ideals embodied in the medieval romance and by resuscitating the myths associated with the plantation tradition, he attempts to bring his Enlightenment ideology with him to Clarendon and begin his project of furthering his progressive agenda in his new Southern locale.

Literary Analysis

To help students recognize the politics of folklore that Chesnutt is engaging, I have them identify places where French's ideals, myths, and beliefs are brought to the surface. For instance, when French first arrives in Clarendon, he hears a young untrained "coloured girl" singing lyrics from *The Bohemian Girl*, a popular 1843 opera: "I dreamt that I dwelt in marble halls / With vassals and serfs at my side" (100). These ethereal lyrics, I argue, are one of the first clues that Colonel French's dream of a New South is really a return to an imaginary Old South reconfigured through Enlightenment reason, plantation mythology, and medieval romance. His new world vision requires the just and reasonable rule of a benevolent master, the reign of right reason, and a status quo in which some are willing and happy serfs and vassals, while others are gracious and loved kings and queens. In these early passages, students can read in *The Colonel's Dream* the beginnings of a criticism of the valorized place of medieval romance in the white folklore and fiction of race.

As the narrative continues, however, the text underscores the degree to which the colonel's dream is enabled by the willful forgetting of the realities of the antebellum South. When French encounters Peter, his family's former house servant, who is pruning the branches away from the French family plots, French is delighted to have found a living relic to serve as witness to his family's former glory. When he meets Laura, an old family friend, they stroll along, with Peter "following the party at a respectful distance." As Laura, French, and Phil cross a bridge into an enchanting knoll, Peter, "seeing himself forgotten, . . . walked past the gate . . . and went, somewhat disconsolately, on his way" (116). For French, the edenic antebellum past is momentarily realized. As he enters the garden of his plantation dreams, however, Peter, unbeknownst to the colonel, is rounded up to serve in the convict labor system. Peter's enslavement is an aspect of the New South that French chooses not to notice.

The following day, when French is finally confronted by Peter's situation, he buys Peter's time and in effect restores the master-slave relationship. Later in the day, when he learns that Nichols, a mulatto barber who has done quite well for himself, has purchased and is living in the French family mansion, he buys back his former home. French in effect is attempting to create the antebellum South of his imagination by repossessing symbols of the plantation past.

To explore further the interrelation between the Old South and the New South that Chesnutt constructs in the text, I have students compare two sets of seemingly conflicting customs: those of French, the paternalistic aristocrat, and of Fetters, the former overseer turned ruthless landowner. In French we see a man reconstructing the sentimental, surface-level customs he associates with his plantation life: the titles, the etiquette, the dress, the dinners, the dances are all ways for him to recapture an authentic, simpler, more honorable life. Fetters abides by a different set of Southern customs: the unspoken rules of race relations that keep blacks in a subservient position and where racism and white supremacy trump progressive ideals of collective uplift. French learns through his interactions with Fetters that there are customs that run deeper than the titles and dining etiquette he reveres, customs that govern race relations and are more ingrained than any law and not beholden to any chivalric code. Chesnutt exposes French's retreat into the customs and traditions of a simpler, nobler era as part of the white folklore that allows the persistence of less savory customs and traditions dictating racial relations in the New South.

In the second half of the narrative, French makes a series of missteps that reveal not only how naive he is regarding the realities of Southern race relations but also how his ignorance of these realities is in fact complicit in perpetuating racial oppression and violence. His medieval romance, for instance, is exposed as a biased, nonegalitarian system in which the select few impose their righteous will on their benighted subjects and display real courtesy only toward those in their charmed circle, while the rest are disregarded or subjugated. French, for example, fails to understand why Fetters will not acquiesce to his honor-based appeal to release a black prisoner, Bud Johnson, from his convict labor contract. But when the son of one of French's fellow aristocrats is arrested for a shooting, French abandons Bud's case to secure the release of the gentleman's son. Near the end of the novel, after Peter dies trying to save Phil, French assumes that his son's sentimental attachment to Peter will justify crossing the most final of color lines. He believes that he can bury Peter alongside his son Phil, who died from a fever shortly after Peter's death, in the white cemetery. He is mistaken. As we have already been told, the men in the town want "no part nor parcel" in French's "sentimental folly" (336). When the town digs up Peter's body and lays it at French's doorstep, the colonel retreats. Confronted with what Dean McWilliams refers to as "the intractability" of racism in the New South, French retires his progressive agenda and returns to New York (176–77).

French's constant misreading of the New South's emotional landscape suggests the inadequacy of his plantation tradition mythology, his medieval romance, and his Enlightenment reason in addressing the racism and prejudice in the New South. It also indicates, as Charles Mills explains, that French does not understand his own role in creating the social system he comes to detest:

> [O]n matters related to race, the Racial Contract prescribes for its signatories an inverted epistemology, an epistemology of ignorance, a particular pattern of localized and global cognitive dysfunction . . . producing the ironic outcome that whites will in general be unable to understand the world they themselves have made. (*Racial Contract* 18)

French seems to understand not at all that the prejudice, racial hierarchy, and class antagonism that stymie his attempts at liberal reform in the South are products of his own making—and his plantation aristocracy ancestors' making.

In the late nineteenth and early twentieth centuries, many African American authors were interested in how the new formalized study of black folklore and culture intersected with questions of race, identity, and national belonging. By situating Chesnutt's work in this turn-of-the-century discourse and by reading his text through a lens that is attentive to the racialized politics of folklore, students can see in *The Colonel's Dream* a critique of the ideologies underlying the formation of folklore studies. In this novel, Chesnutt does something quite extraordinary: he focuses his literary and ethnographic gaze on unveiling white forms of folklore, including both the conscious enactments of idealized customs and traditions associated with the myth of the Old South and the less romanticized but perhaps more deeply entrenched customs and traditions that dictated race relations in the New South. Reading *The Colonel's Dream* in this literary, historical, and cultural context, students and teachers gain new insights into Chesnutt's literary engagement with folklore, fiction, and race and are introduced to new ways of identifying and interpreting the significance of folklore as a powerful cultural force.

NOTE

¹*Folklore* carries multiple connotations, from popular conceptions of it as myths or lies to academic definitions in which it signals both the communicative processes and cultural materials of a group. The term also designates the organized field devoted to studying those processes and materials. Historically *folklore* has been more closely associated with certain racial-ethnic groups than with others, but more recent trends in folklore studies have insisted that all groups have folklore and that individuals can participate in many different folk groups, often simultaneously. In this essay, I use the term *folklore* instead of terms like *folkloristics* or *folk life* to mean the historical and cultural milieu in which Chesnutt is engaging with and interrogating the concept. Similarly, terms like *dialect* and *vernacular* have circulated widely in Chesnutt studies. *Vernacular* gained particular prominence in the 1980s and 1990s after critics like Henry Louis Gates, Bernard Bell, and Houston Baker promoted their theories for the study of African American expressive culture, in which *vernacular* refers to oral-verbal strategies emerging from everyday African American expressivity. The term *dialect* signals the vast popularity of dialect fiction in the postbellum United States. Gavin Jones, for instance, argues that "dialect literature constitutes a distinct but critically neglected movement in American letters . . . worthy of study on its own terms." He further asserts, "[D]ialect writing is defined by a strong thematic interest in the cultural and political issues surrounding questions of linguistic variety. To an unprecedented degree, the social and personal significance of dialect provides the very framework around which late-nineteenth century works are structured" (2). Although there is overlap between *folklore, vernacular,* and *dialect,* each of these terms indicates a slightly different analytic for interpreting Chesnutt's fiction and foregrounds different aspects of the historical, cultural, and literary context in which Chesnutt was working.

American Sentimentalism and
The Colonel's Dream

Katherine Adams

Published in 1905, Charles Chesnutt's *The Colonel's Dream* is at once immensely readable and closely engaged with its literary and historical moment—
a combination that appeals to both students and teachers. For these qualities,
and more, Chesnutt's third novel, the last to be published in his lifetime, de-
serves a place on American literature syllabi. Though it may never achieve the
popularity of Chesnutt's earlier works, *Dream* has much to offer in graduate
and advanced undergraduate courses. Besides addressing many of the topics we
already teach in conjunction with *The House behind the Cedars*, *The Marrow
of Tradition*, and the short fiction—racial identity and injustice, regional and
national politics, tensions between Southern tradition and social reform—the
novel raises questions about economic violence, racial whiteness, and the relation between sentiment and racial discourse in turn-of-the-century United
States culture.

   The Colonel's Dream tells the story of ex-Confederate officer, Henry French,
as he attempts to rescue his childhood hometown from economic and social
atrophy. Having gone north after the war and made his fortune in the textile
industry, French returns to Clarendon, North Carolina, at the novel's outset and
invests in a defunct cotton mill. He begins to rebuild it with local materials and
labor, confident that industrialization will bring Clarendon back to life. Ultimately thwarted by local reactionaries, he returns north a bitter man and abandons Clarendon to decay. His story provides historical insight into Jim Crow
segregation, white racial terrorism, convict labor leasing, national reunion, New
Southern progressivism, and Old Southern exceptionalism. It also exemplifies
and complicates multiple literary traditions. For example, the juxtaposition of
Clarendon with New York comments suggestively on the local color genre, and
French's dual North-South affiliations puts a new twist on the conventional
outsider-looking-in protagonist. Chesnutt's analysis of transregional cotton
production invites comparison with other economic novels, like William Dean
Howells's *A Hazard of New Fortunes* (1889) and Frank Norris's *The Octopus*
(1901). *Dream* also illuminates the complex relation between social realism and
sentimentalism. Its assessment of the latter is especially rich, enabling students
to explore a cultural force that influenced political, legal, intellectual, and aesthetic practice across the nineteenth century and into the twentieth, shaping
ideas about race throughout.

   Drawing on my experiences with graduate and advanced undergraduate
students, this essay outlines approaches for teaching *Dream* in the context of
United States sentimentalism and its intersecting discourses on sympathy, race,
and reform. I begin with Chesnutt's ambivalence about sentimental literature,

showing how I promote discussion on topics including the failure of French's sentiment-driven reforms, the novel's metareflection on reform literature's unintended effects, and the limits of interracial sympathy. In this, I propose, the novel comments on a century-long tradition of appeals to moral feeling and puts Chesnutt into conversation with contemporary black writers who similarly enlist and resist sentimental conventions. It also challenges the sentimental opposition between affective and market relations. I conclude with the problematic of intraracial sympathy. *Dream* builds on Chesnutt's analysis in earlier works that use mixed-race characters to expose the color line as a social fiction and dramatize its injurious effects. In this novel, race is again presented as a cultural construct, produced by and productive of structural injustice, but the emphasis shifts from racialized blood to racial sympathy—a distinct but closely related form of essentialist racial evidence. Using *Dream* to investigate the interdependent logics of biology and affect introduces students to a dimension of United States racial discourse that has been largely overlooked.

Self-Conscious Sentimentalism

For many black authors working after the Civil War, sentimentalism was the obvious choice for reform writing. The appeals to sympathy, the heightened representations of violence and injustice, and the sharply delineated moral logics that shaped antebellum antislavery and temperance narratives remained relevant in the postbellum and progressive eras—partly to counter the racist sentimentalism of works like Thomas Dixon's *The Clansman*. The most important frame for teaching late-nineteenth-century black sentimentalism is the legacy established by antebellum writers like Frances Harper, Frederick Douglass, and William Wells Brown, who influenced—and continued to publish alongside—the postbellum generation. My approach to this tradition emphasizes the ambivalence that characterizes it from the start. Drawing on scholarship by Frances Smith Foster, Joycelyn Moody, and P. Gabrielle Foreman, I point students to the double-voiced sentimentalism of works by Harper, Harriet Jacobs, and Harriet Wilson. We explore the metadiscursivity of Brown's *Clotel* (1853) and apply James Baldwin's insights about the violence of sentimentalism's Manichaean worldview in "Everybody's Protest Novel" (1949) to writing from nineteenth-century and contemporary United States contexts.

Like other black writers, Chesnutt both recognized and questioned the power of sentimental writing. This ambivalence registers humorously in his 1890s conjure tales, where a frame narrative puts sentimentalism's manipulative effects on display. Featuring Julius McAdoo, a freedman whose stories about the tragic past excite his white employers' sympathy and largesse, pieces like "Po' Sandy" and "Dave's Neckliss" simultaneously convey slavery's horrors and cast sentimental tactics in a cynical light. They pair satisfyingly with Howells's famous 1900 review, which congratulates Chesnutt for avoiding sentiment in favor of a "passionless handling" that makes racial themes universally accessible ("Mr. Charles" 699). Students are quick to recognize that Howells misses the complexity of Chesnutt's realism and, specifically, its ironic treatment of accessible racialized experience.

A somewhat darker assessment of interracial sympathy emerges from Chesnutt's nonfiction writing. In early essays like "An Inside View of the Negro Question" (1889), Chesnutt writes with seeming optimism: "The Negro . . . knows that he can not hope to succeed in the battle for his rights without the sympathy and cooperation of the vast majority of white people all over the country" (*Charles W. Chesnutt: Essays* 64). A decade later, however, he predicts in "A Complete Racial Amalgamation" (1900) that racial progress will be confined to the North because only there can blacks depend on a "field of moral sympathy" (134); and, in "The Negro's Franchise" (1901), he contrasts "white men in the South who think themselves the friends of the Negro" against "the sentiment of the white community toward the Negro [that is] found in its laws" (164). Prefacing *Dream* with passages from these stories and essays helps prepare students for the novel's complex treatment of sentimental readerships and interracial sympathy and for its focus on the intersections among sentimentalism, legal culture, and region.

Even minimal preparation enables students to recognize Chesnutt's meta-references to the sentimental and plantation traditions. Concentrated in the early chapters, where Colonel French reunites nostalgically with the places and people he left behind, these include the ballad sung by the daughter of the black family who own French's childhood home (*Colonel's Dream* 100); the antebellum memories that French exchanges with Laura Treadwell, his love interest (122–24); the Uncle Remus tales recited to the colonel's son, Phil, by Peter French (216–19); and Peter himself, the colonel's loyal former slave whom Chesnutt writes as if he were a caricature from those same tales. Reading these examples closely, my students consider why Chesnutt includes so many examples of sentimental representation. They ask why he links Peter's stories to death (told during visits to Clarendon's cemetery, they dwell on ghosts and dead French ancestors and lead indirectly to an accident that kills both Peter and Phil) and why the colonel's nostalgia is so often linked to blindness ("[Y]ou see us through a haze of tender memories," Laura chides [127]). We examine Phil's deathbed scene, which recalls Little Eva's famous exit from *Uncle Tom's Cabin* by featuring a plea for racial unity: like Eva, who converts her "dear [enslaved] friends" so as to see them again in heaven (Stowe 287), Phil makes his father promise to bury Peter beside him in the family plot (*Colonel's Dream* 326). What are we to make of this conspicuous allusion? Or of the ensuing episode, where a racist mob protests this "sentimental folly" (336) by digging up Peter's coffin and leaving it on the colonel's front porch? Do these scenes imply an ironic rejection of Stowe's utopian vision? Do they criticize its racialist logic? Do they protest its tragic nonrealization in United States culture?

A core principle of nineteenth-century sentimentalism was that an absolute opposition should exist between market relations and affective relationships, between commoditized and noncommoditized domains. Initially, *Dream* appears to share the sentimentalist's horror toward violations of this rule. The story opens with Colonel French collapsing during negotiations with a predatory Wall Street consortium while "mercifully shield[ing]" his business partner, Mrs. Jerviss, from similar injury: "[B]eing a woman [he] liked—she would be spared needless anxiety" (87). Here market forces are incompatible with human feeling, friendship, or femininity. When we head south, the point is reinforced with jarring reminders of what Stowe refers to as "living property" (30)—the ultimate boundary violation—when French recalls that his father "valued" Peter "more than his own son," when Peter proudly confirms, "I wuz wuth five hundred dollahs any day in de yeah" (*Colonel's Dream* 106), and, later, when a spurned lover complains, "Don't you suppose I have any feelings, even if I ain't much account? Ain't I worth as much as a trip up North?" (120).

But *Dream* soon disrupts this clear logic of incommensurable domains. Chapter 8, where Colonel French witnesses a convict labor auction, is an excellent place to begin understanding how. Called *reenslavement* by nineteenth-century reformers, the convict leasing system farmed out prisoners (overwhelmingly African Americans) to private businesses as unpaid labor. Chesnutt's portrait of the practice registers, initially, as another dystopian example of human relationships profaned by market dynamics—especially when Peter, having been arrested for vagrancy in a previous scene, comes up for bid. But the episode takes an intriguing turn when French intervenes by buying Peter's time himself, "a purchase which his father had made, upon terms not very different, fifty years before" (144). Peter's sentimental value promotes his market value instead of being compromised by it: "[French's] interest in the fate of the other prisoners had been merely abstract; in old Peter's case it assumed a personal aspect." With the addition of the auctioneer's metadiscursive gloss—"I thought, suh, that you looked like a No'the'n man. That bein' so, doubtless you'd like somethin' on the Uncle Tom order"—Chesnutt links the transaction to both slavery and the consumption of sentimental literature (143). These linkages multiply in the following chapter, where French purchases his childhood home from the black family who has lived there twenty years. Hearing the current owner, a barber named William Nichols, describe his affection for the house causes French to recall a series of "romantic" scenes from his own early residency—youthful merriment, his mother's final blessing, his first confession of love—and he writes a check on the spot (154–55). He then restores the house to its antebellum condition and hosts an antebellum costume party to celebrate:

> [T]he stream of ready money thus put into circulation by the colonel, soon permeated all the channels of local enterprise. The barber, out of his profits, began the erection of a row of small houses for coloured tenants. This gave employment to masons and carpenters, and involved the sale and purchase of considerable building material. General trade felt the influ-

ence of the enhanced prosperity. Groceries, dry-goods stores and saloons, did a thriving business.   (162)

Rich with implications about the commoditization of nostalgia and how it informs the interregional economics of national reunion, the auction and house-warming plots provide fertile material for reconsidering the sentimental opposition between affective and market value as well as between Old Southern tradition and New Southern economic development. Also, as the above passage indicates, there are interesting questions to pursue about how racialized power structures this sentimental economy. Nichols profits from French's purchase and uses the proceeds to support other black businesses, much as Julius McAdoo trades his sentimental narrative commodities to benefit his community. Yet both examples also illustrate the pattern of black labor and white ownership that typically drives production and consumption of United States sentiment. Hence, perhaps, the parody of transracial sympathy that appears later, when French offers to purchase yet another black convict, Bud Johnson, whom he wishes to rescue from an abusive overseer. The offer is rejected on the pretense that the overseer "loves [Bud] so well" that the prisoner cannot be released: "There's no accountin' for these vi'lent affections, but they're human natur', and they have to be 'umored" (284).

The foregoing may seem to imply that *Dream* rejects sentiment as a basis for moral action or justice, as though antebellum literary strategies have been rendered impotent by progressive era cynicism and commoditization. Finally, however, the novel's position is less straightforward. If sentimentalism blinds Colonel French, it also guides him—partly through the good offices of Laura Treadwell, who supports his reform project with "sympathy that was more than intellectual—that reached down to sources of spiritual strength and inspiration" (226). Could this reunionist union-in-the-making represent a normative horizon such as Gillian Brown finds in *Uncle Tom's Cabin*, where sentimental protocols cross into the political and economic spheres as moral correctives? As we have seen, French's projects fail, and French abandons both Laura and the South. But the narrator's tone of regret ("And so the colonel faltered, and, having put his hand to the plow, turned back" [358]) suggests that he gave up too soon. I like to raise this possibility in my classes, both to resist the overenthusiastic antisentimentalism of twenty-first-century readers and to introduce ideas that will be important for Du Bois's *Quest of the Silver Fleece* (1911), which follows *Dream* in my graduate seminar, U.S. Sentimentalism. Another novel about economic justice, *Quest* focuses on black sharecroppers in Alabama and combines Marxist critique with a highly sentimentalized love plot. Nearly all the criticism on this work dismisses the romance as an outdated indulgence that undermines the social realism. I encourage students, sometimes by assigning Maurice Lee's excellent article on *Quest*, to consider how Du Bois puts the two discourses into conversation. We compare *Quest* and *Dream* as narratives in which economic analysis, realism, and sentimentalism operate as complementary structures of meaning.

Another complicating factor is the reference to *Dream* that appears in Chesnutt's 1906 speech "Age of Problems," in which Chesnutt likens his novel's protagonist to "the writer in the *Atlantic Monthly*, who signs himself 'Nicholas Worth'" and who, "[l]ike the Colonel in my novel," returned home to the South to "help heal the wounds of slavery and of war" (*Charles W. Chesnutt: Essays* 244). The writer in question is Walter Hines Page, Chesnutt's longtime editor and publisher, whose pseudonymous *Autobiography of Nicholas Worth*—a work openly based on Page's own life and opinions—had been serialized in the *Atlantic* earlier that year (its title later as a book was *The Southerner*). That Chesnutt compares Colonel French with Page is fascinating in a number of respects. First, it encourages a favorable view of French, his intended reforms, and even his moral feeling—Chesnutt quotes a long passage from *The Autobiography* in which Page denounces Southern racial violence as a failure of crossracial sympathy. However, Page's racial politics were far from progressive, and his paternalistic representations of black people in *The Autobiography*—including the passage Chesnutt cites—are often quite offensive. One wonders if Chesnutt's comparison might also signify in the opposite direction, if the ambivalent portrait of French might cast a critical light on Page and his recently published work.

Feeling Race

Questions about intraracial sympathy stand at the center of *Dream*'s engagement with sentimentalism. Like blood, feeling was a form of racial evidence for nineteenth-century Americans, invoked as proof of racial essence and difference. To introduce this issue I use Justice Henry Billings Brown's majority opinion from the 1896 Supreme Court ruling on *Plessy v. Ferguson*. Many students are familiar with this case and its infamous "equal but separate" determination (*Transcript*), and some know that Homer Plessy's blood—one eighth of it from African descent—figured prominently in the arguments. Most, however, are surprised that Brown based his decision also on racial feeling, citing the unassailable "natural affinities" that proscribed racial mixing (*Transcript*). I like to assign the court documents with Chesnutt's "The Courts and the Negro," which contrasts Brown's defense of racial aversion with the ethic of moral sympathy, lamenting that even this new alienation of rights would not awaken "the heart and conscience of the nation" (*Charles W. Chesnutt: Essays* 267).

For context in black literary culture, Harper's *Iola Leroy* (1892) pairs wonderfully with *Dream*. Harper celebrates her heroine's black racial loyalty but also implies that it is chosen and situational: Iola feels that slavery is good until she discovers her African heritage and experiences enslavement. Teaching *Dream* alongside Pauline Hopkins's magazine novel *Of One Blood* (1902–03) is also effective. *Of One Blood* imagines a transhistorical and transcontinental flow of intraracial affect—a diasporic black sympathy—through which family and racial origins are felt in dreams and visions, under hypnosis, and through music. Hopkins's take on racial feeling is fascinating for how it does and does not correlate with blood ("one blood" designates, simultaneously, the human race, the black race, and one specific black family), and for its profound unreliability (guided by feeling, the protagonist marries his sister and trusts his villainous brother).

Chesnutt addresses intraracial sympathy frequently in his nonfiction. Unlike Harper and Hopkins, he concerns himself primarily with white affect and the entrenched prejudice that, he came to believe, could be "uprooted" only by amalgamation and the elision of visible racial difference (*Charles W. Chesnutt: Essays* 224). For Chesnutt, it seems, black blood was less indelible than white feeling. In his speech "Race Prejudice," delivered to the African American Boston Literary and Historical Association in 1905, he theorizes white racial feeling as "natural" but also "primitive" and diseased (222, 223, 224). He addresses the unnatural continuation of white prejudice in the South, where it is "deliberately and designedly stimulated for political purposes" (222)—a claim that directly frames the scene in *Dream* where a town leader raises a lynch mob (a "sympathetic following") to protect white supremacy (*Colonel's Dream* 336). About black racial affect Chesnutt was skeptical. In *Marrow*, for example, where William Miller sits in the black car musing on the competing claims of racial and class allegiance, his lack of brotherly feeling for a group of manual laborers seems to privilege class over race. In "Race Prejudice," Chesnutt goes further, dismissing black pride as an idea created to reify black difference and justify segregation. "Race Integrity," he argues, is "a modern invention of the white people to perpetuate the color line. It is they who preach it, and it is their racial integrity which they wish to preserve" (*Charles W. Chesnutt: Essays* 231–32).

Colonel French is the focal point for *Dream*'s interrogation of racial affect. From the outset he represents the hope that white prejudice can be overcome. He possesses "one of those rare natures of whom it may be truly said that they are men, and that they count nothing of what is human foreign to themselves" (105). Yet, as Chesnutt observes in "Age of Problems" (1906), the "merely fellow feeling" of sympathy seldom includes the recognition of equality that characterizes true "friendship" (*Charles W. Chesnutt: Essays* 245). When Laura worries about French's occupying his childhood home "after a coloured family," for example, French waves off her racial aversion but also reassures her: "There were always Negroes in it when we were there—the place swarmed with them" (*Colonel's Dream* 158). In fact, he purchases the house in order to privilege his white family feeling over Nichols's: as the barber fondly recalls raising his children there, "this display of sentiment [jars] the colonel's sensibilities" and makes the colonel "want the monopoly of association" (156, 158). I encourage students to explore how Chesnutt aligns white racial affect with control of geographic and cultural space. Much like Brown's "equal but separate" SCOTUS ruling,

French's "monopoly of associations" regarding the house enacts a segregation-ist agenda by displacing the Nichols family to a black neighborhood, an out-come later echoed in the eviction of Peter's corpse from Clarendon's all-white cemetery.

Also worth considering is the affective transformation of French as he travels from Manhattan to North Carolina. Like William Miller's identity in *Marrow*, French's identity shifts as he crosses from one region to another and the nar-rator automatically switches from "Mr." to "Colonel." But where Miller's jour-ney illustrates the racializing intersection of regional geography with embodi-ment—once below the Mason-Dixon Line, his African blood cannot occupy the white car—French seems to be remade by regionalist feeling: "The mere act of leaving New York . . . set in motion old currents of feeling, which, moving slowly at the start, gathered momentum as the miles rolled by, until his heart leaped forward to the old Southern town which was his destination" (93).

Comparing the two train scenes in conjunction with their common refer-ence to *Plessy* initiates discussion about feeling and blood as overlapping foun-dations of racial essence, and about the mutually constitutive relations among feeling, identity, space, and power. Is it whiteness that French feels as he enters the South's affective field? Maybe so, given that the title "Colonel" suggests he rejoins the Confederacy on entering its former dominion. How might this change relate to the "monopoly" held by white racial feeling over both private and public spaces in the postbellum South? *Dream* provides several illustra-tions for consideration. When French hires a black supervisor at the mill, he confronts the "sensitiveness" of white labor. "Even a healthy social instinct," he reflects, "might be perverted into an unhealthy and unjust prejudice" (259). And, in chapter 18, another ex-Confederate, General Thornton, who has aban-doned the Republican ticket after meeting a black voter at the polls, explains, "I could stand the other party in the abstract, but not in the concrete . . . call it prejudice—call it what you like—it's human nature" (236).

These disheartening conclusions point to a final line of inquiry that inevitably arises among *Dream*'s readers: What possibilities, if any, does the novel offer for change? Here is a world where the democratizing promises of law, free la-bor, and suffrage are trumped by white racism justified as ineluctable "human nature"; where moral sympathy has been commoditized; where "deep-seated feelings" from before the war, as the colonel recognizes, remain "a smoldering fire capable always of being fanned into flame" (259–60). Reviewers criticized the novel's pessimism in 1905, accusing Chesnutt of writing "a *cul de sac* sort of ending . . . leading the reader up to a dark, blank wall, and there leaving him" ("Dream"), and twenty-first-century students often express similar disappoint-ment. It can help to play devil's advocate here, drawing material from *Dream*'s final chapter, which imagines a day when "the sun of liberty shall shine alike upon all men" (355) and reminds us that "other hands have taken up the fight which the colonel dropped" (358). Taking a different approach, I sometimes assign these original reviews (available at Berea College's *Charles Chesnutt Digital Archive* www.chesnuttarchive.org/Reviews/contemp_reviews.html) to give students critical distance from their own sense of entitlement to a hopeful conclusion. What are the racial politics of imposing that sentimental demand on and requiring that sentimental labor from a writer like Chesnutt? The novel itself leads us to ask such questions and provides a framework in which to examine them.

Economics, Race, and Social (In)Justice: Teaching *The Colonel's Dream*

Francesca Sawaya

Charles W. Chesnutt's novel *The Colonel's Dream* has been a puzzle to critics and teachers alike. In his other major novels, *The House behind the Cedars* and *The Marrow of Tradition*, Chesnutt creates complex, multivocal accounts of race relations, using a wide range of black and white characters. In *The Colonel's Dream*, however, he focuses almost entirely on elite white perspectives and particularly the perspective of the eponymous colonel. Colonel French is a Southerner from a slave-owning family who fought for the Confederacy and then made his fortune as a corporate capitalist in the North before deciding to return to his hometown of Clarendon. Motivated by "the best of intentions," he dreams of economic and social reform in the South, of replacing racial conflict and poverty with "the trinity of peace, prosperity and progress" (*Colonel's Dream* 311, 190). Nevertheless, he explicitly refuses the possibility that such economic and social reform will involve "strict justice" between blacks and whites, because that would involve too "great [a] sacrifice" to white self-interest (234). Why, students might wonder, would an African American novelist devote an entire novel to the views and experiences of a character with such a limited perspective on race? In addition, even with the most modest and moderate goals, the colonel fails spectacularly at every effort he makes to create "peace, prosperity and progress," apparently exacerbating the racial violence in Clarendon. As a result, readers sometimes see the novel as a botch, as an experiment with perspective that charts failure and that itself fails.

Whiteness studies, however, helps students enter Chesnutt's brilliant and complex novel. Emerging as a recognized field of scholarly endeavor in the 1990s, whiteness studies examines the history of the social and cultural construction of white identity and power, in relation to the construction of other raced identities, in order to contribute to antiessentialist, antiracist debates and political movements. David Roediger points out that although whiteness studies became a named field of academic study very recently, there is a long and rich tradition in black thought that precedes this naming and that has analyzed the social and cultural construction of whiteness. This tradition, Roediger argues, emerged out of necessity and an intellectual and political commitment to antiessentialist, antiracist struggle but also out of what he describes as curiosity, even compassion (11–12). It was neglected, bell hooks says, because white people believe that "black people cannot see them" and because ignorance about black people's knowledge—including their knowledge of the social and cultural construction of whiteness—is an "imperative of racial domination" (qtd. in Roediger 6). One measure of this suppression, Roediger adds, is that the "serious 'white life' novel" by black writers has been underexamined (8).

The Colonel's Dream provides an opportunity to examine a "white life" novel by a black writer who saw that understanding the construction of whiteness was a necessity in his day for whites and blacks alike and whose profound political commitments were undergirded by both his intellectual curiosity and his clear-eyed but encompassing compassion.

The time in which Chesnutt wrote has been called the nadir of race relations, but it has also been called the age of incorporation. Central to white power at the turn of the century was the emergent corporation, which was transforming every aspect of American life.[1] Many Americans then believed that corporate capitalism was a progressive force that would work to ameliorate racial conflict. For example, the most successful black leader of the period, Booker T. Washington, gained Northern and Southern white financial and ideological support by arguing that corporate capitalism was an innately equalizing force. "When it comes to business, pure and simple . . . the Negro is given a man's chance," he famously said (155). He appeared to subordinate the fight for legal and political rights to a pursuit of business success: "The wisest among my race understand that the agitation of questions of social equality is the extremest folly" (153).

Chesnutt was friendly with Washington but disagreed adamantly in both his private letters to him and in his fiction that corporate capitalism was egalitarian or that a focus on business rather than legal and political rights would lead to social justice. Like many progressives of the period, Chesnutt argued that the collusion between corporations and government in the Gilded Age, and the inordinate power held by these corporations, had betrayed the nation's political ideals of democracy and equality. He focused particularly on the ways that this collusion was betraying the antiracist political movements of the time. The richness and complexity of *Dream*; its fascinating intertextual dialogue with other American literary texts of its time; its anticipation of the themes that would galvanize American novels of the future; and its relevance to debates today about the relation of economics, race, and social justice make it important and exciting reading for students and teachers alike.

Mining the Garrison: Chesnutt's Philosophy of Writing

I like to begin any discussion of Chesnutt's work with his journals. Chesnutt prepared himself meticulously for his career as a writer and was deeply self-conscious about his goals. His journals provide a provocative starting point for thinking about the broad social and political situation for a black intellectual at the turn of the twentieth century. I often use his entry of 29 May 1880, in which the young Chesnutt commits himself to a writing career. Saying that he "feel[s] an influence that [he] cannot resist calling [him] to the task," he writes:

> If I do write, I shall write for a purpose, a high holy purpose. . . . The
> object of my writings would be not so much the elevation of the colored

people as the elevation of the whites,—for I consider the unjust spirit of caste which is so insidious as to pervade a whole nation, and so powerful as to subject a whole race and all connected with to scorn and social ostracism—I consider this a barrier to the moral progress of the American people; and I would be one of the first to head a determined, organized crusade against it. Not a fierce indiscriminate onslaught; not an appeal to force, for this is something that force can but slightly affect; but a moral revolution which must be brought about in a different manner. . . . [T]he subtle almost indefinable feeling of repulsion toward the negro, which is common to most Americans—and easily enough accounted for—, cannot be stormed and taken by assault; the garrison will not capitulate: so their position must be mined, and we will find ourselves in their midst before they think it.   (*Journals* 139–40)

Students are always surprised and intrigued by this remarkable entry. Chesnutt describes himself as writing for a white, not a black or mixed, audience. He explicitly reverses the usual tropes of civilization and savagery of the time, in which whites saw themselves as responsible for educating and morally elevating "savages" at home and abroad. It is whites, not blacks, Chesnutt argues, who need to be civilized. At the same time, his attitude toward lower-class blacks is tinged by his relatively elite class status: he describes white racism as "unjust" but also says it is "easily enough accounted for." Nonetheless, he sees literature as providing a kind of ethical education, as high, holy work that can transform people's unjust beliefs and feelings. All these topics lead to fruitful classroom debate, but I find that students are most intrigued by his paradoxical description of writing as far more effective than force in the fight against racism, even as it is a form of strategic force, in which a black writer mines the garrison of white feeling. They are also intrigued by the metaphor of white racism as a garrison of feeling, a heavily protected defensive fort of emotions and subjectivity. We debate the question of whether or not literature can work, as Chesnutt imagines, both subtly and yet powerfully. Can literature be this transformative and politically revolutionary? And what techniques would an author use to create change?

The central question for us when we discuss *The Colonel's Dream*, therefore, is, How does Chesnutt construct and depict white perspectives on race relations in order to mine the garrison of white feelings and thoughts? What kinds of white perspective does he choose and why? What are the limitations to those perspectives and how are those limitations made evident to the reader? This line of inquiry leads us to consider not only perspective but also narrative structure. We analyze, first, how Chesnutt imagines and describes the perspectives of the colonel and the other elite white characters in his social circle. Then we track the different narrative strands he weaves together. This essay deals only with the colonel's perspective and with one narrative strand—his attempt to reform Clarendon. But by taking into account the perspectives of other characters and different narrative strands, students can begin to understand the brilliant ways in which Chesnutt links historical and institutional matrices to subjective or affective states, demonstrating how inadequate corporate capitalist ideology and practice are in transforming race relations and structural inequality.

Capitalism, Paternalism, Philanthropy

Chesnutt describes the colonel as a product of both the South and the North, and he describes the divisions as well as the links between elites in those two regions. On the one hand, the colonel served on the Confederate side in the Civil War and loses his fortune and his family. I ask students to think about what Chesnutt focuses on in depicting elite Southern culture and also what a loss of status and family means. I ask them to compare his depictions of the Southern white elite with those by white writers with whom they may be familiar (Mark Twain, Ellen Glasgow, William Faulkner, Flannery O'Connor). In *Dream*, as in all his fiction, Chesnutt shows the displaced Southern elite imagining themselves as benevolent paternalists, committed to noblesse oblige and working to chivalrously protect those beneath them. He is deeply interested in conceptions of inequality that are unexamined, in the evasions and self-deceptions that lie behind the attempts of displaced elites to regain their power ideologically and practically over both blacks and what he describes as the class of newly ascendant poor whites.[2] At the same time, Chesnutt demonstrates how noblesse oblige can function as a residual historical formation in the culture of corporate capitalism and of genocidal racism and how it can have unpredictable, sometimes even useful, results.

On the other hand, the colonel has also become an elite Northerner. After the war, he was offered employment by a Northern relative sympathetic to the Confederacy, which again highlights the links as much as divisions between North and South. The colonel makes his fortune as a capitalist—the story opens in medias res with his negotiating the sale of his bagging company to the "bagging trust" (85). Once the negotiation is complete and he has accrued his millions, he decides "to do something for humanity" (189), returning to the South to begin that process. But if Chesnutt connects the colonel's benevolent paternalism to his Southern roots, he also links it to Northern corporate capitalism, suggesting that Southern and Northern elites are not so different. In many ways, the colonel is a familiar Northern figure of the Gilded Age. A wealthy industrialist turned philanthropist, he evokes real business titans of the time who turned to philanthropy (Andrew Carnegie, Henry Clay Frick, John D. Rockefeller), as well as fictional ones (Hank Morgan of Mark Twain's *A Connecticut Yankee in King Arthur's Court*, Adam Verver of Henry James's *The Golden Bowl*, Frank Cowperwood of Theodore Dreiser's *Trilogy of Desire*). The colonel is also a figure who anticipates modern black novelists' depictions of Northern liberal white paternalist philanthropists—for example, Ralph Ellison's *Invisible Man* and Richard Wright's *Native Son*.[3]

Chesnutt criticizes both Southern and Northern white elites and the collusion between them: the colonel's reform efforts partake of both old-fashioned Southern paternalism and a more modern Northern capitalist paternalism. The colonel engages in personal efforts to help individual blacks in his employ and in the employ of his elite white friends, but at the same time he attempts to create structural change that borrows from corporate capitalism and its forms of paternalism. In one of his first such actions, he decides to reopen a disused mill in Clarendon:

> To a man of action, like the colonel, the frequent contemplation of the unused water power, which might so easily be harnessed to the car of progress, gave birth, in time, to a wish to see it thus utilized, and the further wish to stir to labour the idle inhabitants of the neighbourhood. . . . And so he planned to build a new and larger cotton mill where the old had stood; to shake up this lethargic community; to put its people to work, and to teach them habits of industry, efficiency and thrift. This, he imagined, would be pleasant occupation for his vacation, as well as a true missionary enterprise. . . .   (178–79)

In language comparable to that used by Twain's Hank Morgan, we see how old-fashioned paternalist noblesse oblige combines with a more modern capitalist paternalism that values social control and the maximizing of profits. The colonel will transform an unprofitable water source into a profitable one and lethargic laborers into well-regulated ones. Chesnutt's touch here is deft and restrained. He does not demonize the colonel but highlights his unexamined belief that social control and maximizing profits are inherently benevolent, progressive, and ethical goals, through the use of quasi-religious, quasi-business language ("a true missionary enterprise"). The colonel's assumption that capitalism is natural, even the work of God, and his condescending self-righteousness in deciding what will benefit the community, is emphasized by his certainty that his efforts will be easily successful and provide a "pleasant occupation for his vacation." Chesnutt then carefully anatomizes in the chapters that follow how the colonel's missionary enterprise meets resistance and fails.

Chesnutt's analysis of the way a combination of Southern and Northern benevolent paternalism and capitalist ideology limits the colonel's perspective and hence his reform efforts are carefully elaborated. The colonel sees the South as economically backward in comparison with the capitalist North and therefore believes himself engaged in a missionary enterprise, but Chesnutt suggests that such a dichotomy is false. First, a slave system and the racial violence that inheres in it are not at all in opposition to rationalized profit making. Indeed, slavery and capitalism can operate simultaneously and support each other. For example, Chesnutt shows that slavery continues in the capitalist present through convict labor. Even the colonel recognizes this as he begins to get a clearer picture of the labor situation in the South. He thinks to himself, "New definitions were given to old words, new pictures set in old frames, new wine poured into old bottles" (260). Second, Southern slavery was different from Northern capitalism but left its historical imprint on both whites and blacks. A commitment to rational self-interest and maximizing profits, Chesnutt demonstrates, can erase neither the past nor its long-term psychological consequences. He carefully analyzes the ways in which certain kinds of emotional or psychological states of being, associated with the history of slavery, maintain their hold against capitalist beliefs, which ignore the past.

Resentment and the desire for revenge is harbored against blacks by their former white owners, while the blacks have their own (more obvious) reasons for anger and resentment against whites. The whites express their feelings through an overpowering and systematic state-based violence, while the blacks resist in any way they can—including guerrilla warfare. Chesnutt's analysis of the history of these emotions, their tenacious hold on the present, and why capitalism, both ideologically and practically, can neither account for nor transform these emotions is again deft and restrained but carefully detailed. The colonel understands and even sympathizes to a degree with the elite and lower-class whites—"[H]e could almost understand why they let their feelings govern their reason and judgment" (261)—and therefore decides to be "patient, and . . . prudent" in his social reform (262). But his patience and prudence, tied as they are to false assumptions about human psychology as always rational and self-interested, can do nothing to change the emotional dynamics in the South and its violent results. If anything, the colonel's prudence exacerbates tensions, and after a series of interracial and intraracial tragedies occur that affect his own family, he precipitously abandons his reform efforts and flees North.

The narrator's ending message of hope, despite the depiction of intractable racial conflict rooted in the past, has puzzled many a reader. In my classes we do a close reading of the last pages of the novel.[4] We examine the colonel's capitalist dream of social reform, which hopes to establish "the trinity of peace, prosperity and progress" (190), as opposed to the narrator's concluding hope, in which "Justice, the seed, and Peace, the flower, of liberty, will prevail throughout all our borders" (359). I ask the students to compare the colonel's three goals with the narrator's two, and we work to expand our analysis of the implications of Chesnutt's subtle criticism of the limitations of capitalist assumptions and ideology. Why is justice missing from the colonel's trinity? Why is it so central to the narrator? What might Chesnutt be saying about the relation between corporate capitalism and justice, or, more to the point, about the lack of relation? Chesnutt was not a socialist, but his account of the inadequacy of corporate capitalism in dealing with history and the history of emotions, and thus social justice, is scathing.

To conclude our discussion, I often return to Chesnutt's description in his journal of his goals as a writer. I ask the students if they feel that his text effectively mines the garrison of white feeling and thought. I also ask the students, since the book mostly poses itself as a realist exploration of the historical forces that shape perspective, if Chesnutt implicitly proposes any solution to the racial conflicts in the North and South or to the continuing problem of white racism. In other words, if historical forces shape—and limit—emotions and perspective, how can change ever occur? If a dominant corporate capitalism limits our views of social justice, what does Chesnutt suggest might transform our perspectival limitations?

NOTES

[1] Rayford Logan first applied the term *nadir* to race relations" (*Negro*). Two classic accounts of the effects of corporate capitalism on American life are Alan Trachtenberg's *The Incorporation of America* and Robert Wiebe's *The Search for Order.*

[2] See particularly *The Marrow of Tradition* for the variety of ways that the paternalist benevolence and lost status of the Southern elite express themselves.

[3] Chesnutt wrote two other "white life" novels, *A Business Career* and *Evelyn's Husband*, both rejected for publication, that anticipate Ellison's and Wright's depictions of Northern corporate capitalist paternalism. Arguably, Chesnutt's Uncle Julius stories are likewise "white life" short stories, showing as they do on the highly limited perspective of a Northern capitalist.

[4] A particularly interesting figure to discuss in the conclusion, and who seems to represent the difficult position of the black intellectual in the period, is Henry Taylor, the schoolteacher who aligned himself with the colonel in his reform efforts. Seen as an enemy of his race by the blacks and thwarted by the whites in his plans for an industrial school, he had to flee the South and work as a porter in the North, which is the "best job" he can find—an indictment of Northern racism (357). This outcome, as well as Taylor's views of the future, are worth analyzing and debating on their own terms, in terms of Chesnutt's position as a black intellectual, or, in more advanced classes, in terms of other figurations of the position of the black intellectual in a dominant white society: W. E. B. Du Bois's *The Souls of Black Folks*, Carter G. Woodson's *The Mis-education of the Negro*, Harold Cruse's *The Crisis of the Negro Intellectual.*

NOTES ON CONTRIBUTORS

Katherine Adams is associate professor and Kimmerling Chair in English at Tulane University. She is the author of *Owning Up: Privacy, Property, and Belonging in US Women's Life Writing* (2009) and essays on race and gender in nineteenth-century United States culture. Her current book project, "Cotton Culture and Blackness after Emancipation," looks at the reimagining of racial capitalism in works by black writers from 1865 to 1923.

Susanna Ashton is professor of English at Clemson University. She is the author of *"I Belong to South Carolina": South Carolina Slave Narratives* and the coeditor, with Rhondda R. Thomas, of *The South Carolina Roots of African American Thought*. Currently she is at work on *A Plausible Man*, a biography of John Andrew Jackson, a fugitive slave, activist, and author.

Margaret D. Bauer is Rives Chair of Southern Literature and Harriot College of Arts and Sciences Distinguished Professor at East Carolina University. She is the author of *The Fiction of Ellen Gilchrist, William Faulkner's Legacy: "What Shadow, What Stain, What Mark," Understanding Tim Gautreaux*, and *A Study of Scarletts: Scarlett O'Hara and Her Literary Daughters*. Her articles include one on Chesnutt's "Po' Sandy."

Ernestine Pickens Glass is professor emerita, Department of English at Clark Atlanta University. She is the author of *Charles W. Chesnutt and the Progressive Movement* (1994), the editor of *Frederick Douglass: A Biography*, by Chesnutt (2001), and the coeditor of *Passing in the Works of Charles W. Chesnutt* (2010). She is the cofounder of the Charles Waddell Chesnutt Association.

William Gleason is Hughes-Rogers Professor of English at Princeton University. He is the author of *The Leisure Ethic: Work and Play in American Literature, 1840–1940, Sites Unseen: Architecture, Race, and American Literature* and of essays on such writers as Chesnutt, Hannah Crafts, and Frederick Douglass.

George Gordon-Smith is visiting assistant professor of English and disability studies at Emory University. His current book project, "Enslaved Bodies: Disability and Race in Early American Literature," examines the role of disability in the development and justification of slavery in the early American republic.

Jennifer Riddle Harding is associate professor of English and director of the First Year Seminar Program at Washington and Jefferson College. She is the author of *Similes, Puns, and Counterfactuals in Literary Narrative* and essays on Chesnutt's short fiction. In 2017, she was thrilled to lecture on Chesnutt at several universities in the Czech Republic as a Fulbright scholar.

Bill Hardwig is associate professor in the English Department at the University of Tennessee. He is the author of *Upon Provincialism: Southern Literature and National Periodical Culture, 1870–1900* (2013) and essays on the reception and publishing history of Chesnutt's fiction, as well as the teaching of his literature.

Sarah Ingle is lecturer in the Department of English at the University of Virginia. She is the author of an essay on mapping the geography of Chesnutt's conjure tales in the Norton Critical Edition of *The Conjure Stories*. She is currently working on a book manuscript titled "Conjured Memories: Race, Place, and Cultural Memory in the American Conjure Tale, 1877–1905."

Kathryn S. Koo is professor of English at Saint Mary's College of California. She is the author of articles on New England slavery and representations of America's founding. Her current research and teaching focus on the intersection of law and literature. She is working on a project on the crime of lynching in twentieth-century American literature.

Gregory Laski is a civilian assistant professor of English at the United States Air Force Academy. In addition to articles in *J19*, *Callaloo*, *Pedagogy*, and other outlets, he is the author of *Untimely Democracy: The Politics of Progress after Slavery* (2017). He is a cofounder of the Democratic Dialogue Project, an exchange between students at the Air Force Academy and Colorado College that seeks to bridge the military-civilian divide.

Janaka Lewis is assistant professor of English at University of North Carolina, Charlotte. She is the author of "Elizabeth Keckley and Freedom's Labor," "Elizabeth Keckley and Lessons of Freedom," and "Civil Discourse: Black Women's Narratives of Freedom and Nation." She is excited to continue conversations on how early African American authors and educators used and taught African American history and literature.

Trinyan Paulsen Mariano is assistant professor of English at Florida State University. She is the author of essays on law and lynching in Chesnutt's *The Marrow of Tradition*, on legal realism in Richard Wright's *Native Son*, and on the legal fictions of race and personhood in Mark Twain's *Pudd'nhead Wilson*. She is currently working on a book about the late-nineteenth-century romantic novel and the emergence of American tort law.

Jeffrey W. Miller is associate professor of English at Gonzaga University. He is the author of essays on authors associated with American realism and naturalism, including Mark Twain, Charles Chesnutt, Pauline Hopkins, and Rebecca Harding Davis. He is currently completing a monograph on citizenship in nineteenth-century United States literary culture.

Shirley Moody-Turner is associate professor of English and African American studies at Pennsylvania State University. She is the author of *Black Folklore and the Politics of Racial Representation* and coeditor of *Contemporary African American Literature: The Living Canon*. In 2015 she was selected as one of three Penn State University Alumni Teaching Fellows.

Marisa Parham is professor of English at Amherst College and director of Five College Digital Humanities. She is the author of *Haunting and Displacement in African-American Literature and Culture* and *The African-American Student's Guide to College* (1999) and the coeditor of *Theorizing Glissant: Sites and Citations*.

Hollis Robbins is a member of the humanities faculty at the Peabody Institute of Johns Hopkins University, on sabbatical leave at the National Humanities Center in Durham, NC. She is the coeditor, with Henry Louis Gates, Jr., of The *Portable Nineteenth-Century African American Women Writers* and is currently completing *Forms of Contention: The African American Sonnet Tradition*.

Francesca Sawaya is professor of English and American studies at the College of William and Mary. She is the author of *Modern Women, Modern Work: Domesticity, Professionalism, and American Writing* and *The Difficult Art of Giving: Patronage, Philanthropy, and the American Literary Market.*

Ryan Simmons is instructor of English at Spokane Falls Community College, where he teaches African American literature, multicultural American literature, and other literature and writing courses. He is the author of *Chesnutt and Realism: A Study of the Novels* (2006) and essays on Zora Neale Hurston, Mark Twain, and others.

Mark Sussman teaches at Hunter College at the City University of New York. His work has appeared in *Novel* and *MELUS*, which gave his essay "Charles W. Chesnutt's Stenographic Realism" honorable mention for the 2016 Katherine Newman Best Essay Award.

Sarah Wagner-McCoy is assistant professor of English and humanities at Reed College. She is one of the editors of *The Complete Writings of Charles W. Chesnutt.* She is currently working on a book titled "Eden Scams: Transatlantic Pastoral and the Realist Novel." She received the 2016 Graves Award in the Humanities, for excellence in teaching.

Brian Yothers is Frances Spatz Leighton Endowed Distinguished Professor of English at the University of Texas, El Paso. He is the author of *Reading Abolition: The Critical Reception of Harriet Beecher Stowe and Frederick Douglass* (2016), *Sacred Uncertainty: Religious Difference and the Shape of Melville's Career* (2015), *Melville's Mirrors: Literary Criticism and America's Most Elusive Author* (2011), and *The Romance of the Holy Land in American Travel Writing, 1790–1876* (2007).

Mary E. Brown Zeigler is associate professor of English language and linguistics at Georgia State University. She was president of the Charles W. Chesnutt Association from 2006 to 2010. She is the author of "Migration and Motivation in the Development of AAVE" (2008) and contributing editor for the special issue of *Studies in the Literary Imagination: Charles Waddell Chesnutt: Placing a Stamp on America* (2010).

WORKS CITED

Abrahams, Roger. "Sincerities: William Wells Newell and the Discovery of Folklore in Late Nineteenth Century America." *Folklore in American Life*, edited by Jane Becker and Barbara Franco, Museum of Our National Heritage, 1998, pp. 61–75.

Allen, James. *Without Sanctuary*, withoutsanctuary.org/main.html.

Andrews, William L. Introduction. C. Chesnutt, *Conjure Tales*, pp. vii–xviii.

——. *The Literary Career of Charles W. Chesnutt*. Louisiana State UP, 1980.

Aristotle. "Justice." *Law and Philosophy: Readings in Legal Philosophy*, edited by Edward Allen Kent, Prentice, 1970, pp. 465–73.

Baldwin, James. "Everybody's Protest Novel." 1949. Gates and McKay, pp. 1654–59.

Bancroft, Hubert Howe. *Popular Tribunals*. Vol. 1. San Francisco, 1887. *Google Books*, books.google.com/books?id=u14mAQAAMAAJ&printsec.

Barry, Peter. *Beginning Theory*. 3rd ed., Manchester UP, 2009.

Baudrillard, Jean. "The Precession of Simulacra." *Simulacra and Simulation*, translated by Seila Faria Glaser, U of Michigan P, 1994, pp. 1–42.

Bauer, Margaret D. "On Flags and Fraternities: Lessons in History in Charles Chesnutt's 'Po' Sandy.'" *Passing in the Works of Charles W. Chesnutt*, edited by Susan Prothro Wright and Ernestine Pickens Glass, UP of Mississippi, 2010, pp. 23–38.

Baynton, Douglas. "Disability and the Justification of Inequality in American History." *The Disability Studies Reader*, 4th ed., edited by Lennard Davis, Routledge, 2013, pp. 17–33.

Bell, Derrick. "*Brown v. Board of Education* and the Interest Convergence Dilemma." Crenshaw et al., pp. 20–29.

——. "The Space Traders." *Dark Matter: A Century of Speculative Fiction from the African Diaspora*, edited by Thomas Sheree, Warner, 2000, pp. 326–55.

Bishir, Catherine W. *North Carolina Architecture*. U of North Carolina P, 1990.

Black on White. Films Incorporated, 1986. Part 5 of *The Story of English*.

Blight, David W. *Beyond the Battlefield: Race, Memory, and the American Civil War*. U of Massachusetts P, 2002.

"Bloody Conflict with Negroes." *Morning Star* (Wilmington, NC), 11 Nov. 1898, p. 1.

Borges, Jorge Luis. *Ficciones*. Translated by Anthony Bonner et al., Grove Press, 1962.

Brodhead, Richard H. Introduction. C. Chesnutt, *Conjure Woman*, pp. 1–22.

Brown, Gillian. *Domestic Individualism: Imagining Self in Nineteenth-Century America*. U of California P, 1992.

Brown, Henry Billings. *Plessy v Ferguson, 163 U.S. 537*. 1896. *The Thin Disguise: Turning Point in Negro History; Plessy v Ferguson; A Documentary Presentation, 1864–96*, edited by Otto H. Olsen, Humanities Press, 1967, pp. 110–11.

Brown, William Wells. *Clotel: or, The President's Daughter.* 1853. Penguin, 2003.

Bulwer-Lytton, Edward. *Last of the Barons.* Saunders and Otley, 1843.

Burnett, Cathleen. "Justice: Myth and Symbol." *Legal Studies Forum*, vol. 11, 1987, pp. 79–94. *HeinOnline*, heinonline.org/HOL/LandingPage?handle=hein .journals/lstf11&div=12&id=&page=.

Byerman, Keith. "Black Voices, White Stories: An Intertextual Analysis of Thomas Nelson Page and Charles Waddell Chesnutt." *North Carolina Literary Review*, vol. 8, 1999, pp. 98–105.

Cary, Elizabeth. "A New Element of Fiction." *Book Buyer*, 1901, pp. 26–28.

Cecelski, David. "'Race Riot'—or Massacre?: What Happened in Wilmington in 1898 and What It Means Today." *News and Observer* (Raleigh), 1 Nov. 1998, pp. 25A–27A.

Cecelski, David, and Timothy B. Tyson, editors. *Democracy Betrayed: The Wilmington Race Riot of 1898 and Its Legacy.* U of North Carolina P, 1998.

Chandler, Karen M. "Charles Chesnutt's Cultural Exchange: Race and the Reading of Melodrama in 'Her Virginia Mammy.'" *South Central Review*, vol. 17, no. 2, Summer 2000, pp. 6–23.

Charity-Hudley, Anne H., and Christine Mallinson. *Understanding English Language Variation in U.S. Schools.* Foreword by William Labov, afterword by Walt Wolfram, Teachers College Press, 2011. Multicultural Education Series.

Chesnutt, Charles. "Baxter's Procrustes." C. Chesnutt, *Portable*, pp. 194–206.

———. "The Bouquet." C. Chesnutt, *Charles W. Chesnutt: Stories*, pp. 239–49.

———. *Charles W. Chesnutt: Essays and Speeches.* Edited by Joseph McElrath, Jr., Robert Leitz, and Jesse Crisler, Stanford UP, 1999.

———. *Charles W. Chesnutt: Stories, Novels, and Essays.* Edited by Werner Sollors, Library of America, 2002.

———. "Charles W. Chesnutt's Own View of His New Story, *The Marrow of Tradition.*" *World* [Cleveland], 20 Oct. 1901, p. 5. Magazine section.

———. *The Colonel's Dream.* Edited by R. J. Ellis, West Virginia UP, 2014.

———. "The Conjurer's Revenge." C. Chesnutt, *Charles W. Chesnutt: Stories*, pp. 46–57.

———. *The Conjure Stories.* Edited by Robert B. Stepto and Jennifer Rae Greeson, W. W. Norton, 2011.

———. *Conjure Tales and Stories of the Color Line.* Edited by William W. Andrews, Penguin Books, 1992.

———. *The Conjure Woman and Other Conjure Tales.* Edited by Richard H. Brodhead, Duke UP, 1993.

———. *Frederick Douglass: The Beacon Biographies of Eminent Americans.* Small, Maynard and Company, 1899.

———. "The Future American." *Boston Evening Transcript*, 18 Aug. 1900, p. 20; 25 Aug. 25, p. 15; 1 Sept, p. 24. Schmidt, p. 553.

———. "Her Virginia Mammy." C. Chesnutt, *Conjure Tales*, pp. 115–32.

———. *The House behind the Cedars.* Edited by Donald B. Gibson, Penguin Books, 1993.

————. "How Dasdy Came Through." *The Short Fiction of Charles W. Chesnutt*, edited by Sylvia Lyons Render, Howard UP, 1974, pp. 249–52.

————. *The Journals of Charles W. Chesnutt*. Edited by Richard M. Brodhead, Duke UP, 2001.

————. *The Marrow of Tradition*. Edited by Nancy Bentley and Sandra Gunning, Palgrave, 2002. Bedford Cultural Edition.

————. *The Marrow of Tradition*. Edited by Werner Sollors, W. W. Norton, 2012. Norton Critical Edition.

————. *The Marrow of Tradition*. Edited by Eric J. Sundquist, Penguin Classics, 1993.

————. "Methods of Teaching." C. Chesnutt, *Charles W. Chesnutt: Essays*, pp. 40–54.

————. Papers, 1864–1938. Fisk U Library Special Collections. Box 9, unpublished works—books, folder 1, "Rena," 39 pp.

————. *The Portable Charles W. Chesnutt*. Edited by William W. Andrews, Penguin Books, 2008.

————. *Selected Writings*. Edited by SallyAnn H. Ferguson, Houghton Mifflin, 2001.

————. "The Sheriff's Children." C. Chesnutt, *Portable*, pp. 71–88.

————. "Sis' Becky's Pickaninny." C. Chesnutt, *Conjure Woman*, pp. 82–93.

————. *Tales of Conjure and the Color Line: Ten Stories*. Edited by Joan R. Sherman, Dover Publications, 1998.

————. *"To Be an Author": Letters of Charles W. Chesnutt, 1889–1905*. Edited by Joseph McElrath, Jr., and Robert Leitz III, Princeton UP, 1997.

————. "The White and the Black." C. Chesnutt, *Charles W. Chesnutt: Essays*, pp. 139–44.

————. "The Wife of His Youth." C. Chesnutt, *Portable*, pp. 59–70.

————. *"The Wife of His Youth" and Other Stories of the Color Line*. Houghton Mifflin, 1899.

Chesnutt, Helen. *Charles Waddell Chesnutt: Pioneer of the Color Line*. U of North Carolina P, 1952.

Colorless Green Ideas Sleep Furiously. Equinox Film, 1995, thehumanlanguage.com/films/one/. Part 1 of *Discovering the Human Language*.

"Conjure." *Encyclopaedia Britannica, Micropaedia*, vol. 3, 1981.

Craft, William. *Running a Thousand Miles for Freedom; or, The Escape of William and Ellen Craft from Slavery*. 1860. *Documenting the American South*, docsouth.unc.edu/neh/craft/menu.html.

Crenshaw, Kimberlé, et al., editors. *Critical Race Theory: The Key Writings That Formed the Movement*. New Press, 1995.

Cruse, Harold. *The Crisis of the Negro Intellectual: A Historical Analysis of the Failure of Black Leadership*. The New York Review of Books, 2005.

Dahl, Robert A. *On Democracy*. Yale UP, 2000.

Dannenberg, Hilary P. *Coincidence and Counterfactuality: Plotting Time and Space in Narrative Fiction*. U of Nebraska P, 2008.

"Democratic Regime Strangling Anarchy." *News and Observer* (Raleigh), 12 Nov. 1898, p. 1.

De Santis, Christopher. "The Dangerous Marrow of Southern Tradition: Charles W. Chesnutt, Paul Laurence Dunbar, and the Paternalist Ethos at the Turn of the Century." *Southern Quarterly*, vol. 38, 2000, pp. 79–97. *ProQuest*, search .proquest.com/docview/1416165899?pq-origsite=gscholar.

Dimock, Wai Chee. *Residues of Justice: Literature, Law, Philosophy*. U of California P, 1996.

Dixon, Thomas. *The Leopard's Spots: A Romance of the White Man's Burden, 1865–1900*. Doubleday, Page, 1902.

Douglass, Frederick. "Lynch Law in the South." *North American Review*, July 1892, pp. 17–24. *Google Books*, books.google.com/books/about/Lynch_Law_in_the _South.html?id=FGakHAAACAAJ.

"Dream Doesn't Come True." *The Globe and Commercial Advertiser* [New York], 9 Sept. 1905, p. 6. *Reviews: The Charles Chesnutt Digital Archive*, www .chesnuttarchive.org/Reviews/ColonelReviews/colonels25.html.

Du Bois, W. E. B. "Postscript: Chesnutt." *The Crisis*, vol. 40, no. 1, Jan. 1933, pp. 20–22.

———. *The Quest of the Silver Fleece, A Novel*. 1911. Harlem Moon, 2004.

———. *The Souls of Black Folk*. Library of America / Penguin Books, 1996.

———. "The Talented Tenth." *The Negro Problem: A Series of Articles by Representative American Negroes of To-day*, James Pott, 1903, pp. 31–76. *Internet Archive*, archive.org/details/negroproblemseri00washrich.

Duncan, Charles. *The Absent Man*. Ohio UP, 1998.

Edmonds, Helen G. *The Negro and Fusion Politics in North Carolina, 1894–1901*. U of North Carolina P, 1954.

Ellis, Clifton, and Rebecca Ginsburg, editors. *Cabin, Quarter, Plantation: Architecture and Landscapes of North American Slavery*. Yale UP, 2010.

Ellison, Curtis W., and E. W. Metcalf, editors. *Charles W. Chesnutt: A Reference Guide*. G. K. Hall, 1977.

Ellison, Ralph. "Change the Joke and Slip the Yoke." *The Partisan Review*, Spring 1958, pp. 212–22.

"English in America." *The Adventure of English, 500 AD to 2000 AD*, vol. 5, Films for the Humanities and Sciences, 2004. PE 1075, A3846 2004, disc 5.

Erkkila, Betsy. "Radical Jefferson." *American Quarterly*, vol. 59, no. 2, 2007, pp. 277–89.

Ewell, Barbara, and Pamela Glenn Menke. Introduction. *Southern Local Color: Stories of Region, Race, and Gender*, U of Georgia P, 2002, pp. xiii–lxvi.

Fabi, M. Guilia. "Reconstructing the Race: The Novel after Slavery." *The Cambridge Companion to the African American Novel*, Cambridge UP, 2004, pp. 34–51.

Fasold, Ralph. "The Relation between Black and White Speech in the South." *American Speech*, vol. 56, 1981, pp. 163–89.

Ferguson, SallyAnn. "Charles W. Chesnutt: An American Signifier." C. Chesnutt, *Selected Writings*, pp. 1–11.

Foreman, Piers Gabrielle. *Activist Sentiments: Reading Black Women in the Nineteenth Century*. Illinois UP, 2009.

Foster, Frances Smith. *Written by Herself: Literary Production by African American Women, 1746–1892*. Indiana UP, 1993.

Fowler, Roger. *Linguistic Criticism*. Oxford UP, 1986.

Franklin, John Hope, and Alfred A. Moss, Jr. *From Slavery to Freedom: A History of African Americans*. 7th ed., McGraw-Hill, 1998.

Fredrickson, George. *The Black Image in the White Mind: The Debate on Afro-American Character and Destiny, 1817–1914*. Harper, 1971.

Freud, Sigmund. "Repression." 1915. *The Standard Edition of the Complete Psychological Works of Sigmund Freud*, edited and translated by James Strachey, vol. 14, Hogarth Press, 1957, pp. 146–58.

Friedman, Ryan Jay. "Between Absorption and Extinction: Charles Chesnutt and Biopolitical Racism." *Arizona Quarterly*, vol. 63, no. 4, 2007, pp. 39–62. *Project Muse*, muse.jhu.edu/article/225253.

Garland-Thomson, Rosemarie. *Extraordinary Bodies: Figuring Physical Disability in American Culture and Literature*. Columbia UP, 1997.

Gaston, Alice. "Interview with Alice Gaston, Gee's Bend, Alabama, 1941." Interview by Robert Sonkin. *Voices from the Days of Slavery, American Memory, The Library of Congress*, hdl.loc.gov/loc.afc/afc9999001.5091b.

Gates, Henry Louis, Jr. *African American Lives 2: The Road Home*. Public Broadcasting Service. *YouTube*, 3 Dec. 2007, www.youtube.com/watch?v=_ILh3BphzUU.

Gates, Henry Louis, Jr., and Nellie Y. McKay, editors. *The Norton Anthology of African American Literature*. 2nd ed., W. W. Norton, 2004.

Gerard, Philip. *Cape Fear Rising*. Blair, 1994.

Giles, James, and Thomas Lally. "Allegory in Chesnutt's *Marrow of Tradition*." *JGE: The Journal of General Education*, vol. 35, 1984, pp. 259–69. *JSTOR*, www.jstor.org/stable/27796970?seq=1#page_scan_tab_contents.

Gilligan, Heather Tirado. "Reading, Race, and Charles Chesnutt's 'Uncle Julius' Tales." *ELH*, vol. 74, no. 1, Spring 2007, pp. 195–215.

Gleason, William. "Chesnutt's Piazza Tales: Architecture, Race, and Memory in the Conjure Stories." *American Quarterly*, vol. 51, no. 1, March 1999, pp. 33–77.

"Good Order Rules." *Morning Star* (Wilmington, NC), 13 Nov. 1898, p. 1.

Goodrich, Alan. "Virtuality." *Theories of Media: Keyword Glossary*, edited by W. J. T. Mitchell, U of Chicago, 2002, csmt.uchicago.edu/glossary2004/virtuality.htm.

Grady, Henry. "The South and her Problems." *The Complete Orations and Speeches of Henry W. Grady*. 1910, pp. 23–64. *Internet Archive*, archive.org/details/completeorations00graduoft.

Green, Lisa J. *African American English: A Linguistic Introduction*. Cambridge UP, 2002.

Greenough, Sarah, editor. *Selected Letters of Georgia O'Keeffe and Alfred Stieglitz: Volume 1, 1915–1933.* Yale UP, 2011. Kindle ed.

Gunning, Sandra. "Mark Twain, Charles Chesnutt, and the Politics of Literary Antiracism." *Race, Rape, and Lynching: The Red Record of American Literature, 1890–1912,* Oxford UP, 1996, pp. 48–76.

Haney Lopez, Ian. "The Social Construction of Race." *Critical Race Theory: The Cutting Edge,* edited by Richard Delgado and Jean Stefancic, Temple UP, 2007, pp. 163–75.

Harding, Jennifer Riddle. "Narrating the Family in Charles W. Chesnutt's 'Her Virginia Mammy.'" *Journal of Narrative Theory,* vol. 423, no. 3, Fall 2012, pp. 309–31.

Hardwig, Bill. *Upon Provincialism: Southern Literature and National Periodical Culture, 1870–1900.* U of Virginia P, 2013.

Harper, Frances Ellen Watkins. *Iola Leroy; or, Shadows Uplifted.* Edited by Hollis Robbins, Penguin Books, 2010.

Heermance, J. Noel. *Charles W. Chesnutt, America's First Great Black Novelist.* Archon Books, 1974.

Holy Bible. Royal Publishers, 1971.

Hopkins, Pauline. *Of One Blood; or, The Hidden Self.* 1903. *The Magazine Novels of Pauline Hopkins,* Oxford UP, 1988, pp. 439–621.

"Horrible Butcheries at Wilmington." *Richmond Planet,* 19 Nov. 1898, pp. 1, 8.

Howells, William Dean. "Mr. Charles W. Chesnutt's Stories." *Atlantic Monthly,* May 1900. *The Atlantic,* www.theatlantic.com/magazine/archive/1900/05/mr-charles -w-chesnutts-stories/306659/.

———. "A Psychological Counter-current in Recent Fiction." *The North American Review,* vol. 173, no. 6, 1901, p. 882.

Ingle, Sarah. "The Terrain of Chesnutt's Conjure Tales." C. Chesnutt, *Conjure Stories,* pp. 149–64.

Irwin, William. "What Is an Allusion?" *The Journal of Aesthetics and Art Criticism,* vol. 59, no. 3, Summer 2001, pp. 287–97.

Jacobs, Harriet. *Incidents in the Life of a Slave Girl, Written by Herself, with Related Documents.* Edited by Jennifer Fleischner, Bedford / St. Martin's, 2010.

Jefferson, Thomas. *Writings.* Edited by Merrill D. Peterson, Library of America, 1984.

Johanningsmeier, Charles. "What We Can Learn from a Better Bibliographical Record of Chesnutt's Periodical Fiction." *North Carolina Literary Review,* vol. 8, 1999, pp. 84–96.

Johnson, James Weldon. Preface. *The Book of American Negro Spirituals,* edited by Johnson, Viking Press, 1925, pp. 11–50.

Jones, Gavin. *Strange Talk: The Politics of Dialect Literature in Gilded Age America.* U of California P, 1999.

Jones, Tommy H. *Tullie Smith House: Original Site and Outbuildings.* Tomitronics, www.tomitronics.com/old_buildings/tulliesmith/originalsite.html.

Kawash, Samira. *Dislocating the Color Line: Identity, Hybridity, and Singularity in African-American Literature.* Stanford UP, 1997.

Keller, Francis Richardson. *An American Crusade: The Life of Charles Waddell Chesnutt.* Brigham Young UP, 1978.

Kirshenbaum, Andrea Meryl. "'The Vampire That Hovers over North Carolina': Gender, White Supremacy, and the Wilmington Race Riot of 1898." *Southern Cultures*, vol. 4, no. 3, 1998, pp. 6–29.

Labov, William. Foreword. Charity-Hudley and Mallinson, pp. xiii–xvi.

Lamb, Charles. "Quatrains: To the Editor of the Every-Day Book." *Miscellaneous Prose (1798–1834),* by Charles Lamb and Mary Lamb, edited by E. V. Lucas, Macmillan, 1913, p. 525.

Laski, Gregory. *Untimely Democracy: The Politics of Progress after Slavery.* Oxford UP, 2017.

Lee, Maurice. "Du Bois the Novelist: White Influence, Black Spirit, and *The Quest of the Silver Fleece.*" *African American Review*, vol. 33, no. 3, Fall 1999, pp. 389–400.

Linton, Simi. "Disability Studies / Not Disability Studies." *Disability and Society*, vol. 13, no. 4, 1998, pp. 525–40.

Litwack, Leon F. *Trouble in Mind: Black Southerners in the Age of Jim Crow.* Vintage Books, 1998.

Logan, Rayford W. *Howard University: The First Hundred Years, 1867–1967.* Howard U, 1968.

———. *The Negro in American Life and Thought: The Nadir, 1877–1901.* Dial Press, 1954.

Mandela, Nelson. Quotations. *African Wisdom, 365 Days a Year,* edited by Wilfred T. Harris and David Smith, Jr., Wisdom Collection Publications, 2010.

Mariano, Trinyan Paulsen. "The Law of Torts and the Logic of Lynching in Charles Chesnutt's *The Marrow of Tradition.*" *PMLA*, vol. 128, no. 3, 2013, pp. 559–74.

"Marrow." *Oxford English Dictionary*, www.oed.com.

The Matrix. Directed by the Wachowski Brothers, Warner Brothers, 1999.

McElrath, Joseph, Jr., et al. Introduction. C. Chesnutt, *Charles W. Chesnutt: Essays,* pp. xxiii–xxxvii.

McFatter, Susan. "From Revenge to Resolution: The (R)evolution of Female Characters in Chesnutt's Fiction." *CLA Journal*, vol. 42, 1998, pp. 194–211.

McWilliams, Dean. *Charles Chesnutt and the Fictions of Race.* U of Georgia P, 2002.

Mills, Charles W. "Contract of Breach: Repairing the Racial Contract." *Contract and Domination*, by Carole Pateman and Mills, Polity, 2007, pp. 106–33.

———. *The Racial Contract.* Cornell UP, 1999.

Mitchell, W. J. T., and Mark B. N. Hansen, editors. *Critical Terms for Media Studies.* U of Chicago P, 2010.

Moody, Joycelyn. *Sentimental Confessions: Spiritual Narratives of Nineteenth-Century African American Women.* U of Georgia P, 2001.

Morrison, Toni. *Playing in the Dark: Whiteness and the Literary Imagination*. Vintage, 1993.

Murphy, Jeffrie G., and Jean Hampton. *Mercy and Forgiveness*. Cambridge UP, 1988.

Najmi, Samina. "Janet, Polly, and Olivia: Constructs of Blackness and White Femininity in Charles Chesnutt's *The Marrow of Tradition*." *Southern Literary Journal*, vol. 32, 1999. *JSTOR*, www.jstor.org/stable/20078249?seq=1#page_scan_tab _contents.

"Negro Rule Ended: Wilmington's Fusion City Officers Forced to Resign." *Washington Post*, vol. 11, Nov. 1898, p. 1.

Newell, William Wells. "The Importance and Utility of the Collection of Negro Folklore." *Southern Workman*, vol. 23, no. 7, 1894, pp. 131–32.

———. "On the Field and Work of a Journal of American Folk-Lore." *Journal of American Folklore*, vol. 1, no. 1, 1888, pp. 3–7.

"Nigger." *The Oxford Dictionary of English Etymology*, edited by C. T. Onions with G. W. S. Friedrichsen and R. W. Burchfield, Oxford UP, 1966.

Nussbaum, Martha C. "Equity and Mercy." *Philosophy and Public Affairs*, vol. 22, no. 2, 1993, pp. 93–125. *JSTOR*, www.jstor.org/stable/2265442?origin=JSTOR -pdf&seq=1#page_scan_tab_contents.

———. *Poetic Justice: The Literary Imagination and Public Life*. Beacon, 1995.

"Occult," definition 3a. *Oxford English Dictionary*, Oxford UP, www.oed.com.

Orban, Maria. "The Fiction of Race: Folklore to Classical Literature." *Charles Chesnutt Reappraised: Essays on the First Major African American Fiction Writer*, edited by David Garrett Izzo and Orban, McFarland and Company, 2009, pp. 81–90.

"Order Is Restored." *Morning Star* (Wilmington, NC), 12 Nov. 1898, p. 1.

"Order Now Reigns." *News and Observer* (Raleigh), 13 Nov. 1898, pp. 1–2.

Page, Thomas Nelson. *In Ole Virginia; or, "Marse Chan" and Other Stories*. J. S. Sanders, 1991.

Page, Walter Hines. *The Southerner: A Novel*. U of South Carolina P, 2008.

Perkins, Dolen. "'White Heat' in Wilmington: The Dialogue between Journalism and Literature in *The Marrow of Tradition*." *North Carolina Literary Review*, vol. 11, 2002, pp. 38–47.

Pickens, Ernestine. *Charles W. Chesnutt and the Progressive Movement*. Pace UP, 1994.

"Plantation Life." *The Making of African American Identity: Vol. I, 1500–1865*. National Humanities Center, nationalhumanitiescenter.org/pds/maai/enslavement/ text3/text3read.htm.

Plato. *The Republic*. Translated by Benjamin Jowett, *The Internet Classics Archive*, classics.mit.edu/Plato/republic.8.vii.html.

Poe, Edgar Allan. *The Portable Edgar Allan Poe*. Edited by J. Gerald Kennedy, Penguin Books, 2006.

Posnock, Ross. "How It Feels to Be a Problem: Du Bois, Fanon, and the 'Impossible Life' of the Black Intellectual." *Critical Inquiry*, vol. 23, no. 2, Winter 1997, pp. 323–49.

Prather, H. Leon, Sr. *We Have Taken a City: Wilmington Racial Massacre and Coup of 1898.* Fairleigh Dickinson UP, 1984.

Princeton Encyclopedia of Poetry and Poetics. 4th ed., Princeton UP, 2012.

Rampersad, Arnold. "White like Me." *New York Times,* 25 Oct. 1998, www.nytimes .com/books/98/10/25/reviews/981025.25rampert.html.

Rawls, John. *A Theory of Justice.* Rev. ed., Harvard UP, 1999.

Render, Sylvia Lyons, editor. *Charles W. Chesnutt.* Twayne Publishers, 1980.

Resnik, Judith, and Dennis Curtis. *Representing Justice: Invention, Controversy, and Rights in City-States and Democratic Courtrooms.* Yale UP, 2011.

Rickford, John R., and Russell J. Rickford. *Spoken Soul: The Story of Black English.* John Wiley and Sons, 2000.

Ricks, Christopher. *Allusion to the Poets.* Oxford UP, 2002.

Roberts, John. "Grand Theory, Nationalism and American Folklore." *Journal of Folklore Research,* vol. 45, no. 1, 2008, pp. 45–54.

Roediger, David. *Black on White: Black Writers on What It Means to Be White.* Shocken Books, 1998.

Rudolph, Kerstin. "A Woman of One's Own Blood: John Walden and the Making of White Masculinity in Charles W. Chesnutt's *The House behind the Cedars.*" *American Literary Realism,* vol. 46, no. 1, Fall 2013, pp. 27–46.

Salazar, James B. *Bodies of Reform: The Rhetoric of Character in Gilded Age America.* New York UP, 2010.

Samuels, Shirley, editor. *The Culture of Sentiment: Race, Gender, and Sentimentality in Nineteenth-Century America.* Oxford UP, 1992.

Sayles, John. *A Moment in the Sun.* McSweeney's, 2011.

Schmidt, Peter. "Walter Scott, Postcolonial Theory, and New South Literature." *Mississippi Quarterly,* vol. 56, no. 4, Fall 2003, pp. 545–54.

Schwark, Sabine. "Questions and Answers." *Law Library Journal,* vol. 73, 1980, pp. 744–46. *HeinOnline,* home.heinonline.org/titles/Law-Journal-Library/ Law-Library-Journal/?letter=L.

Schwartz, Daniel R., editor. *The Dead.* By James Joyce. Bedford / St. Martin's, 1994. Case Studies in Contemporary Criticism.

Scott, Walter. *Ivanhoe: A Romance.* Project Gutenberg, 30 Aug. 2016, www.gutenberg .org/files/82/82-h/82-h.htm.

Sedlack, Robert P. "The Evolution of Charles Chesnutt's *The House behind the Cedars.*" *College Language Association Journal,* vol. 19, Dec. 1975, pp. 125–35.

Shakespeare, William. *The Norton Shakespeare.* Edited by Stephen Greenblatt et al., W. W. Norton, 1997.

Shapiro, Ian. *Democratic Justice.* Yale UP, 1999.

Siebers, Tobin. *Disability Theory.* U of Michigan P, 2008.

Smitherman, Geneva. *Black Talk: Words and Phrases from the Hood to the Amen Corner.* Houghton Mifflin, 1994.

Sollors, Werner. *African American Writing: A Literary Approach.* Temple UP, 2016.

"Some Tales of Conjuring." *Los Angeles Times*, 9 Apr. 1899, Illustrated Magazine Section, pp. 13–14.

Steelman, Bennett L. "Black, White, and Gray: The Wilmington Race Riot in Fact and Legend." *North Carolina Literary Review*, vol. 2, no. 1, 1994, pp. 70–82.

Stepto, Robert B. "'The Simple but Intensely Human Inner Life of Slavery': Storytelling, Fiction, and the Revision of History in Charles W. Chesnutt's 'Uncle Julius Stories.'" *History and Tradition in Afro-American Culture*, edited by Günter H. Lenz, Campus Verlag, 1984, pp. 29–55.

Stowe, Harriet Beecher. *Uncle Tom's Cabin*. 1852. Bantam Books, 1981.

Sundquist, Eric J. "Charles Chesnutt's Cakewalk." Sundquist, *To Wake*, pp. 271–456.

———. "Charles Chesnutt's Cakewalk." C. Chesnutt, *Marrow* [Sollors], pp. 472–86.

———. Introduction. C. Chesnutt, *Marrow* [Sundquist], pp. vii–xliv.

———. *To Wake the Nations: Race in the Making of American Literature*. Harvard UP, 1998.

Thomas, Brook. "The Legal Argument of Chesnutt's Novels." C. Chesnutt, *Marrow* [Sollors], pp. 427–51.

Thorne, Jack [David Bryant Fulton]. *Hanover; or, The Persecution of the Lowly: Story of the Wilmington Massacre. Documenting the American South*, U Library, U of North Carolina, Chapel Hill, docsouth.unc.edu/nc/thorne/menu.html.

Trachtenberg, Alan. *The Incorporation of America*. Hill and Wang, 1982.

Transcript of Plessy v. Ferguson (1896). Our Documents, ourdocuments.gov/doc.php ?doc=52&page=transcript.

Truth, Sojourner. "Ar'n't I a Woman?" Gates and McKay, pp. 246–49.

Twain, Mark. *The Adventures of Huckleberry Finn*. 3rd ed., edited by Thomas Cooley, W. W. Norton, 1999.

———. *Life on the Mississippi*. 1883. Harper and Brothers, 1901.

Tyson, Timothy B. "The Ghosts of 1898: Wilmington's Race Riot and the Rise of White Supremacy." *News and Observer* (Raleigh), 19 Nov. 2006, section H.

Tyson, Timothy B., and David Cecelski. Introduction. Cecelski and Tyson, *Democracy*, pp. 3–13.

Umfleet, LeRae S. *A Day of Blood: The 1898 Wilmington Race Riot*. North Carolina Office of Archives and History, 2009.

Viramontes, Helena Maria. "Miss Clairol." *The American Short Story and Its Writer: An Anthology*, edited by Ann Charters, Bedford / St. Martin's, 1999, pp. 1178–82.

Vlach, John Michael. *Back of the Big House: The Architecture of Plantation Slavery*. U of North Carolina P, 1993.

Waddell, Alfred Moore. "The Story of the Wilmington, N.C., Race Riots." *Collier's Weekly*, 26 Nov. 1898, pp. 3–5.

Ward, Candace, editor. *Great Short Stories by American Women*. Dover, 1996.

Warren, Kenneth. *Black and White Strangers: Race and American Literary Realism*. U of Chicago P, 1993.

Washington, Booker T. *Up from Slavery*. 1901. Signet, 2010.

Weinrib, Ernest. "The Gains and Losses of Corrective Justice." *Duke Law Journal*, vol. 44, 1994, pp. 277–97. *Duke Law*, scholarship.law.duke.edu/cgi/viewcontent .cgi?article=3264&context=dlj.

Wells, Ida B. "Lynch Law in America." *The Arena*, vol. 23, no. 1, Jan. 1900, pp. 15–24. U of Washington, courses.washington.edu/spcmu/speeches/idabwells.htm.

White, Michael. "Coup." *North Carolina Literary Review*, vol. 18, 2009, pp. 146–47.

Whites, LeeAnn. "Love, Hate, Rape, Lynching: Rebecca Latimer Felton and the Gender Politics of Racial Violence." Cecelski and Tyson, pp. 143–62.

Wiebe, Robert. *The Search for Order*. Hill and Wang, 1967.

Wiley, Ralph. *Why Black People Tend to Shout: Cold Facts and Wry Views from a Black Man's World*. Penguin Books, 1991.

Williams, Raymond. *Keywords: A Vocabulary of Culture and Society*. Rev. ed., Oxford UP, 1983.

Wilmington Race Riot Commission. *1898 Wilmington Race Riot—Final Report, May 31, 2006*. North Carolina Office of Archives and History, www.history .ncdcr.gov/1898-wrrc/report/report.htm.

Wolfram, Walt, and Natalie Schilling-Estes. "Social and Ethnic Dialects." *American English: Dialects and Variation*, Blackwell, 2002, pp. 151–84.

Wolkomir, Michelle J. "Moral Elevation and Egalitarianism: Shades of Gray in Chesnutt's *The Marrow of Tradition*." *CLA Journal*, vol. 36, 1993, pp. 245–59. *CLA Journal*, www.clascholars.org/resources/cla-journal/.

Wonham, Henry B. *Charles W. Chesnutt: A Study of the Short Fiction*. Twayne Publishers, 1998.

Woodson, Carter G. *The Mis-education of the Negro*. Seven Treasures Publications, 2010.

Worden, Daniel. "Birth in the Briar Patch: Charles W. Chesnutt and the Problem of Racial Identity." *Southern Literary Journal*, vol. 41, no. 2, Spring 2009, pp. 1–20.

Zeigler, Mary B. "Something to Shout About: AAVE as a Linguistic and Cultural Treasure." *Sociocultural and Historical Contexts of African American Vernacular English*, edited by Sonja Lanehart, John Benjamins, 2001, pp. 164–85.

INDEX